KURTIS J. WIEBE & TYLER JENKINS

PETER PANZERFAUST™

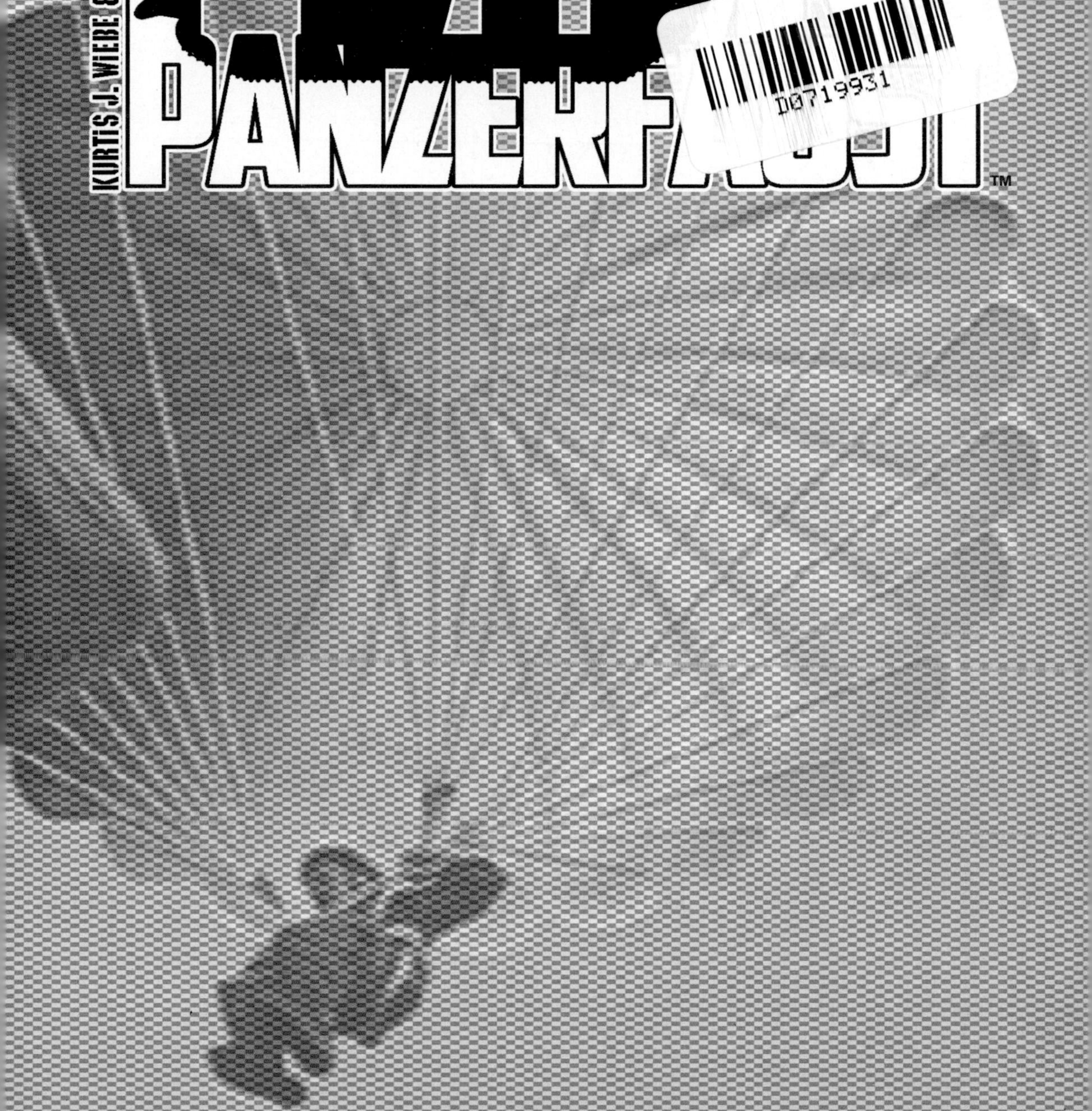

Shadowline™
image®
www.ShadowlineOnline.com

PETER PANZERFAUST VOLUME ONE: THE GREAT ESCAPE

First Printing September, 2012

ISBN: 978-1-60706-582-1

Published by Image Comics, Inc. Office of publication: 2134 Allston Way, Second Floor, Berkeley, California 94704. Copyright © 2012 KURTIS WIEBE and TYLER JENKINS. Originally published in single magazine form as PETER PANZERFAUST #1-5. All rights reserved. PETER PANZERFAUST™ (including all prominent characters featured herein), its logo and all character likenesses are trademarks of KURTIS WIEBE and TYLER JENKINS, unless otherwise noted. Image Comics® and its logos are registered trademarks of Image Comics, Inc. Shadowline and its logos are ™ and © 2012 Jim Valentino. No part of this publication may be reproduced or transmitted, in any form or by any means (except for short excerpts for review purposes) without the express written permission of Mr. Wiebe and/or Jenkins. All names, characters, events and locales in this publication are entirely fictional. Any resemblance to actual persons (living or dead), events or places, without satiric intent, is coincidental. For information regarding the CPSIA on this printed material call: 203-595-3636 and provide reference # RICH – 446308. PRINTED IN USA. International Licensing: foreignrights@imagecomics.com.

 COMICS PRESENTS

CO-CREATORS

KURTIS WIEBE TYLER JENKINS
WORDS PICTURES

ALEX SOLLAZZO ED BRISSON
COLORS LETTERS

LAURA TAVISHATI MARC LOMBARDI
EDITS COMMUNICATIONS

JIM VALENTINO
PUBLISHER/BOOK DESIGN

JADE DODGE-EDITS CHAPTER ONE

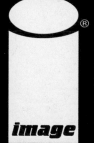

A
Shadowline™
PRODUCTION

IMAGE COMICS, INC.
Robert Kirkman - chief operating officer
Erik Larsen - chief financial officer
Todd McFarlane - president
Marc Silvestri - chief executive officer
Jim Valentino - vice-president

Eric Stephenson - publisher
Todd Martinez - sales & licensing coordinator
Jennifer de Guzman - pr & marketing director
Branwyn Bigglestone - accounts manager
Emily Miller - administrative assistant
Jamie Parreno - marketing assistant
Sarah deLaine - events coordinator
Kevin Yuen - digital rights coordinator
Tyler Shainline - production manager
Drew Gill - art director
Jonathan Chan - design director
Monica Garcia - production artist
Vincent Kukua - production artist
Jana Cook - production artist

www.imagecomics.com

www.ShadowlineOnline.com
Follow SHADOWLINECOMICS on f FACEBOOK and 🅑 TWITTER

"To the memory of J.M. Barrie
for creating a magical world that the child in all of us can explore."

Kurtis J. Wiebe

"To my wife, Hilary.
          To my Family.
                    To grand adventure and wild heroics."

Tyler Jenkins

CHAPTER ONE

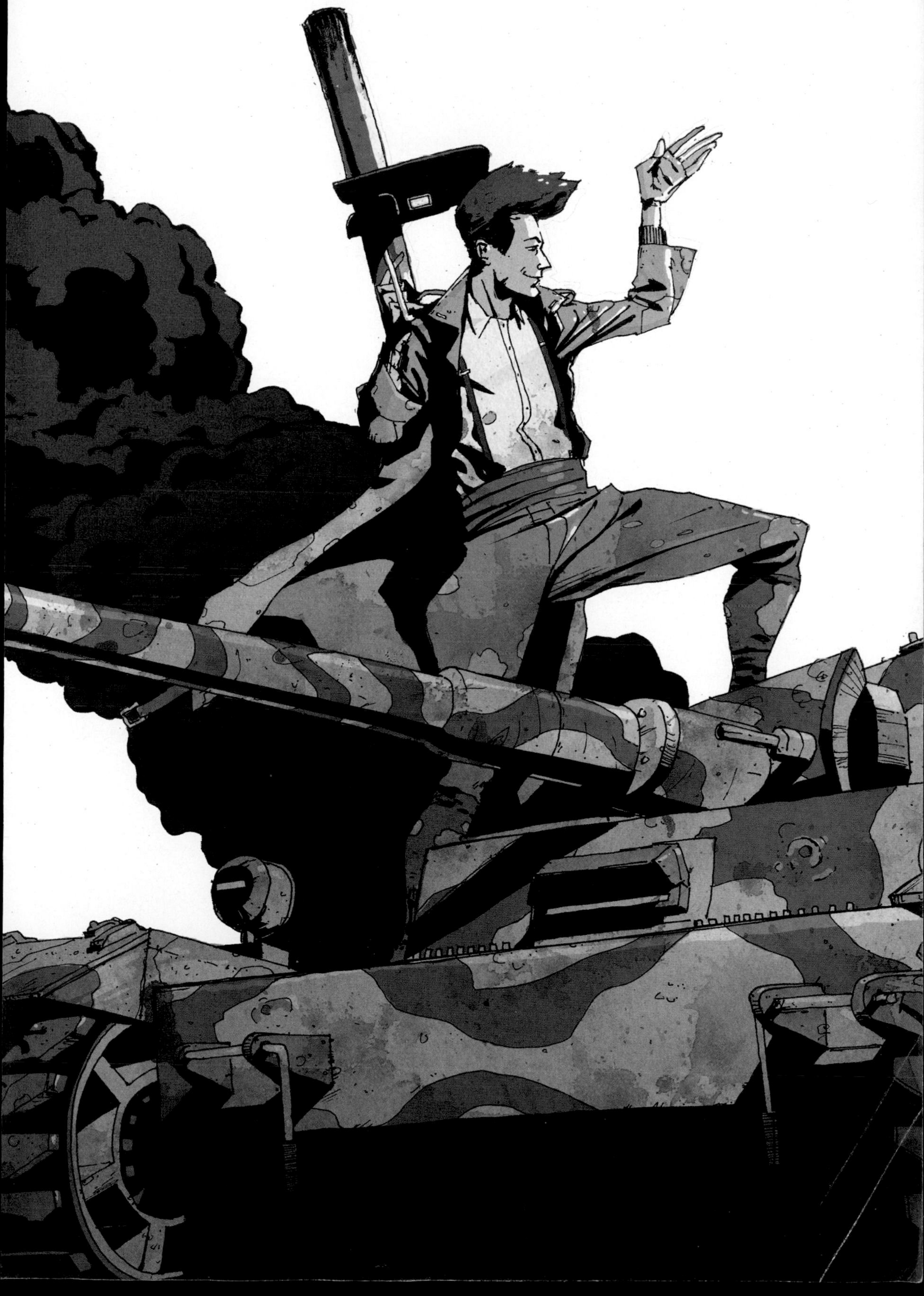

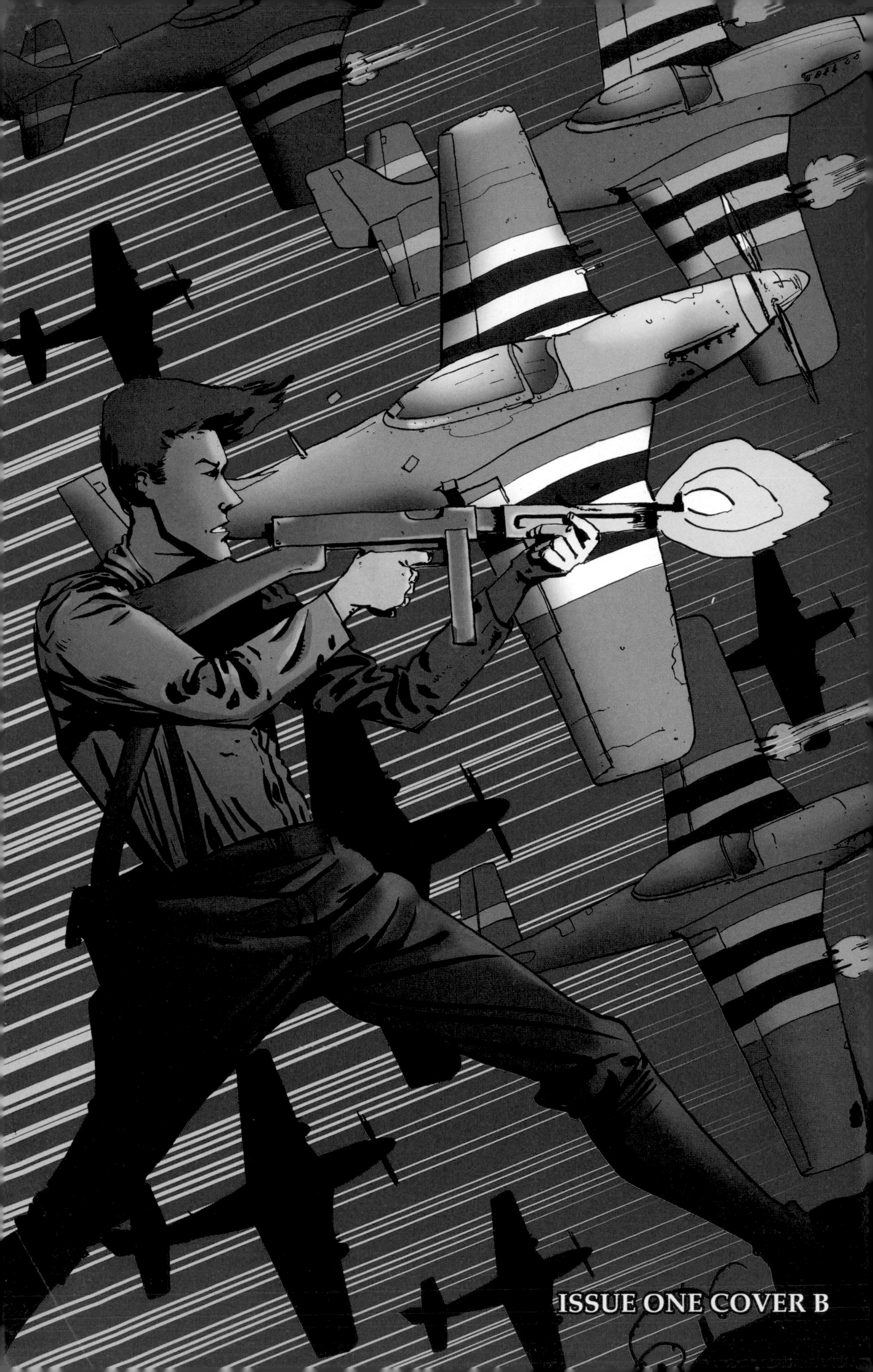
ISSUE ONE COVER B

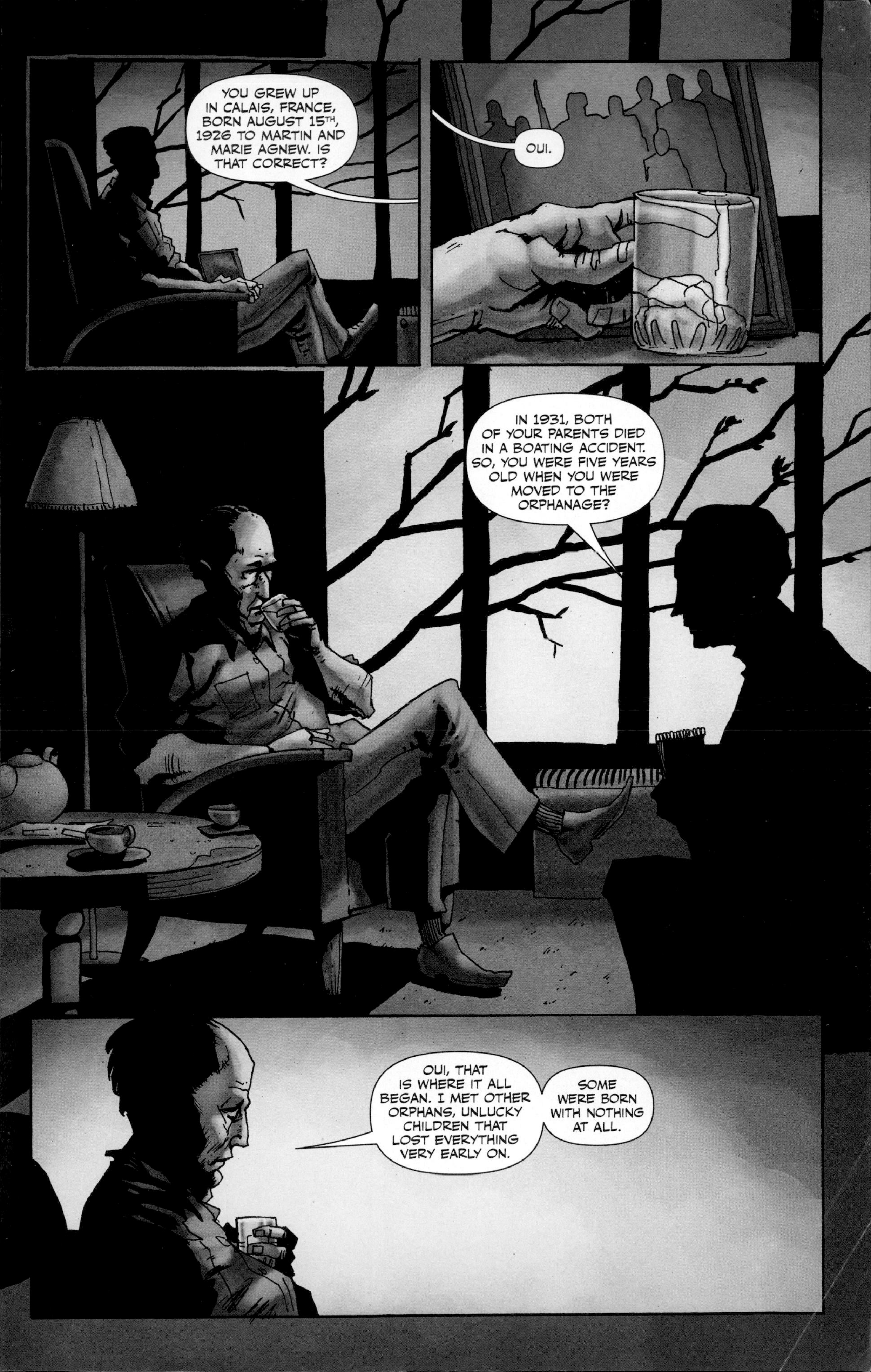
YOU GREW UP IN CALAIS, FRANCE, BORN AUGUST 15TH, 1926 TO MARTIN AND MARIE AGNEW. IS THAT CORRECT?
OUI.
IN 1931, BOTH OF YOUR PARENTS DIED IN A BOATING ACCIDENT. SO, YOU WERE FIVE YEARS OLD WHEN YOU WERE MOVED TO THE ORPHANAGE?
OUI, THAT IS WHERE IT ALL BEGAN. I MET OTHER ORPHANS, UNLUCKY CHILDREN THAT LOST EVERYTHING VERY EARLY ON.
SOME WERE BORN WITH NOTHING AT ALL.

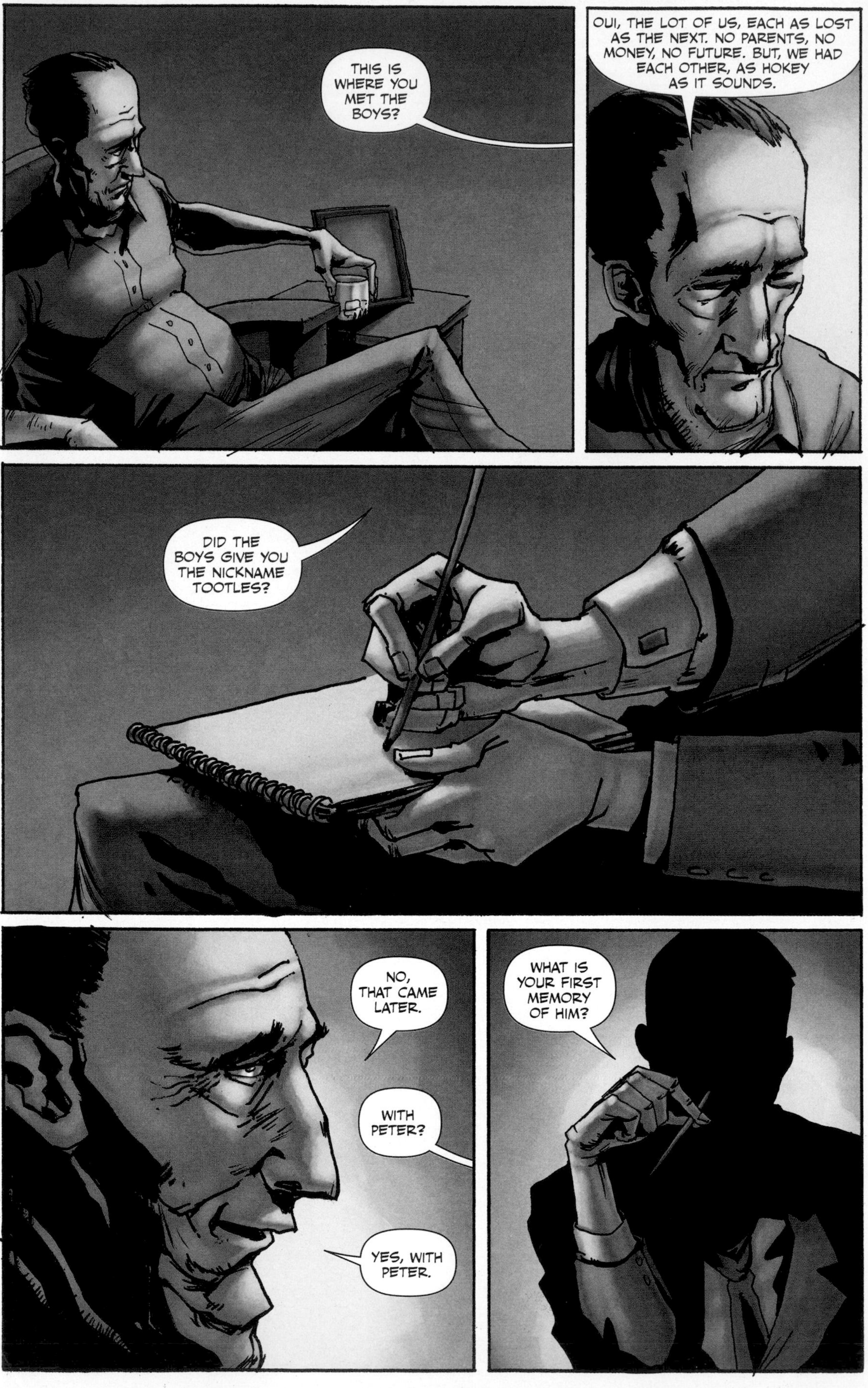
THIS IS WHERE YOU MET THE BOYS?
OUI, THE LOT OF US, EACH AS LOST AS THE NEXT. NO PARENTS, NO MONEY, NO FUTURE. BUT, WE HAD EACH OTHER, AS HOKEY AS IT SOUNDS.
DID THE BOYS GIVE YOU THE NICKNAME TOOTLES?
NO, THAT CAME LATER.
WITH PETER?
YES, WITH PETER.
WHAT IS YOUR FIRST MEMORY OF HIM?

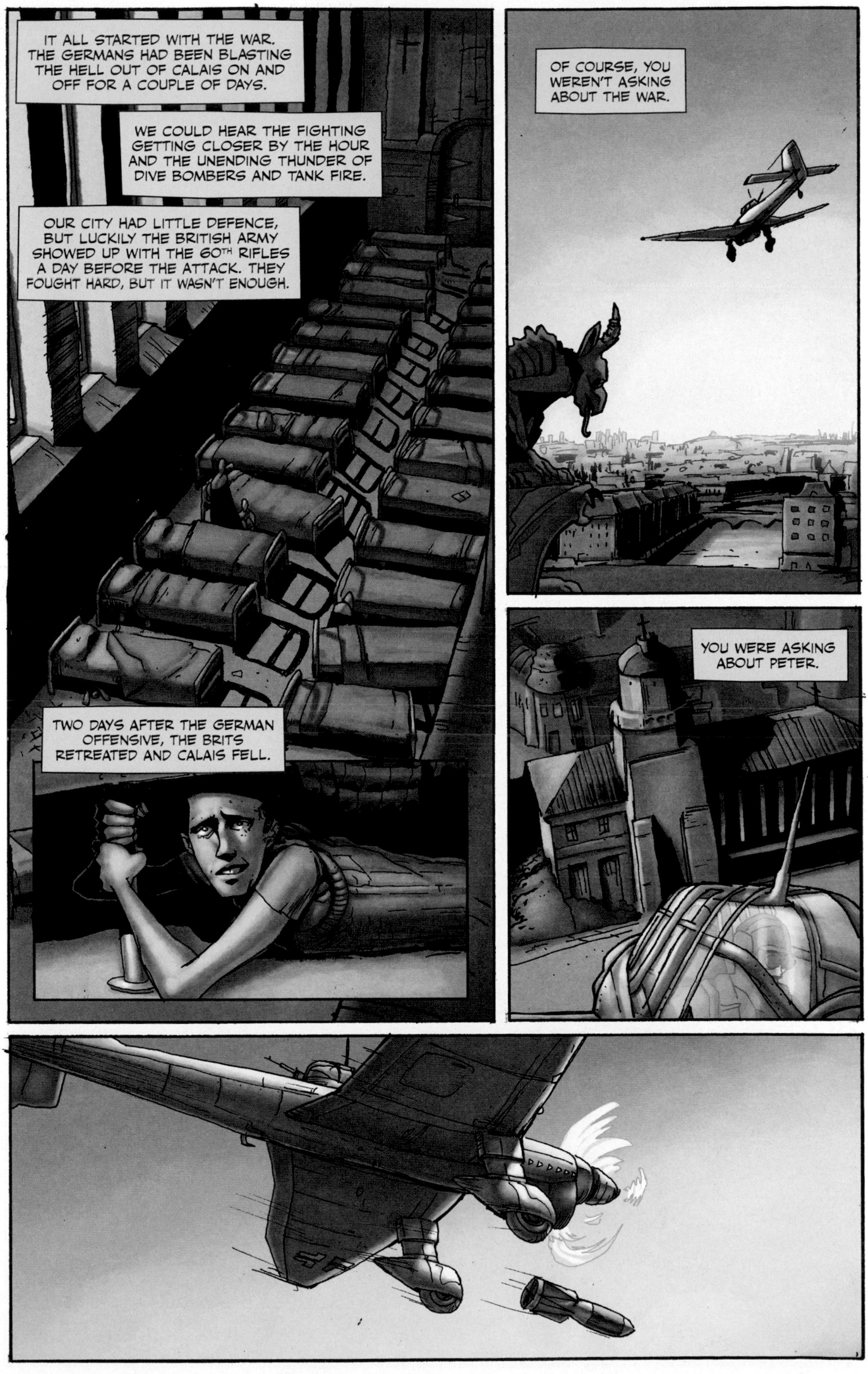
IT ALL STARTED WITH THE WAR. THE GERMANS HAD BEEN BLASTING THE HELL OUT OF CALAIS ON AND OFF FOR A COUPLE OF DAYS.
WE COULD HEAR THE FIGHTING GETTING CLOSER BY THE HOUR AND THE UNENDING THUNDER OF DIVE BOMBERS AND TANK FIRE.
OUR CITY HAD LITTLE DEFENCE, BUT LUCKILY THE BRITISH ARMY SHOWED UP WITH THE 60TH RIFLES A DAY BEFORE THE ATTACK. THEY FOUGHT HARD, BUT IT WASN'T ENOUGH.
TWO DAYS AFTER THE GERMAN OFFENSIVE, THE BRITS RETREATED AND CALAIS FELL.
OF COURSE, YOU WEREN'T ASKING ABOUT THE WAR.
YOU WERE ASKING ABOUT PETER.

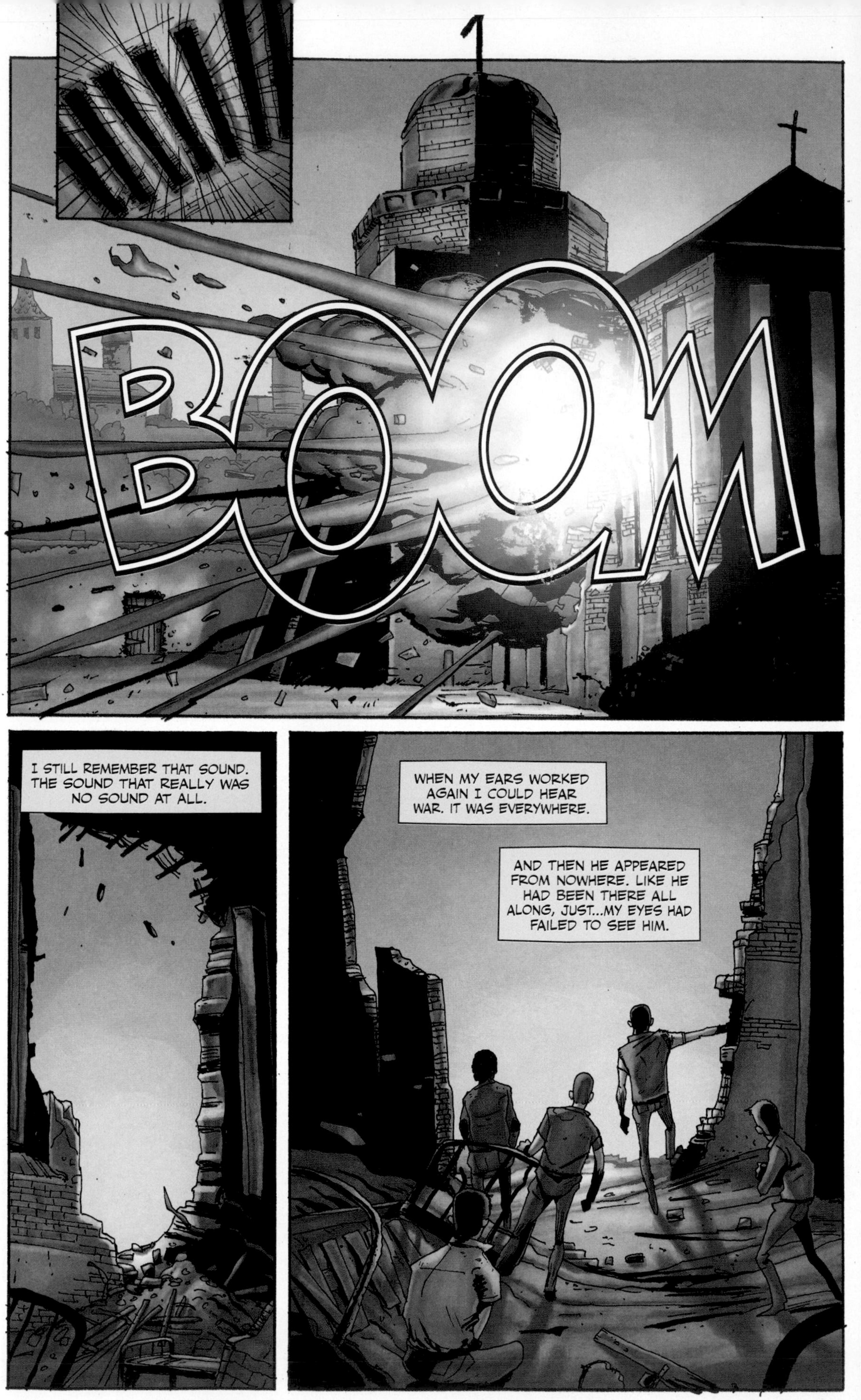
BOOM
I STILL REMEMBER THAT SOUND. THE SOUND THAT REALLY WAS NO SOUND AT ALL.
WHEN MY EARS WORKED AGAIN I COULD HEAR WAR. IT WAS EVERYWHERE.
AND THEN HE APPEARED FROM NOWHERE. LIKE HE HAD BEEN THERE ALL ALONG, JUST...MY EYES HAD FAILED TO SEE HIM.

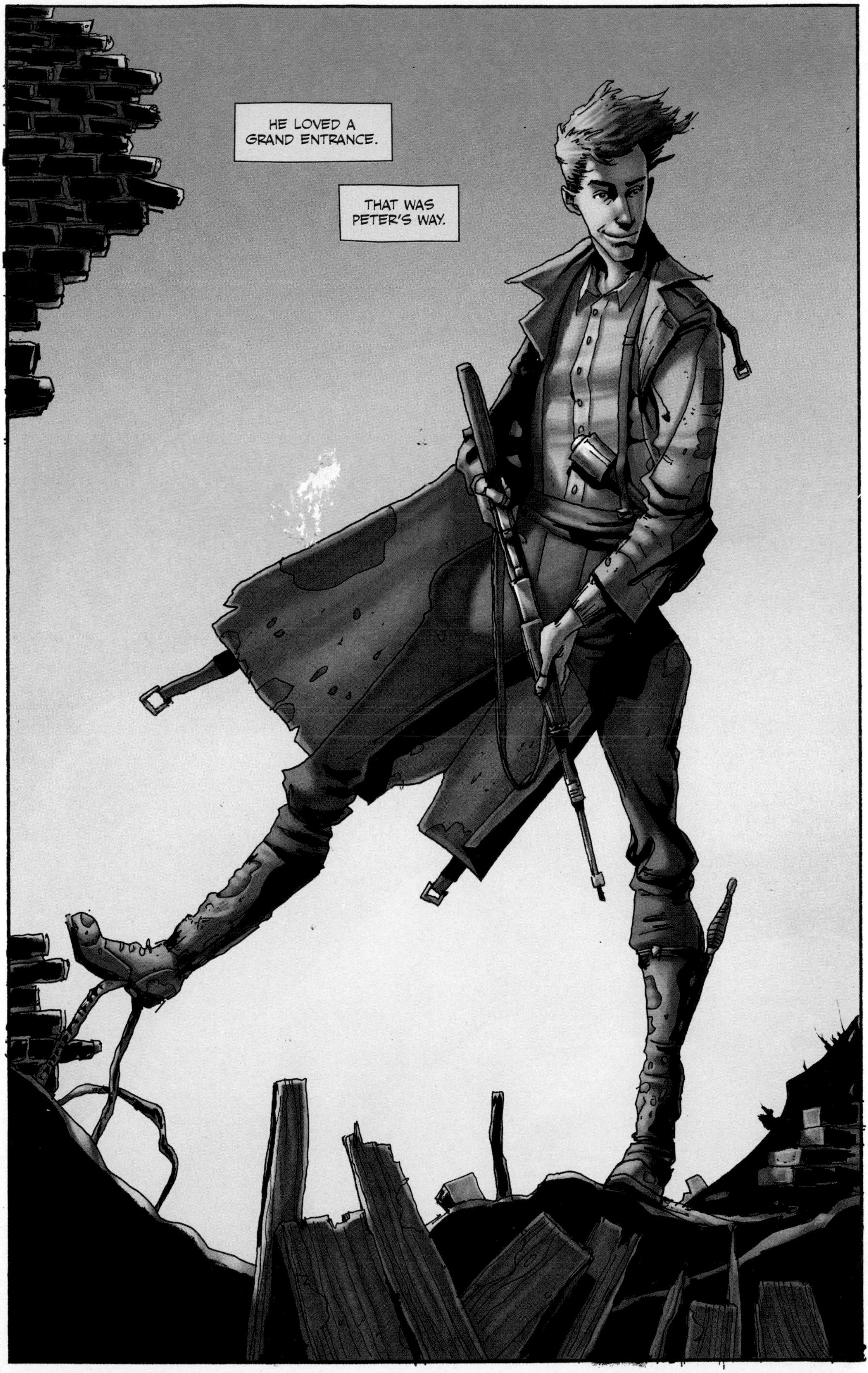
HE LOVED A GRAND ENTRANCE.
THAT WAS PETER'S WAY.

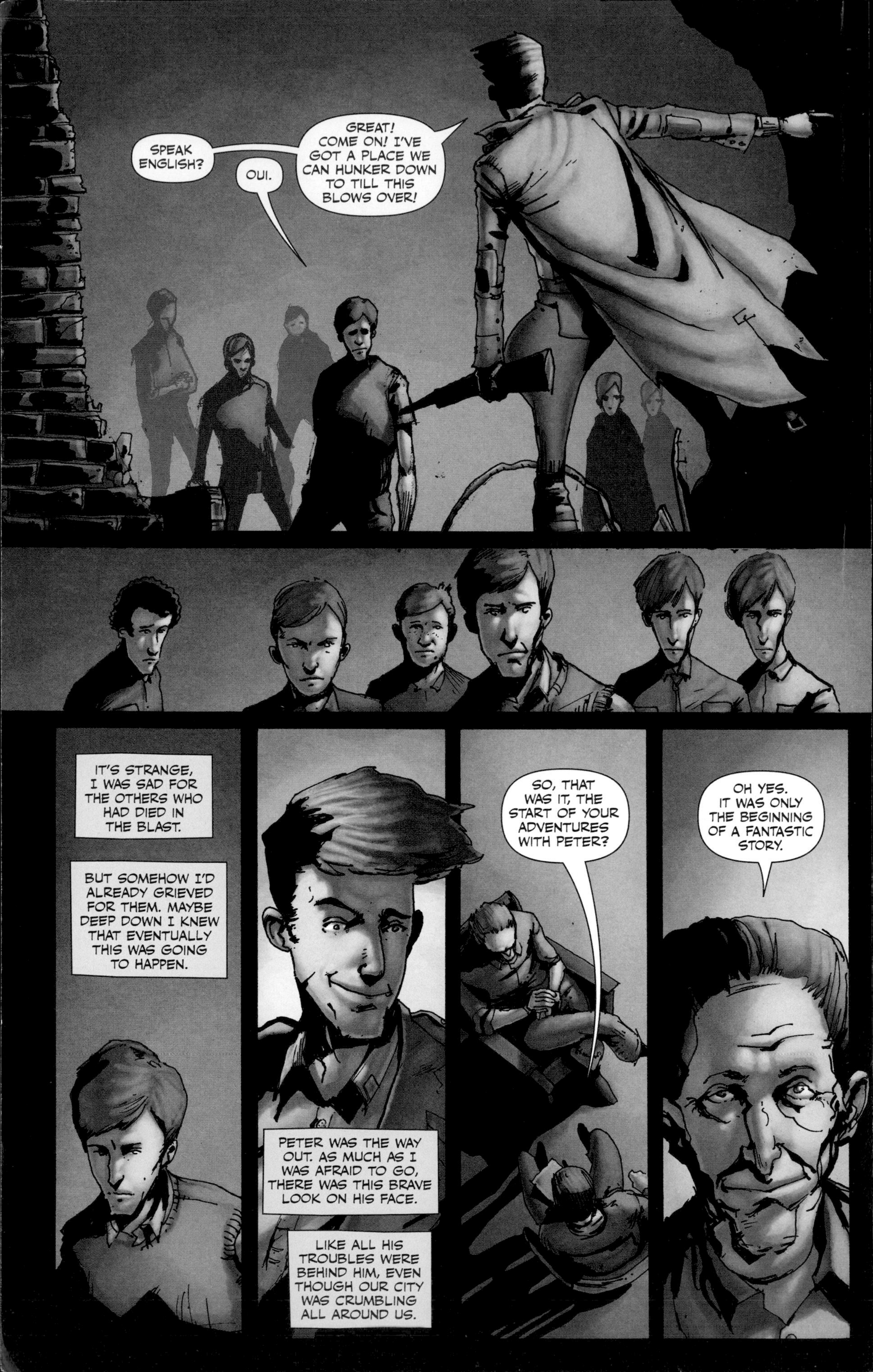
SPEAK ENGLISH?
OUI.
GREAT! COME ON! I'VE GOT A PLACE WE CAN HUNKER DOWN TO TILL THIS BLOWS OVER!
IT'S STRANGE, I WAS SAD FOR THE OTHERS WHO HAD DIED IN THE BLAST.
BUT SOMEHOW I'D ALREADY GRIEVED FOR THEM. MAYBE DEEP DOWN I KNEW THAT EVENTUALLY THIS WAS GOING TO HAPPEN.
PETER WAS THE WAY OUT. AS MUCH AS I WAS AFRAID TO GO, THERE WAS THIS BRAVE LOOK ON HIS FACE.
LIKE ALL HIS TROUBLES WERE BEHIND HIM, EVEN THOUGH OUR CITY WAS CRUMBLING ALL AROUND US.
SO, THAT WAS IT, THE START OF YOUR ADVENTURES WITH PETER?
OH YES. IT WAS ONLY THE BEGINNING OF A FANTASTIC STORY.

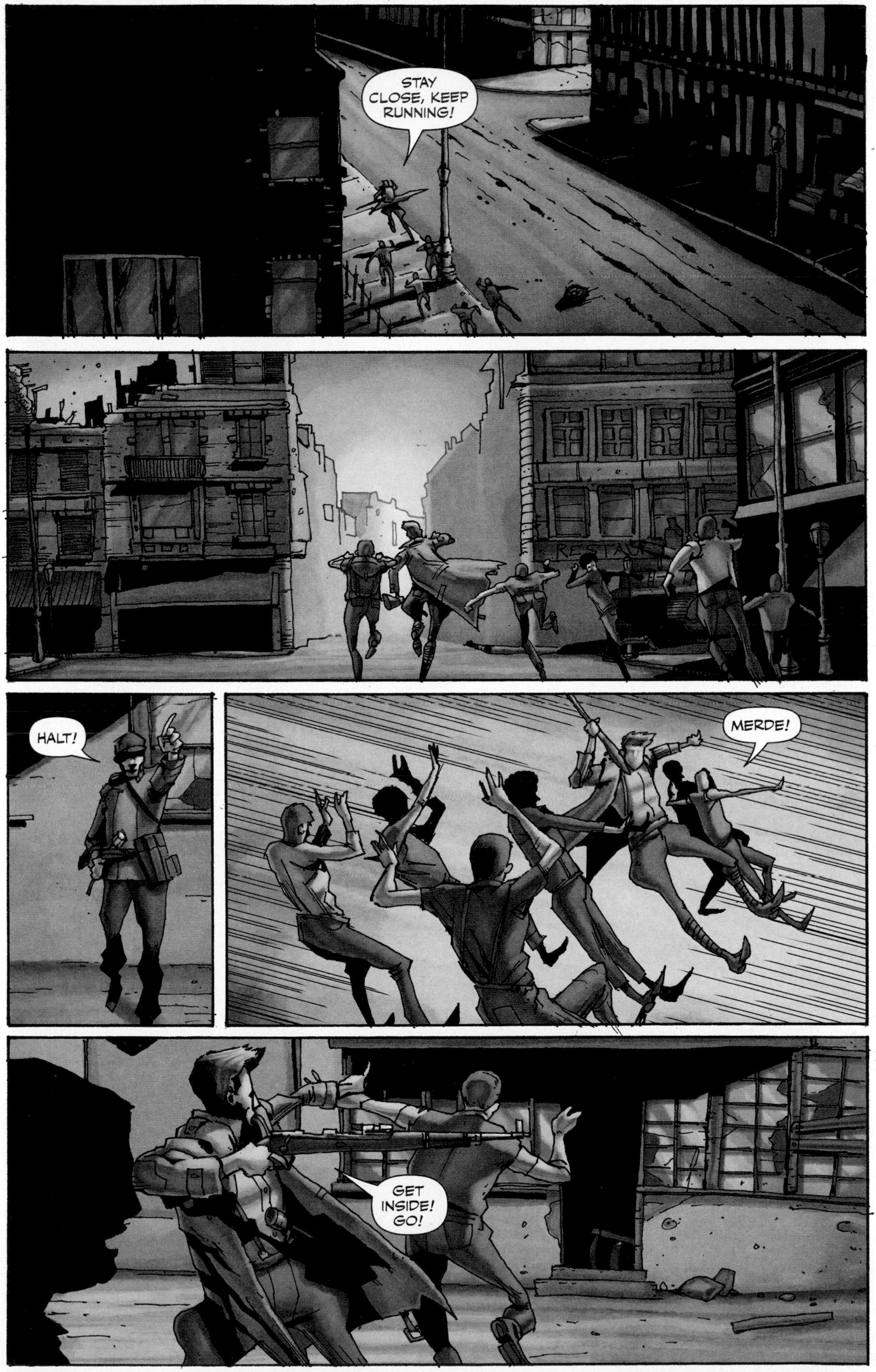
STAY CLOSE, KEEP RUNNING!
RESTAU
HALT!
MERDE!
GET INSIDE! GO!

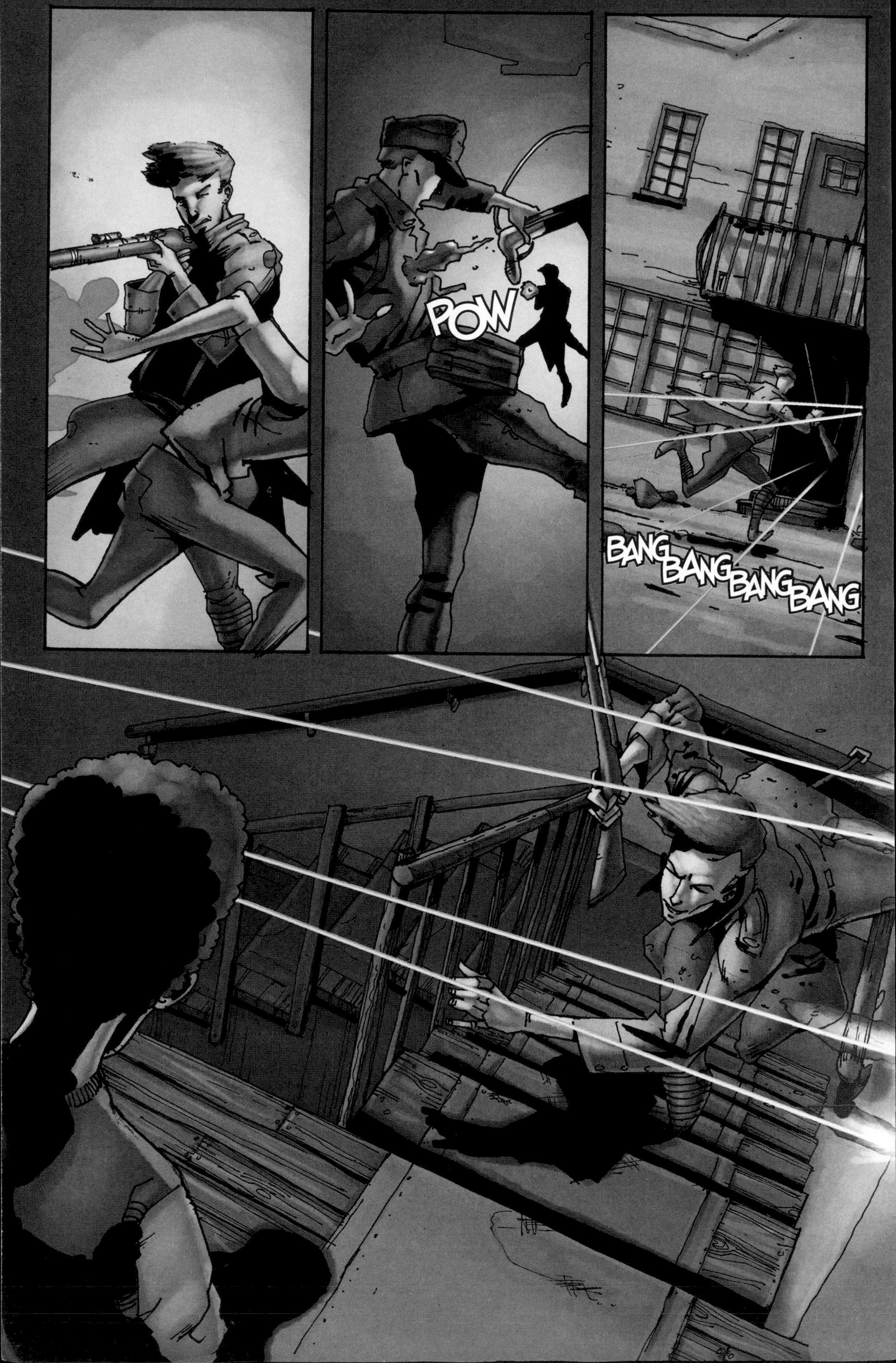
POW
BANG BANG BANG BANG

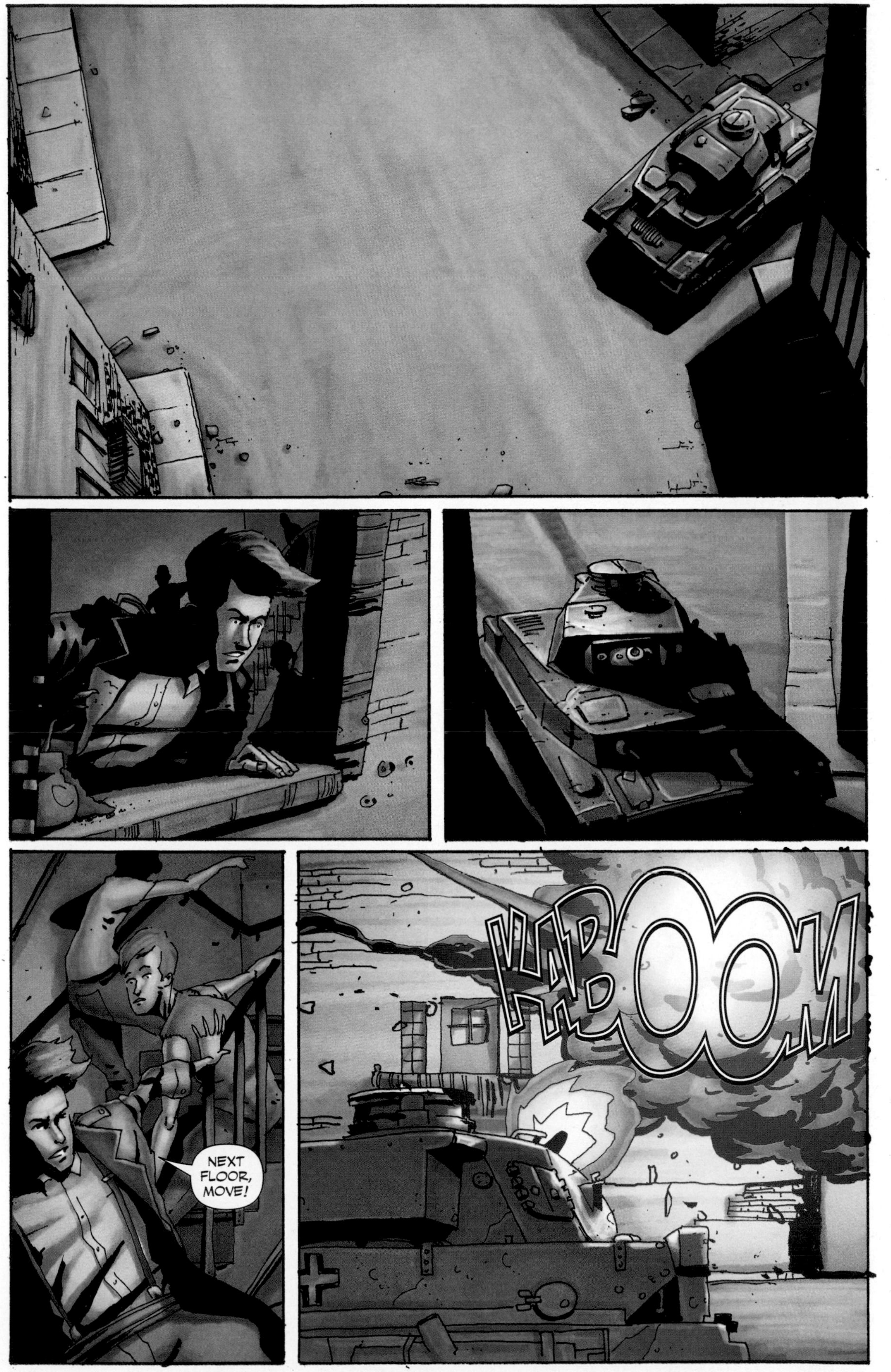
NEXT FLOOR, MOVE!
KABOOM

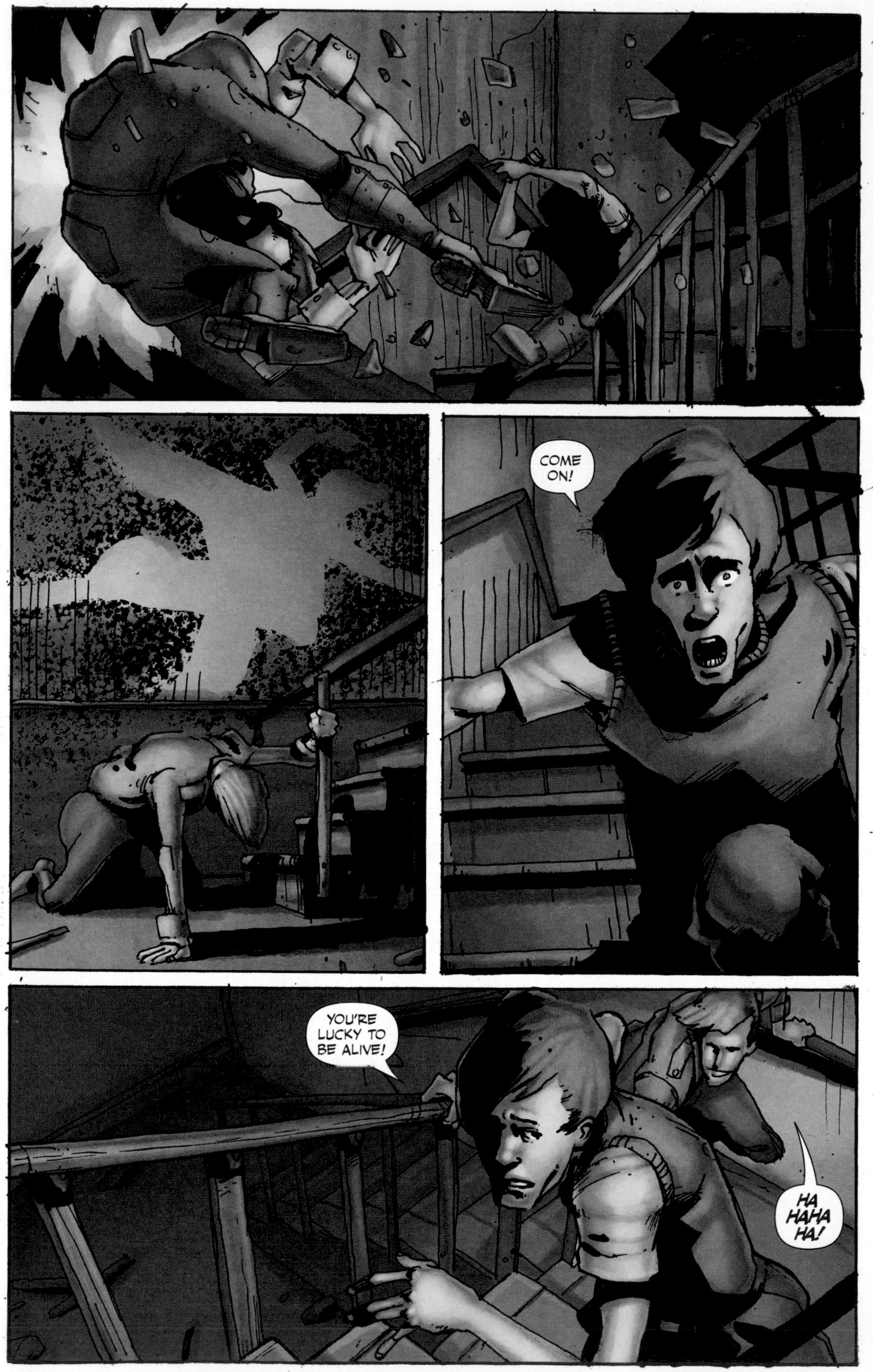
COME ON!
YOU'RE LUCKY TO BE ALIVE!
HA HAHAHA HA!

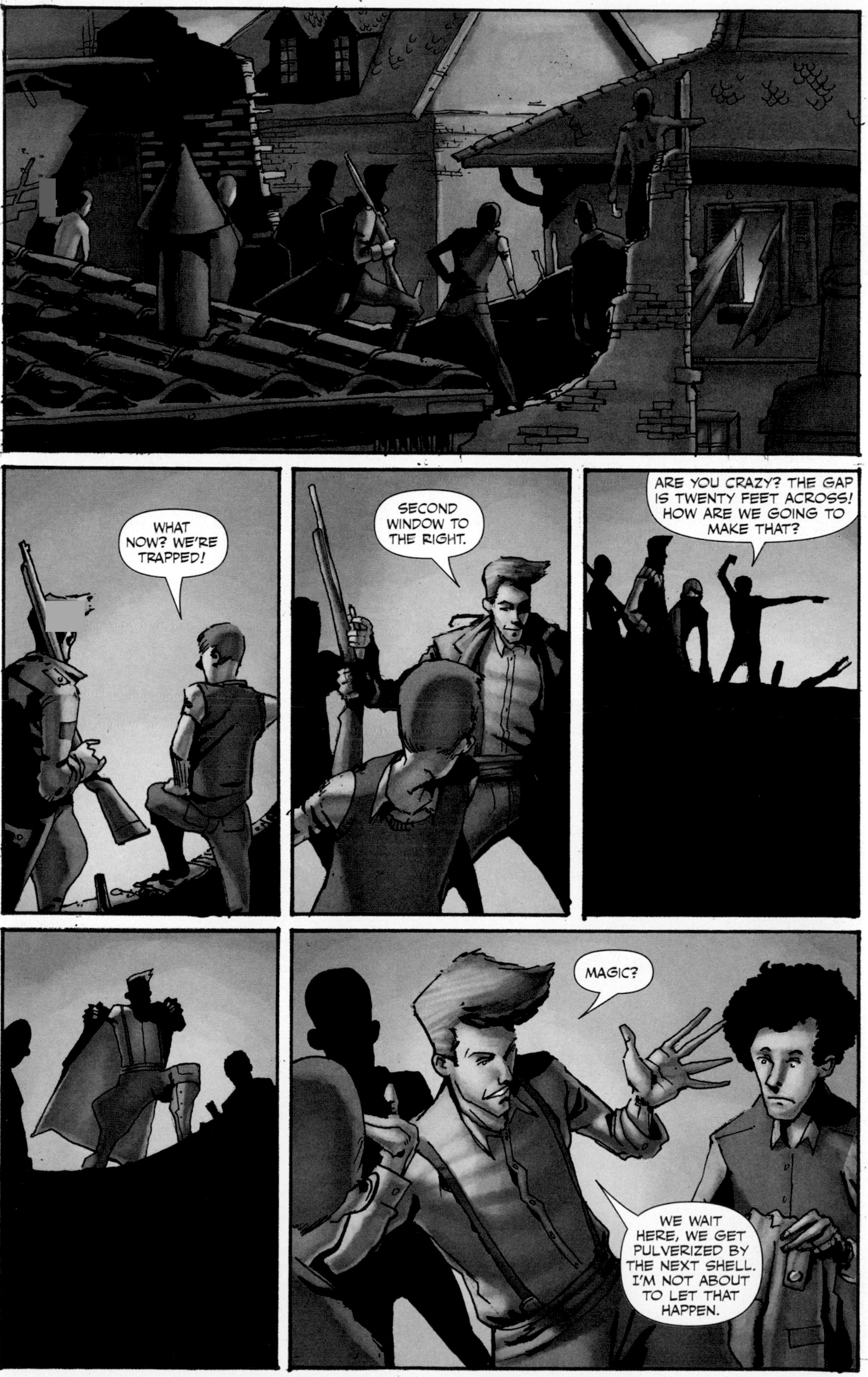
WHAT NOW? WE'RE TRAPPED!
SECOND WINDOW TO THE RIGHT.
ARE YOU CRAZY? THE GAP IS TWENTY FEET ACROSS! HOW ARE WE GOING TO MAKE THAT?
MAGIC?
WE WAIT HERE, WE GET PULVERIZED BY THE NEXT SHELL. I'M NOT ABOUT TO LET THAT HAPPEN.

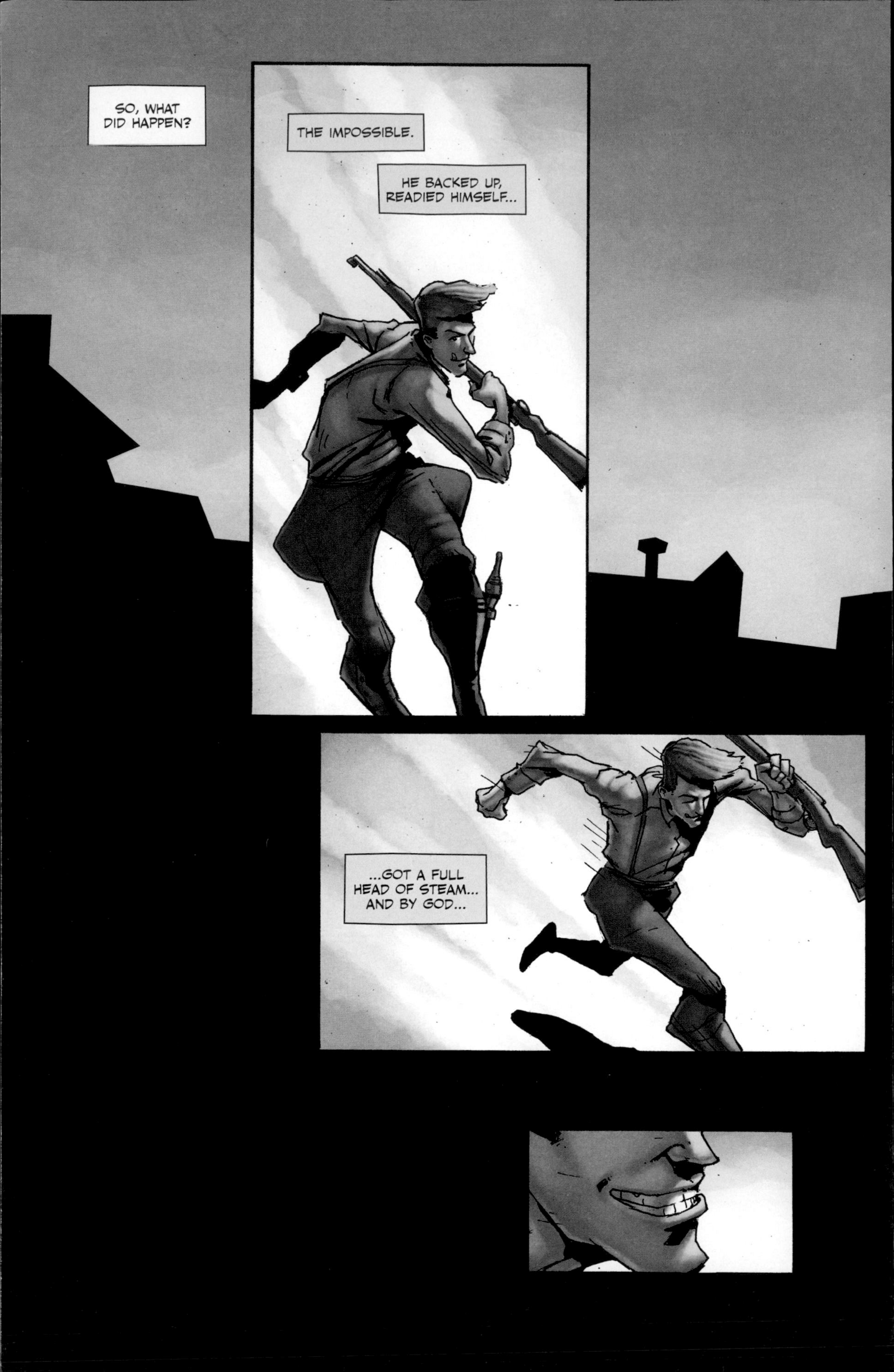
SO, WHAT DID HAPPEN?
THE IMPOSSIBLE.
HE BACKED UP, READIED HIMSELF...
...GOT A FULL HEAD OF STEAM... AND BY GOD...

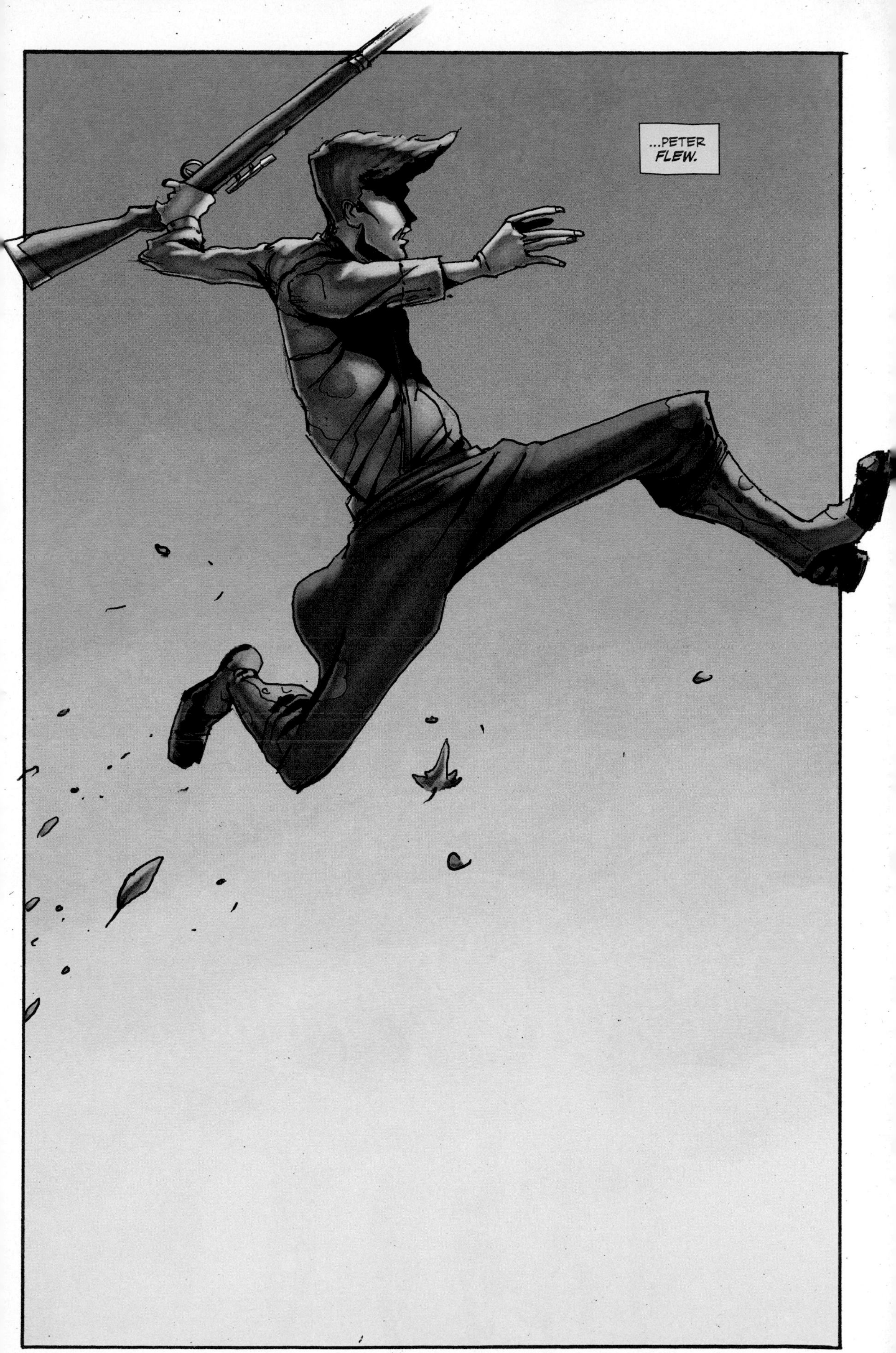
...PETER FLEW.

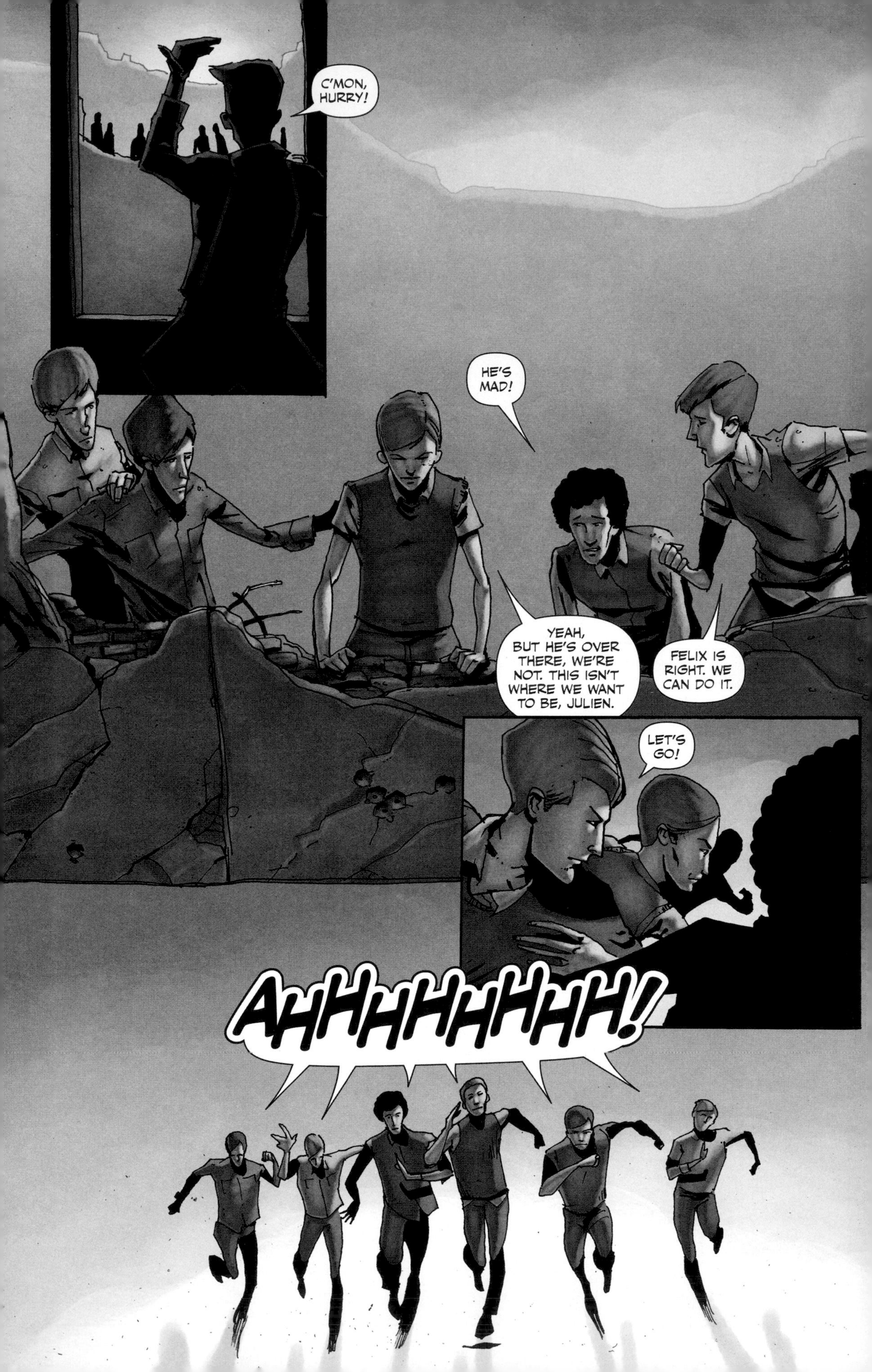
C'MON, HURRY!
HE'S MAD!
YEAH, BUT HE'S OVER THERE, WE'RE NOT. THIS ISN'T WHERE WE WANT TO BE, JULIEN.
FELIX IS RIGHT. WE CAN DO IT.
LET'S GO!
AHHHHHHHH!

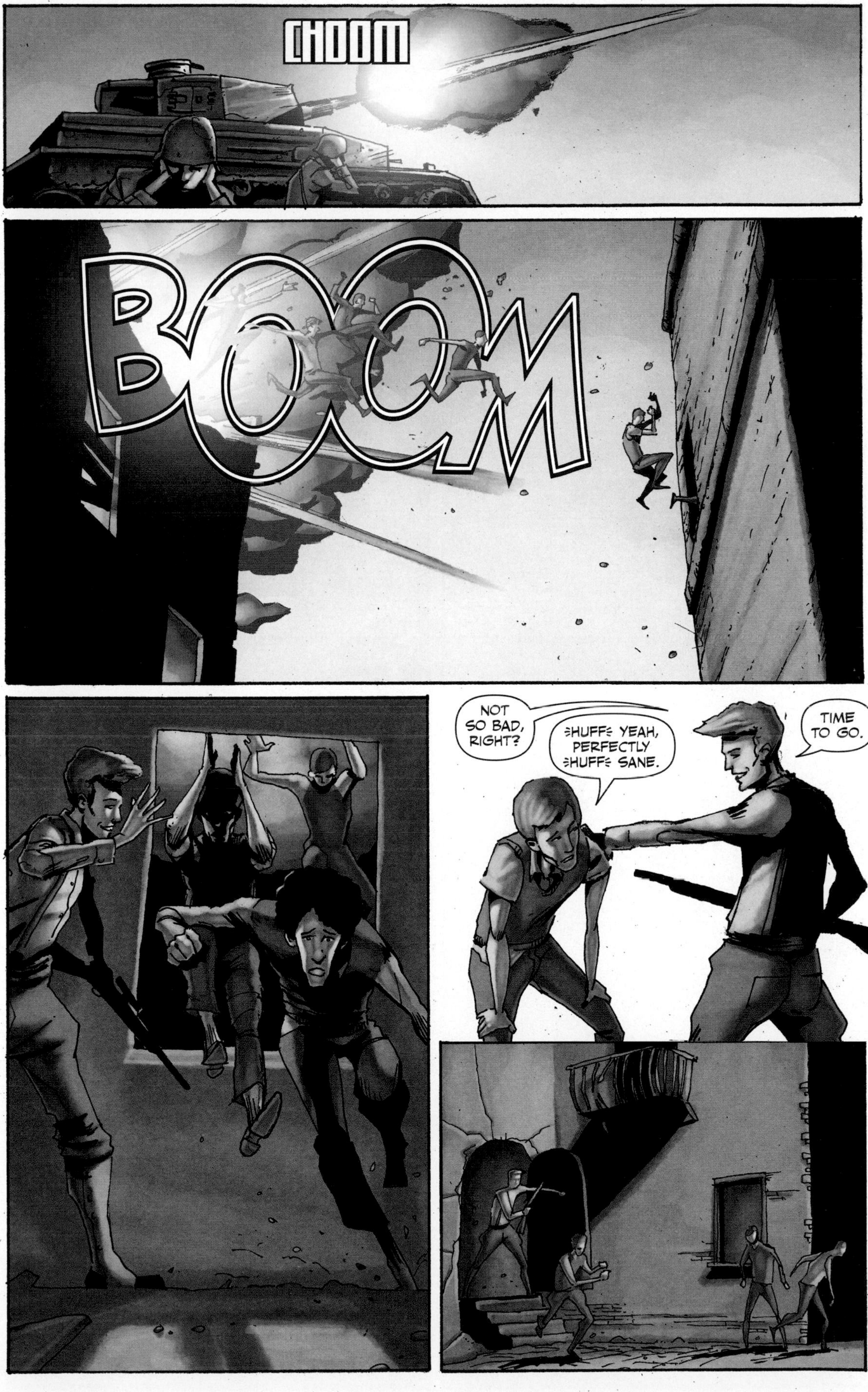
CHOOM
BOOM
NOT SO BAD, RIGHT?
=HUFF= YEAH, PERFECTLY =HUFF= SANE.
TIME TO GO.

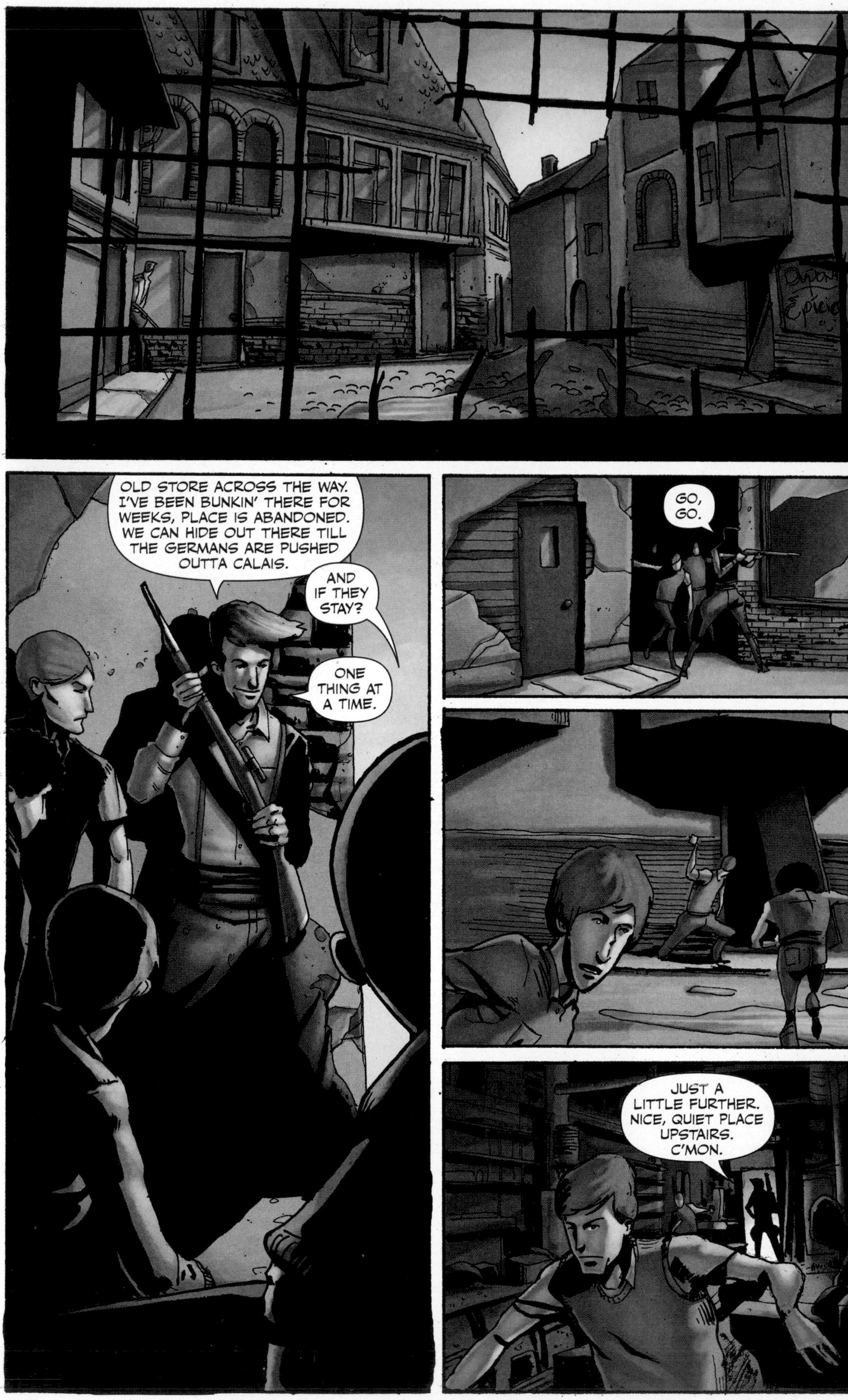
OLD STORE ACROSS THE WAY. I'VE BEEN BUNKIN' THERE FOR WEEKS, PLACE IS ABANDONED. WE CAN HIDE OUT THERE TILL THE GERMANS ARE PUSHED OUTTA CALAIS.
AND IF THEY STAY?
ONE THING AT A TIME.
GO, GO.
JUST A LITTLE FURTHER. NICE, QUIET PLACE UPSTAIRS. C'MON.

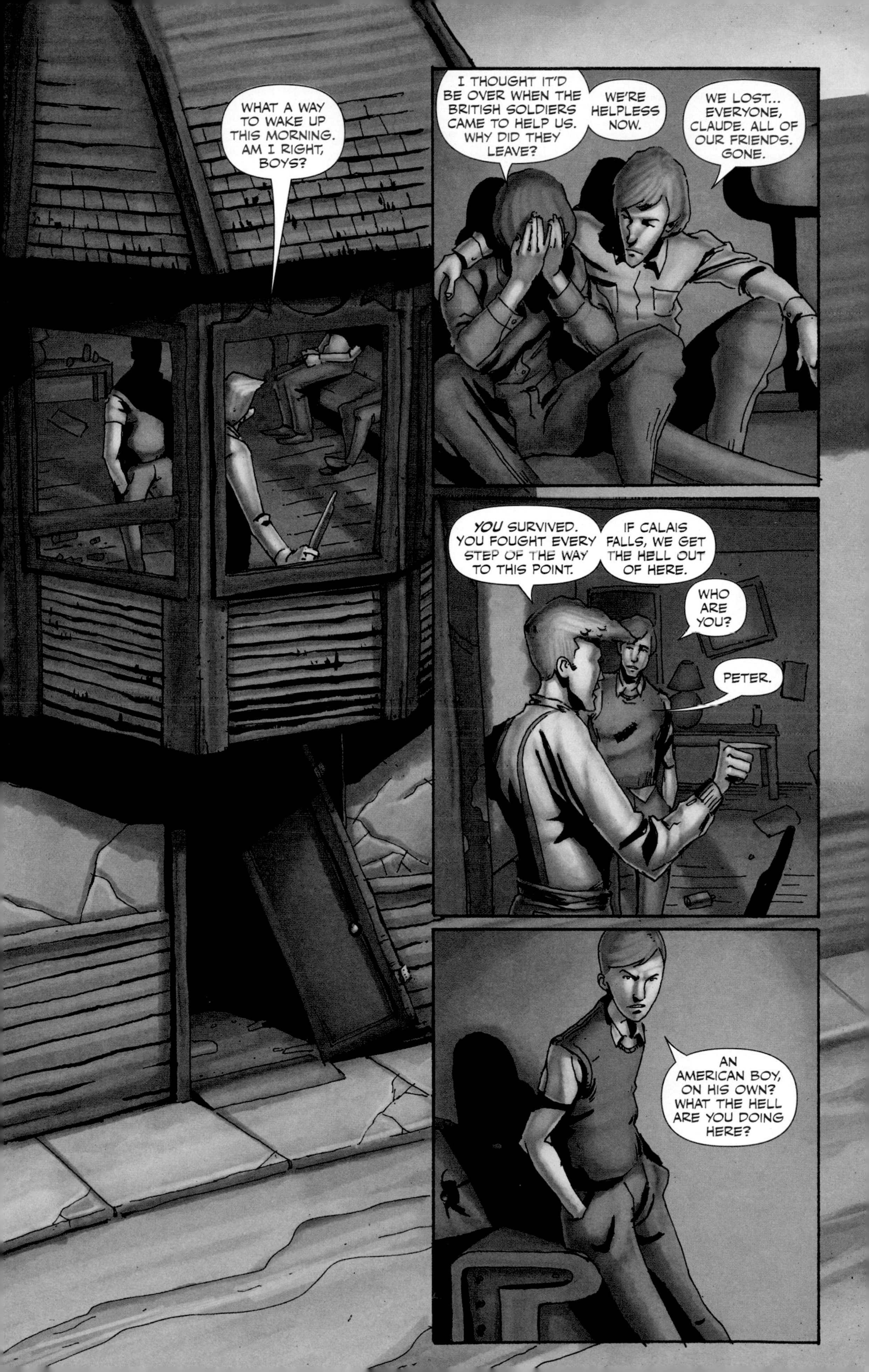
WHAT A WAY TO WAKE UP THIS MORNING. AM I RIGHT, BOYS?
I THOUGHT IT'D BE OVER WHEN THE BRITISH SOLDIERS CAME TO HELP US. WHY DID THEY LEAVE?
WE'RE HELPLESS NOW.
WE LOST... EVERYONE, CLAUDE. ALL OF OUR FRIENDS. GONE.
YOU SURVIVED. YOU FOUGHT EVERY STEP OF THE WAY TO THIS POINT.
IF CALAIS FALLS, WE GET THE HELL OUT OF HERE.
WHO ARE YOU?
PETER.
AN AMERICAN BOY, ON HIS OWN? WHAT THE HELL ARE YOU DOING HERE?

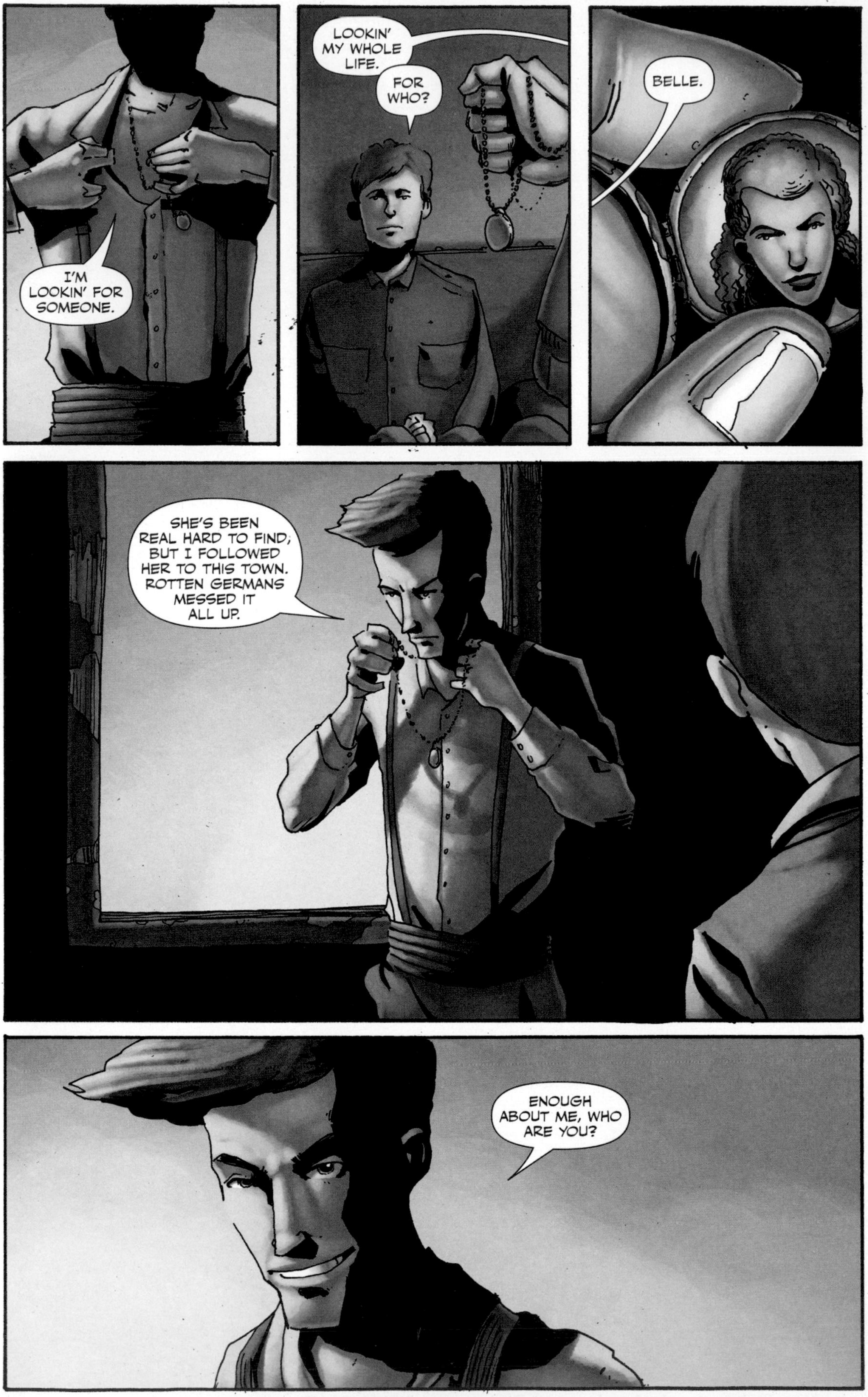
I'M LOOKIN' FOR SOMEONE.
LOOKIN' MY WHOLE LIFE.
FOR WHO?
BELLE.
SHE'S BEEN REAL HARD TO FIND; BUT I FOLLOWED HER TO THIS TOWN. ROTTEN GERMANS MESSED IT ALL UP.
ENOUGH ABOUT ME, WHO ARE YOU?

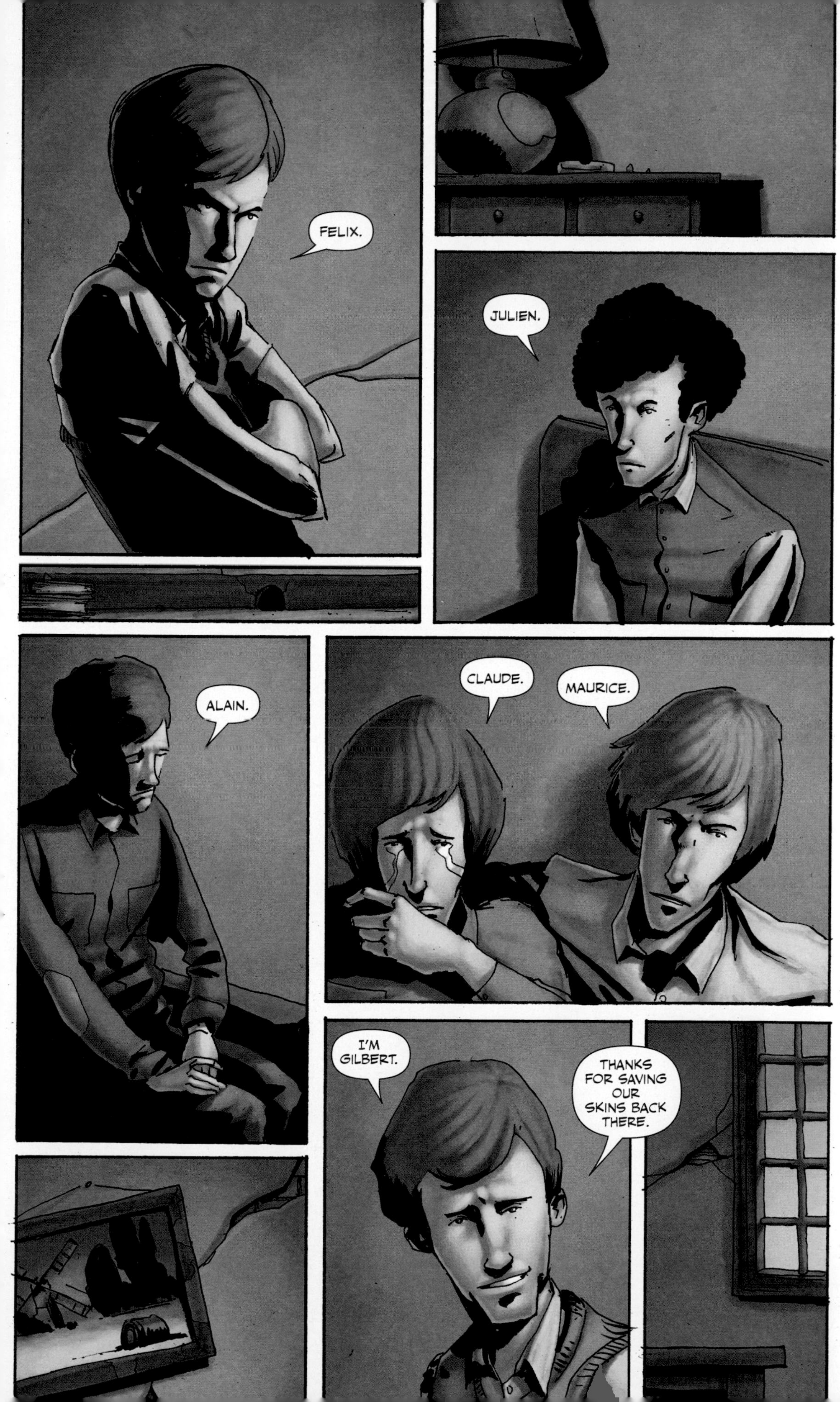
FELIX.
JULIEN.
ALAIN.
CLAUDE.
MAURICE.
I'M GILBERT.
THANKS FOR SAVING OUR SKINS BACK THERE.

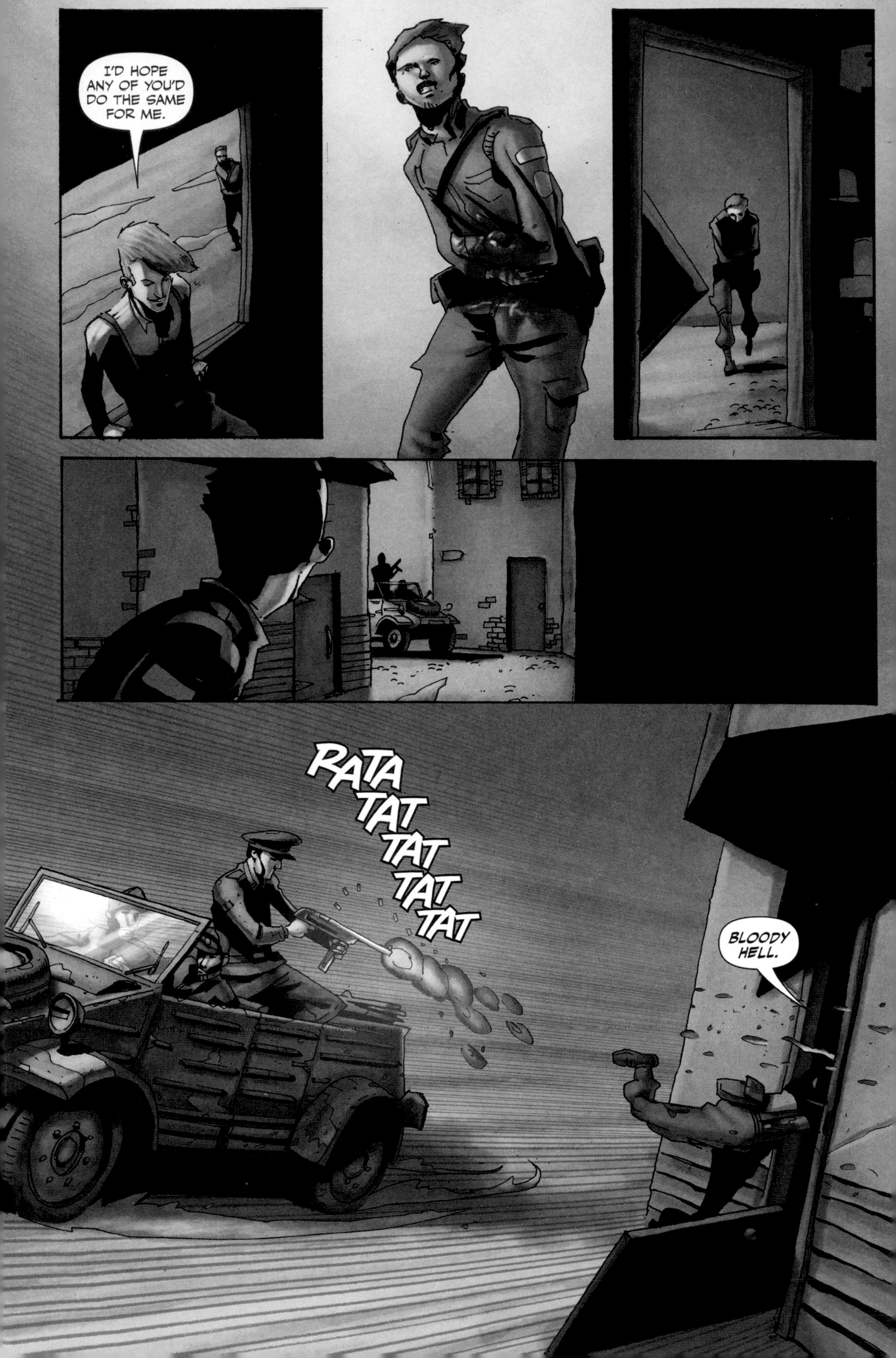
I'D HOPE ANY OF YOU'D DO THE SAME FOR ME.
RATA TAT TAT TAT TAT
BLOODY HELL.

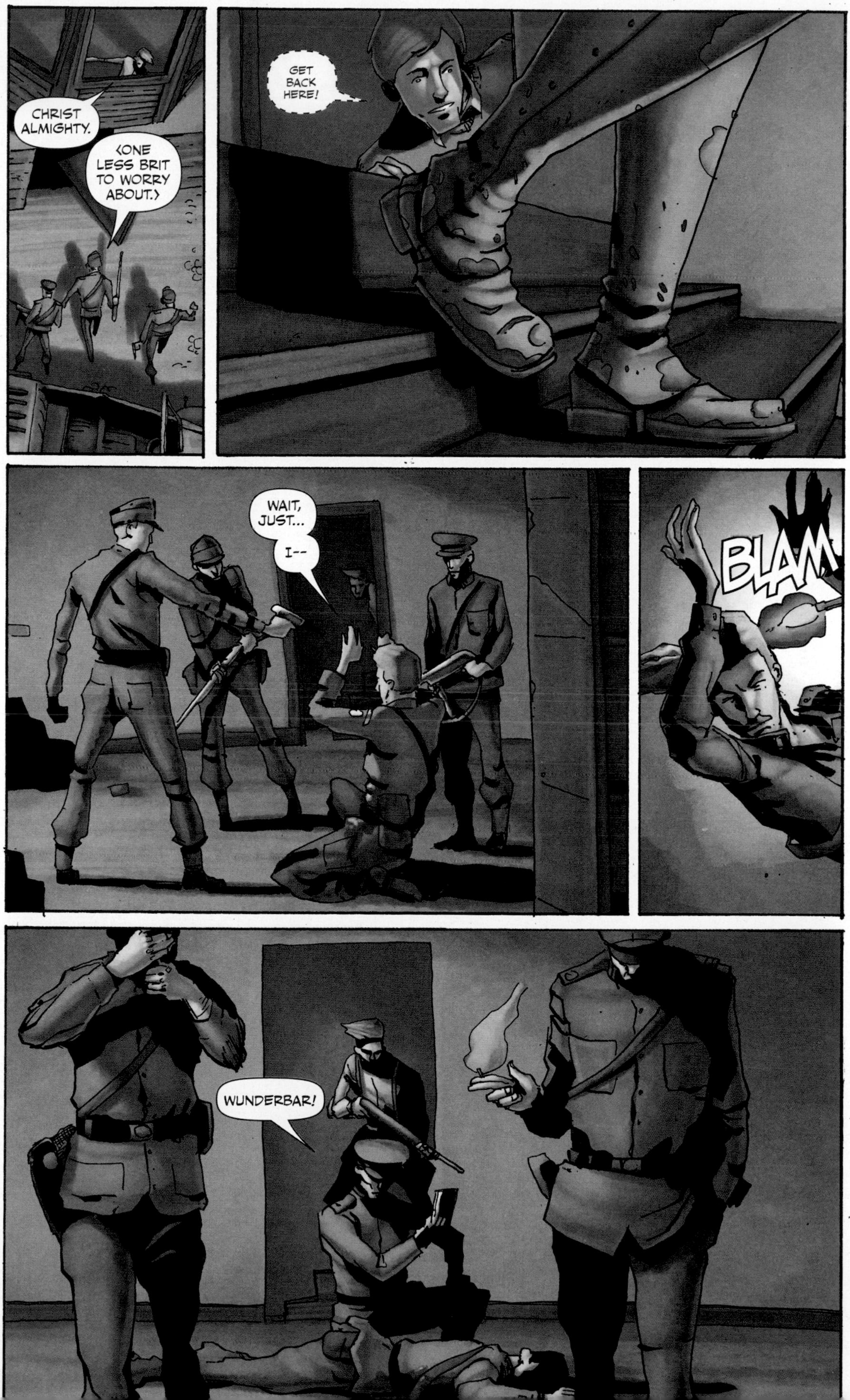
CHRIST ALMIGHTY.
<ONE LESS BRIT TO WORRY ABOUT.>
GET BACK HERE!
WAIT, JUST...
I--
BLAM
WUNDERBAR!

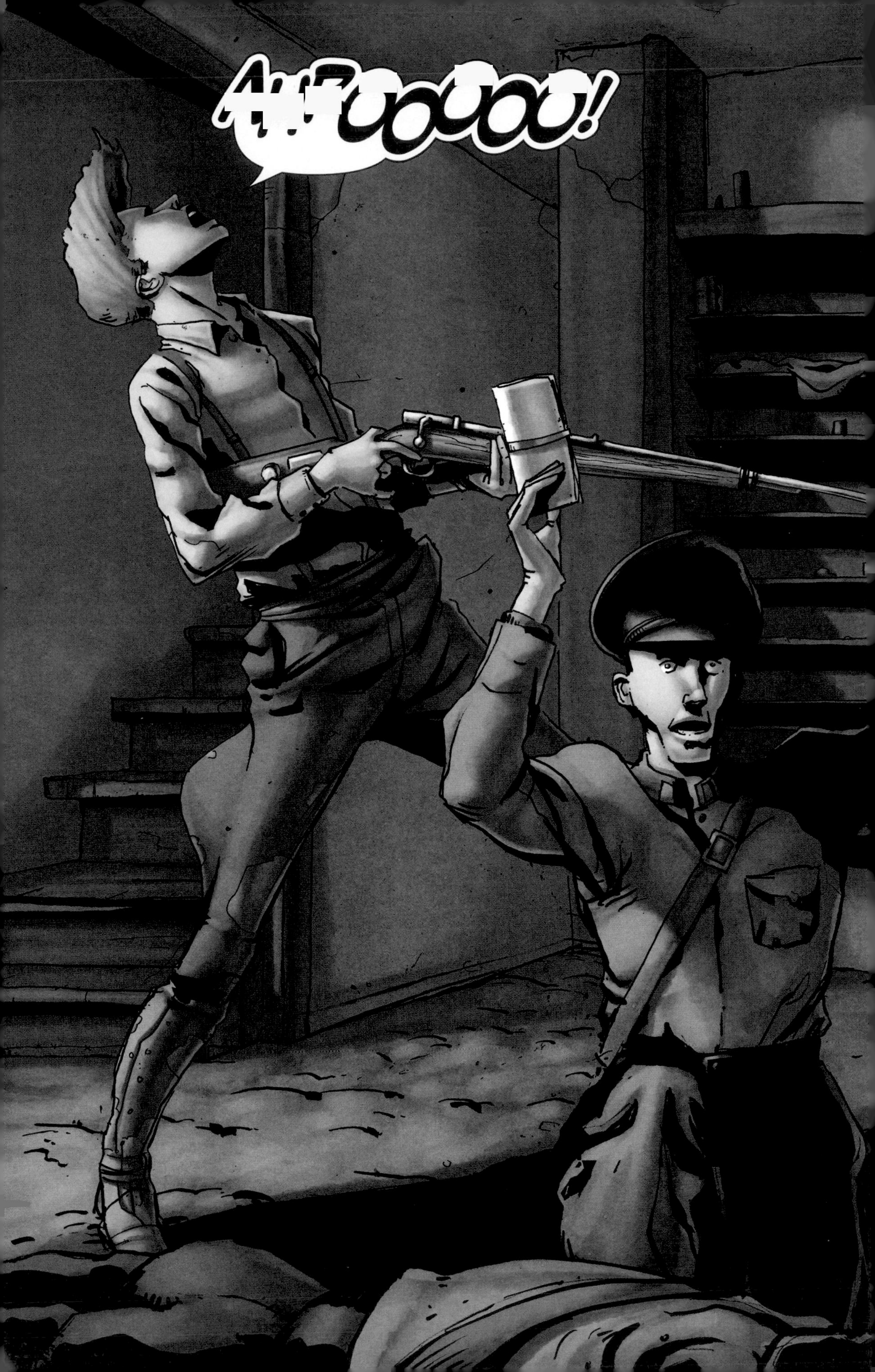

CHAPTER TWO

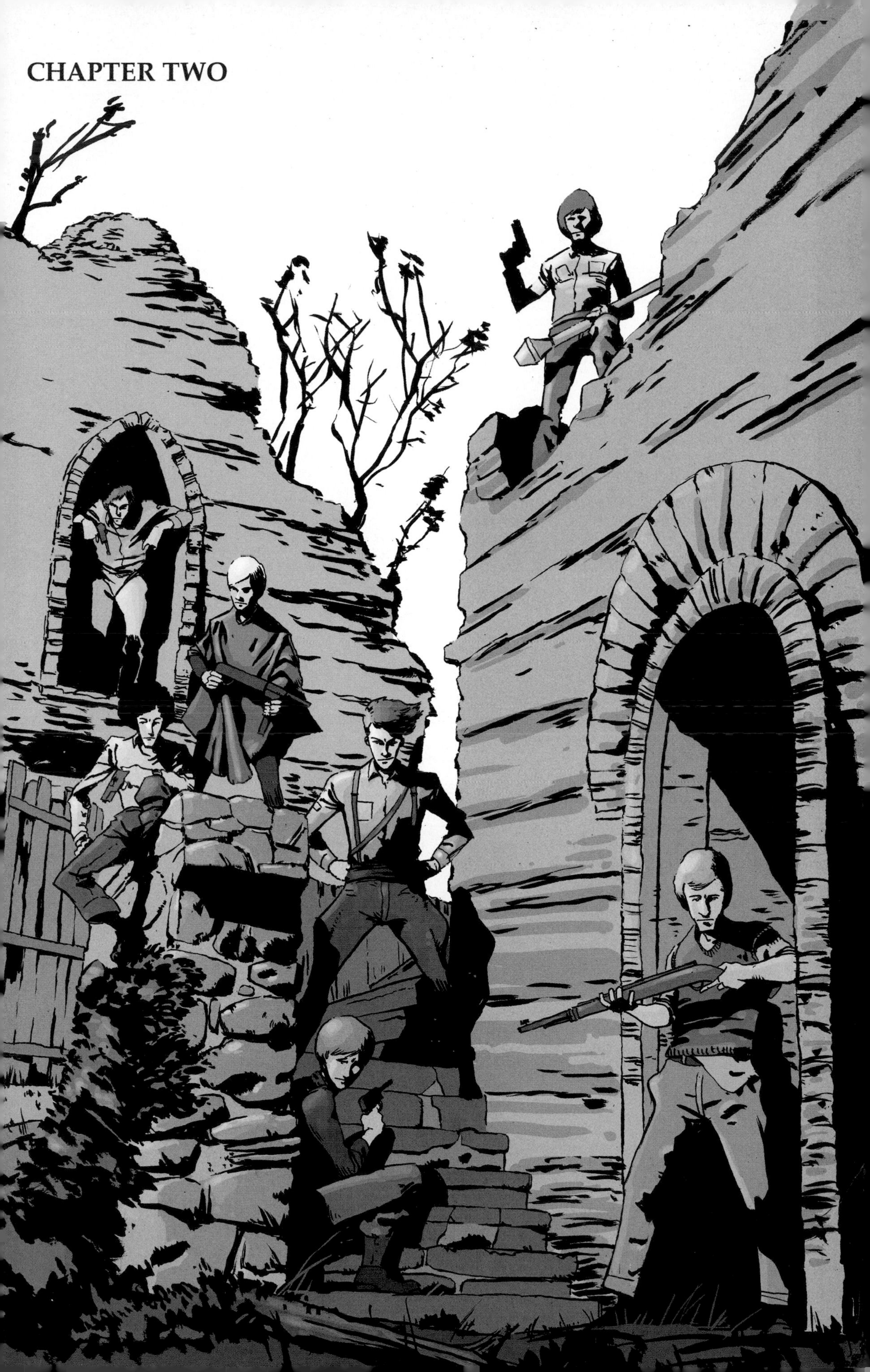

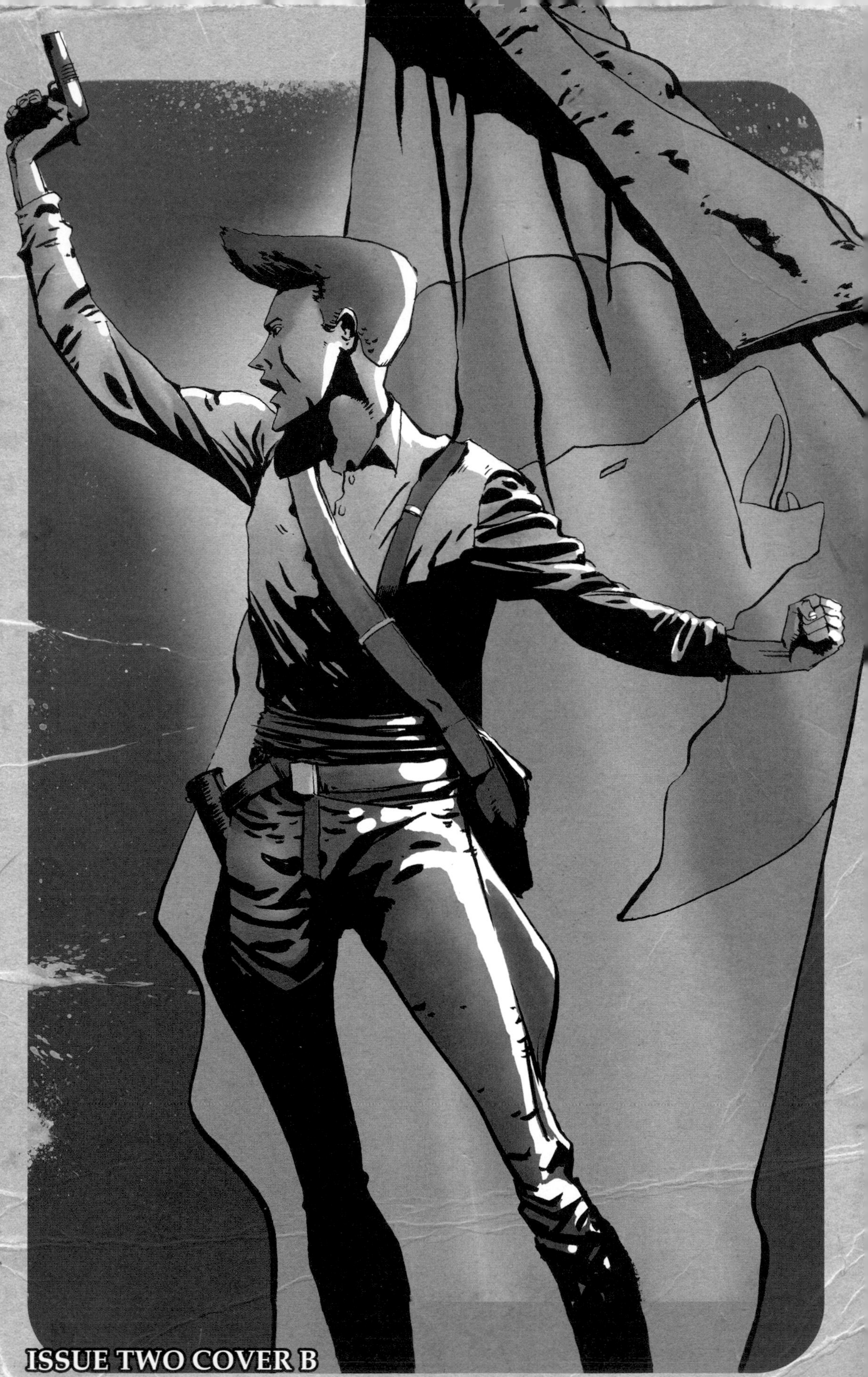

ISSUE TWO COVER B

ANY IDEA WHY HE DID THE WOLF CRY?

HAH, HE WAS A BIT OF A BRAGGART, I'M AFRAID. IT BECAME A SORT OF SYMBOL LATER, A CALLING CARD TO LET THE NAZIS KNOW WE WERE COMING.

HOW DID HIS ACTIONS MAKE YOU FEEL?

ALIVE. ... SCARED, BUT SO ALIVE.

I NEVER FELT TRULY SAFE WITH HIM. HE WAS AN ERRATIC YOUNG MAN. I...

HMM.

HAVE YOU EVER BEEN CHASED BY A DOG?

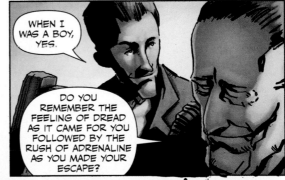

WHEN I WAS A BOY, YES.

DO YOU REMEMBER THE FEELING OF DREAD AS IT CAME FOR YOU FOLLOWED BY THE RUSH OF ADRENALINE AS YOU MADE YOUR ESCAPE?

HAH! I DO, ACTUALLY.

THAT IS WHAT BEING AROUND PETER WAS LIKE, MR. PARSONS...

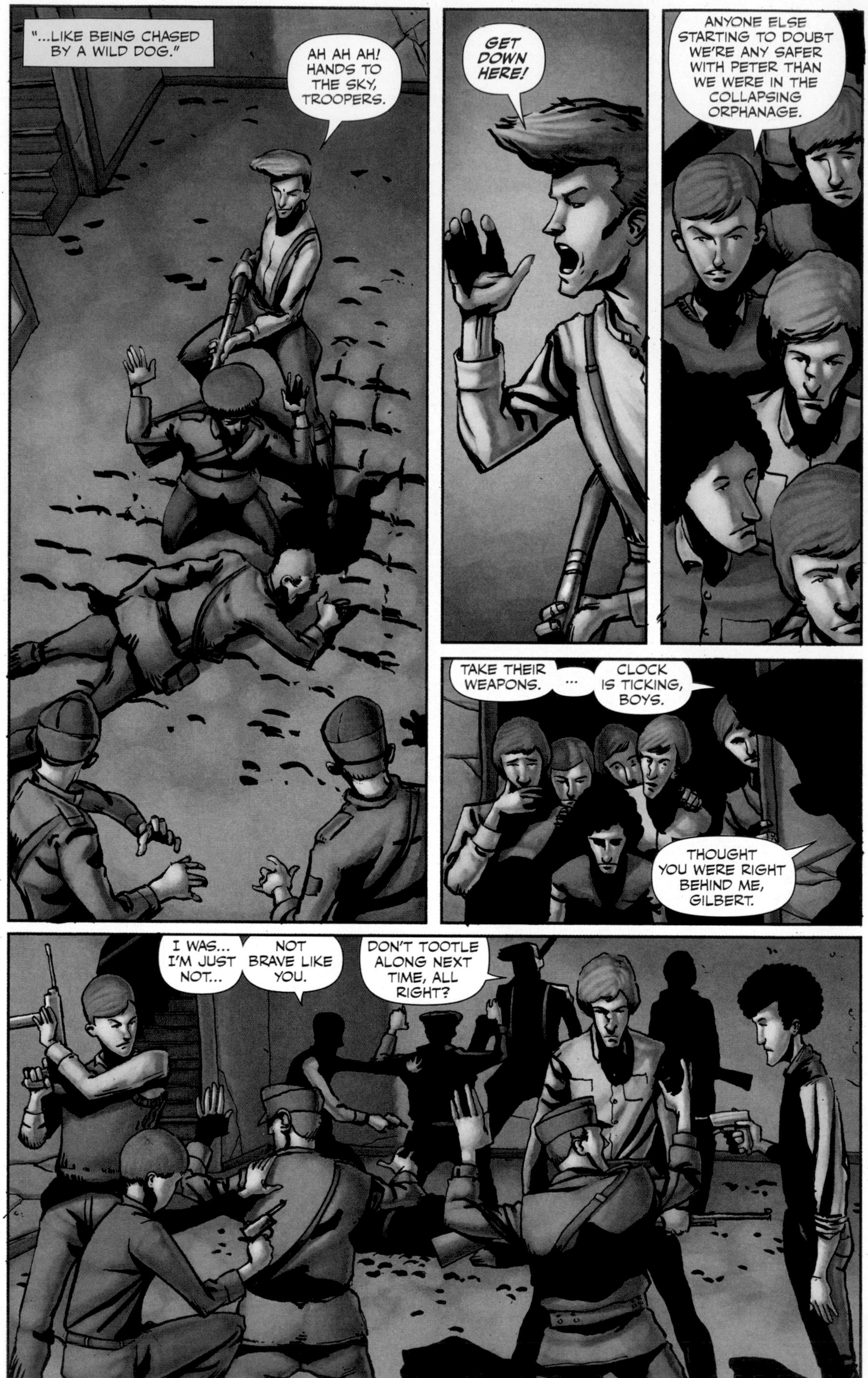
"...LIKE BEING CHASED BY A WILD DOG."
AH AH AH! HANDS TO THE SKY, TROOPERS.
GET DOWN HERE!
ANYONE ELSE STARTING TO DOUBT WE'RE ANY SAFER WITH PETER THAN WE WERE IN THE COLLAPSING ORPHANAGE.
TAKE THEIR WEAPONS.
...
CLOCK IS TICKING, BOYS.
THOUGHT YOU WERE RIGHT BEHIND ME, GILBERT.
I WAS... I'M JUST NOT...
NOT BRAVE LIKE YOU.
DON'T TOOTLE ALONG NEXT TIME, ALL RIGHT?

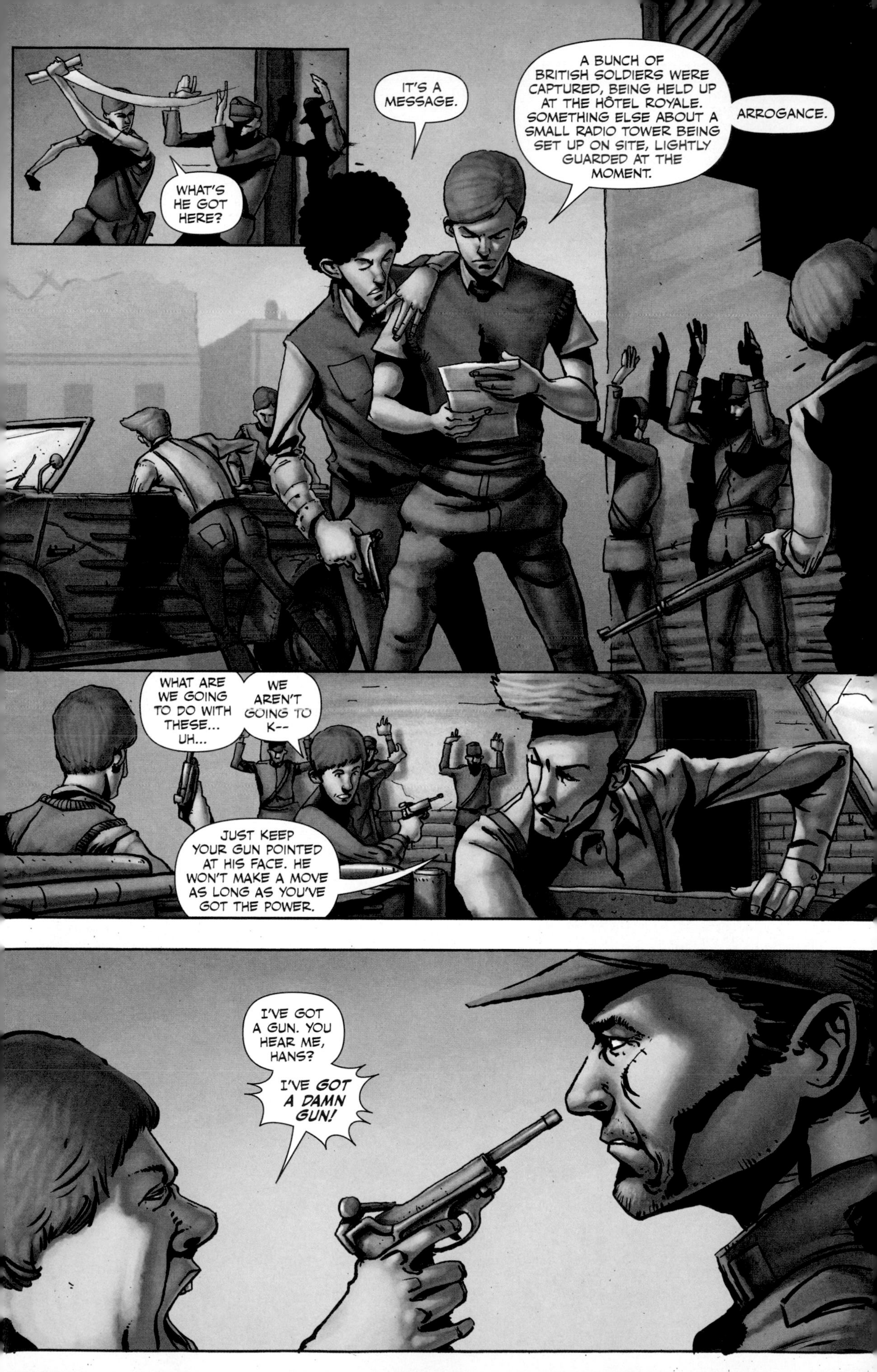
WHAT'S HE GOT HERE?
IT'S A MESSAGE.
A BUNCH OF BRITISH SOLDIERS WERE CAPTURED, BEING HELD UP AT THE HÔTEL ROYALE. SOMETHING ELSE ABOUT A SMALL RADIO TOWER BEING SET UP ON SITE, LIGHTLY GUARDED AT THE MOMENT.
ARROGANCE.
WHAT ARE WE GOING TO DO WITH THESE... UH...
WE AREN'T GOING TO K--
JUST KEEP YOUR GUN POINTED AT HIS FACE. HE WON'T MAKE A MOVE AS LONG AS YOU'VE GOT THE POWER.
I'VE GOT A GUN. YOU HEAR ME, HANS?
I'VE *GOT A DAMN GUN!*

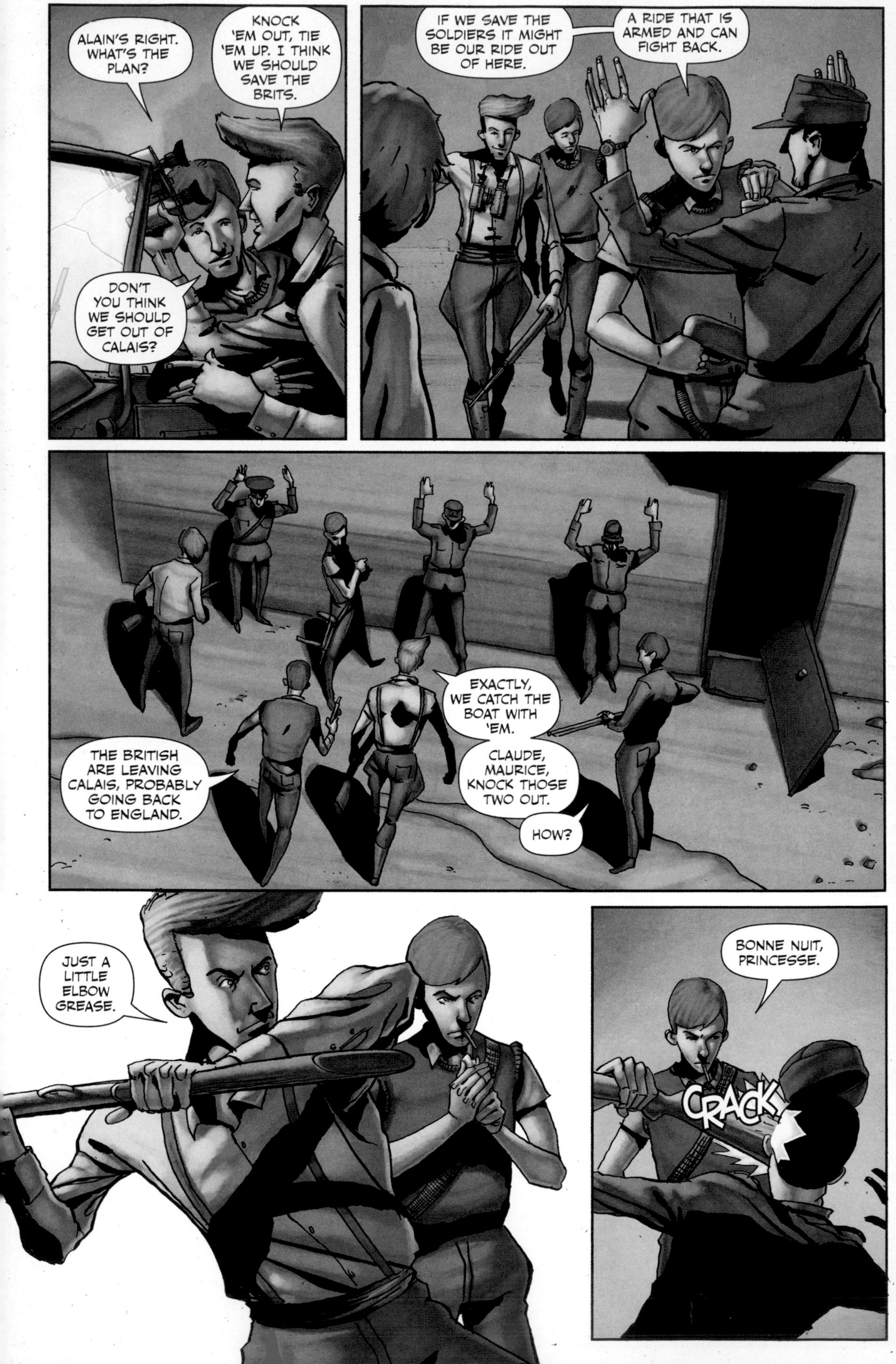
ALAIN'S RIGHT. WHAT'S THE PLAN?
KNOCK 'EM OUT, TIE 'EM UP. I THINK WE SHOULD SAVE THE BRITS.
DON'T YOU THINK WE SHOULD GET OUT OF CALAIS?
IF WE SAVE THE SOLDIERS IT MIGHT BE OUR RIDE OUT OF HERE.
A RIDE THAT IS ARMED AND CAN FIGHT BACK.
THE BRITISH ARE LEAVING CALAIS, PROBABLY GOING BACK TO ENGLAND.
EXACTLY, WE CATCH THE BOAT WITH 'EM.
CLAUDE, MAURICE, KNOCK THOSE TWO OUT.
HOW?
JUST A LITTLE ELBOW GREASE.
BONNE NUIT, PRINCESSE.
CRACK!

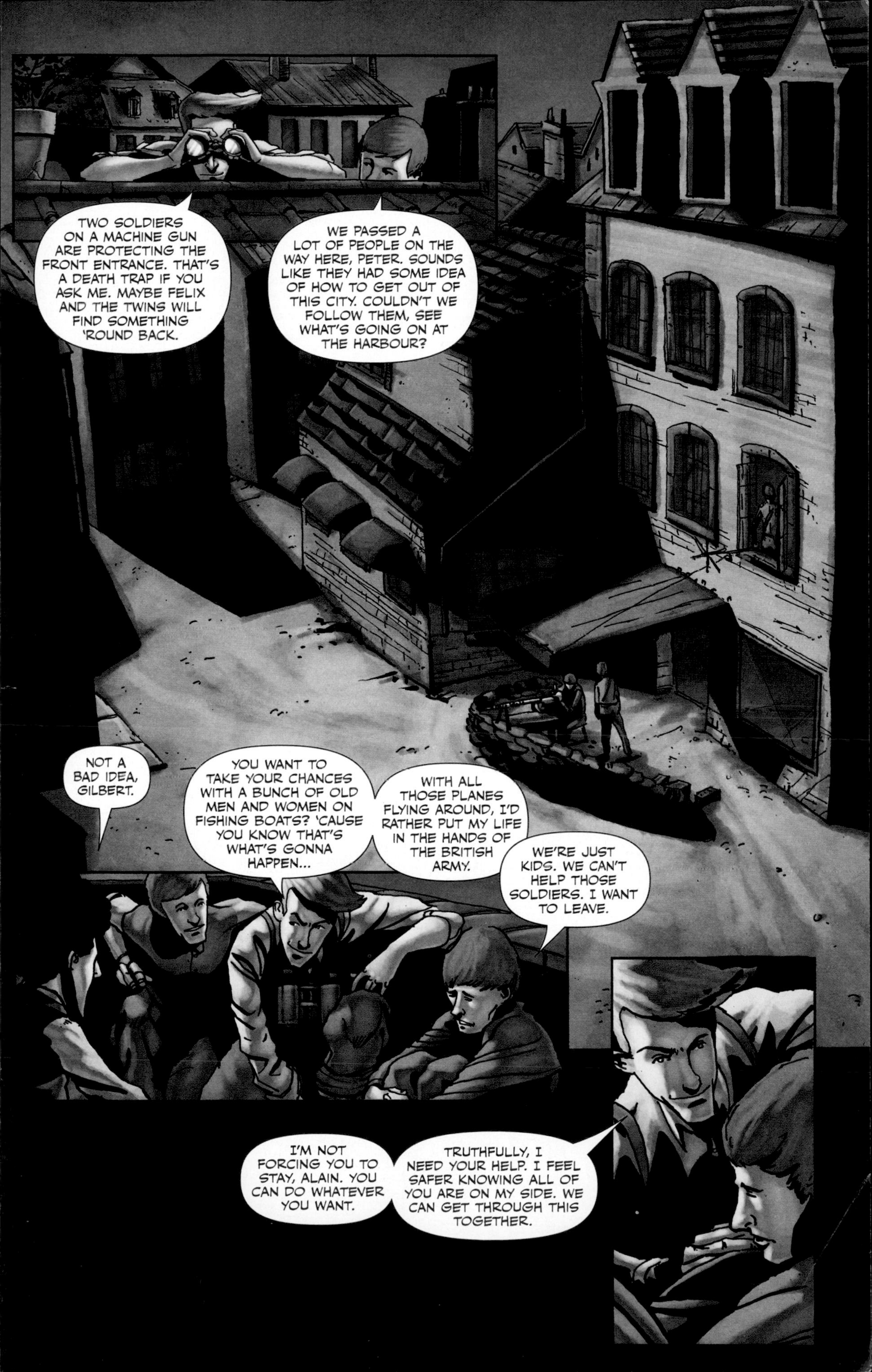
TWO SOLDIERS ON A MACHINE GUN ARE PROTECTING THE FRONT ENTRANCE. THAT'S A DEATH TRAP IF YOU ASK ME. MAYBE FELIX AND THE TWINS WILL FIND SOMETHING 'ROUND BACK.
WE PASSED A LOT OF PEOPLE ON THE WAY HERE, PETER. SOUNDS LIKE THEY HAD SOME IDEA OF HOW TO GET OUT OF THIS CITY. COULDN'T WE FOLLOW THEM, SEE WHAT'S GOING ON AT THE HARBOUR?
NOT A BAD IDEA, GILBERT.
YOU WANT TO TAKE YOUR CHANCES WITH A BUNCH OF OLD MEN AND WOMEN ON FISHING BOATS? 'CAUSE YOU KNOW THAT'S WHAT'S GONNA HAPPEN...
WITH ALL THOSE PLANES FLYING AROUND, I'D RATHER PUT MY LIFE IN THE HANDS OF THE BRITISH ARMY.
WE'RE JUST KIDS. WE CAN'T HELP THOSE SOLDIERS. I WANT TO LEAVE.
I'M NOT FORCING YOU TO STAY, ALAIN. YOU CAN DO WHATEVER YOU WANT.
TRUTHFULLY, I NEED YOUR HELP. I FEEL SAFER KNOWING ALL OF YOU ARE ON MY SIDE. WE CAN GET THROUGH THIS TOGETHER.

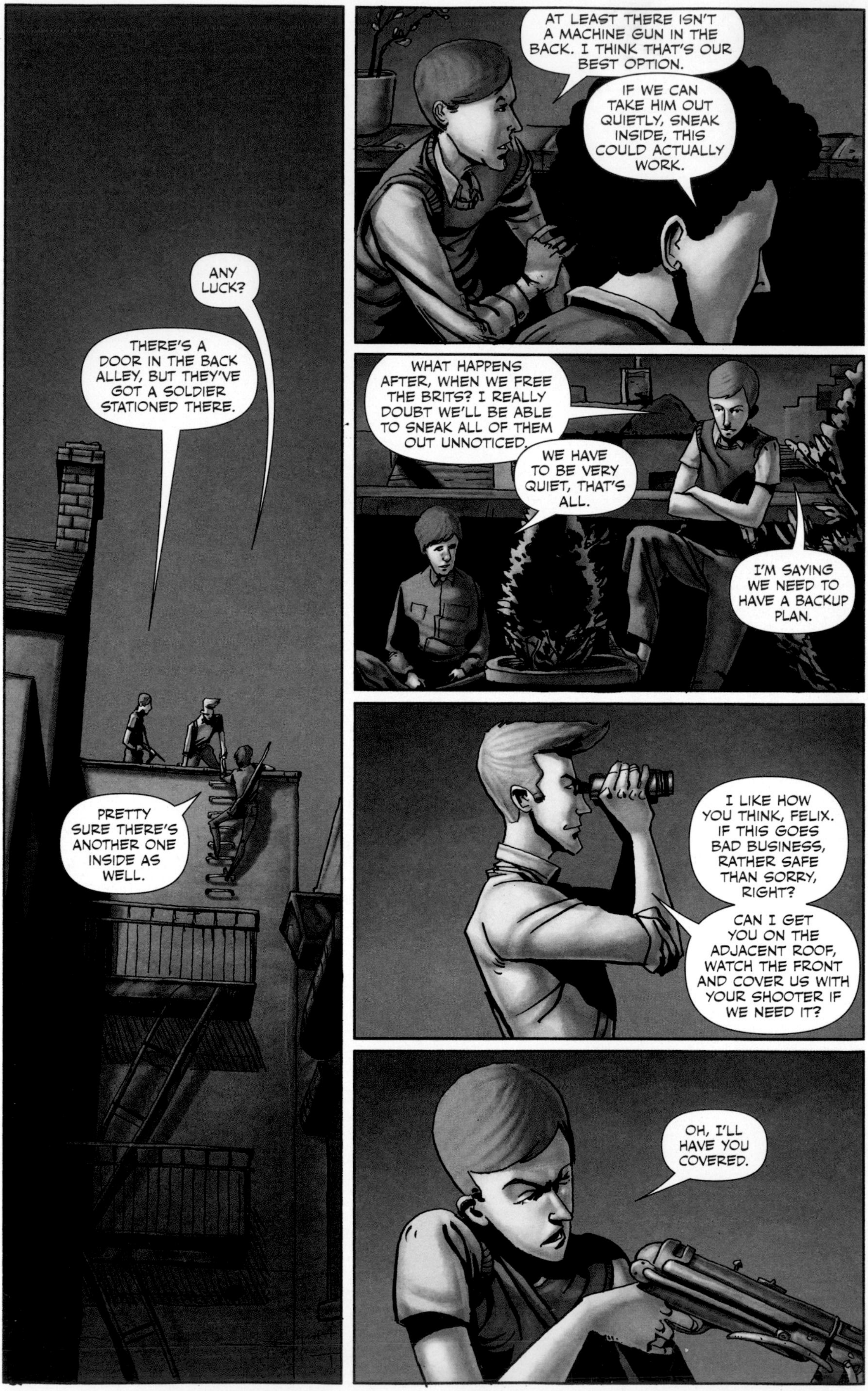
ANY LUCK?
THERE'S A DOOR IN THE BACK ALLEY, BUT THEY'VE GOT A SOLDIER STATIONED THERE.
PRETTY SURE THERE'S ANOTHER ONE INSIDE AS WELL.
AT LEAST THERE ISN'T A MACHINE GUN IN THE BACK. I THINK THAT'S OUR BEST OPTION.
IF WE CAN TAKE HIM OUT QUIETLY, SNEAK INSIDE, THIS COULD ACTUALLY WORK.
WHAT HAPPENS AFTER, WHEN WE FREE THE BRITS? I REALLY DOUBT WE'LL BE ABLE TO SNEAK ALL OF THEM OUT UNNOTICED.
WE HAVE TO BE VERY QUIET, THAT'S ALL.
I'M SAYING WE NEED TO HAVE A BACKUP PLAN.
I LIKE HOW YOU THINK, FELIX. IF THIS GOES BAD BUSINESS, RATHER SAFE THAN SORRY, RIGHT?
CAN I GET YOU ON THE ADJACENT ROOF, WATCH THE FRONT AND COVER US WITH YOUR SHOOTER IF WE NEED IT?
OH, I'LL HAVE YOU COVERED.

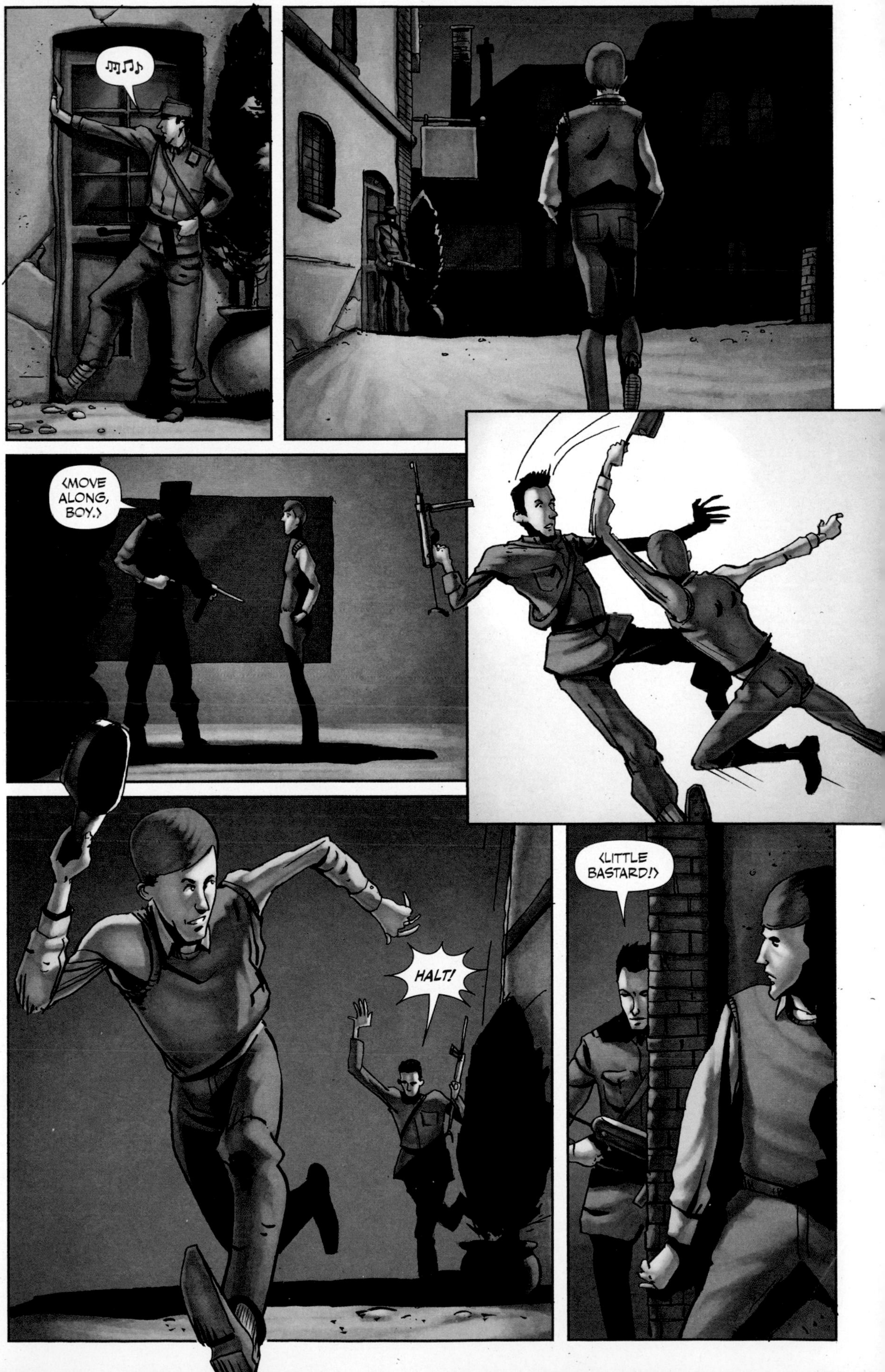
<MOVE ALONG, BOY.>
HALT!
<LITTLE BASTARD!>

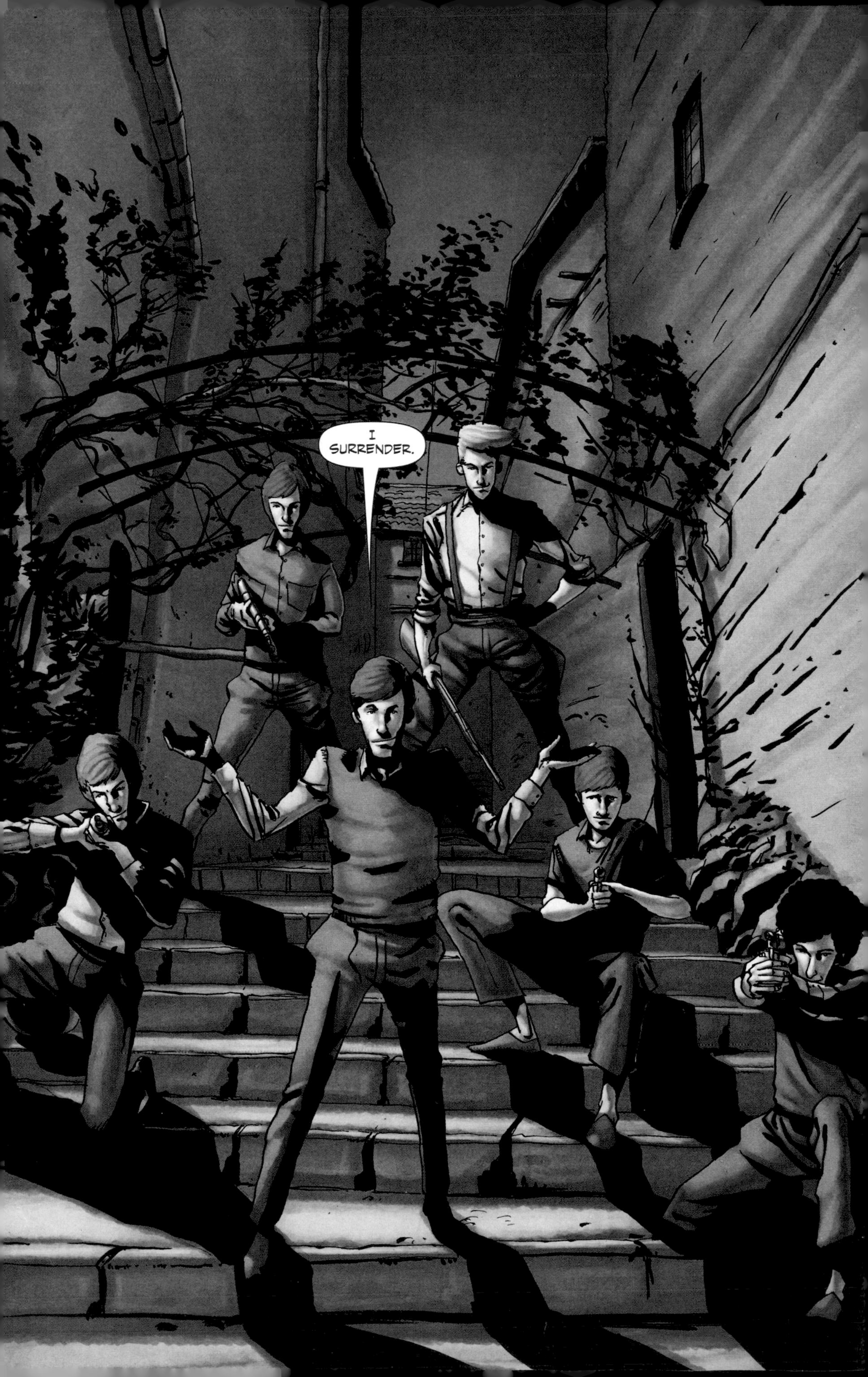
I SURRENDER.

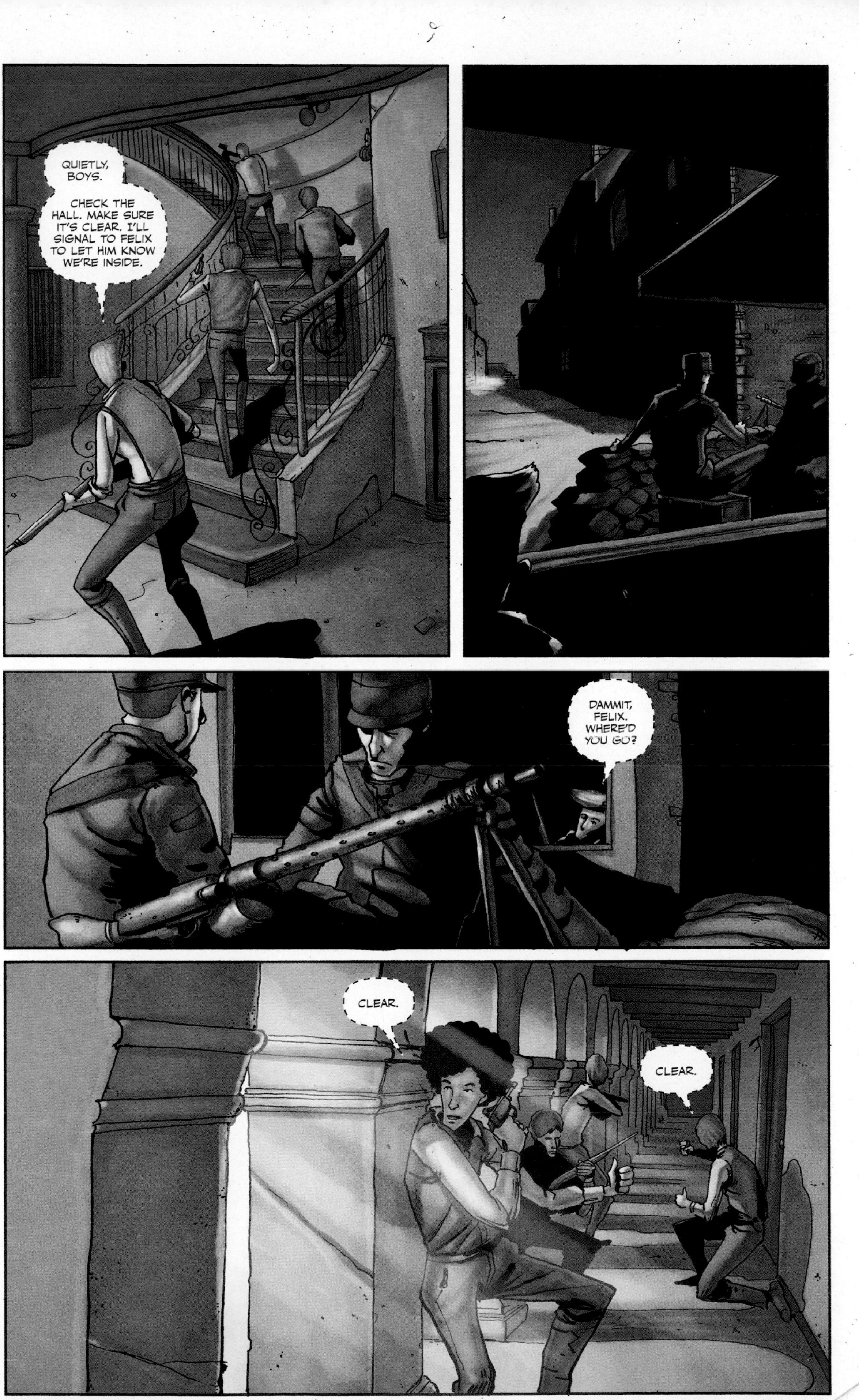
QUIETLY, BOYS.
CHECK THE HALL. MAKE SURE IT'S CLEAR. I'LL SIGNAL TO FELIX TO LET HIM KNOW WE'RE INSIDE.
DAMMIT, FELIX. WHERE'D YOU GO?
CLEAR.
CLEAR.

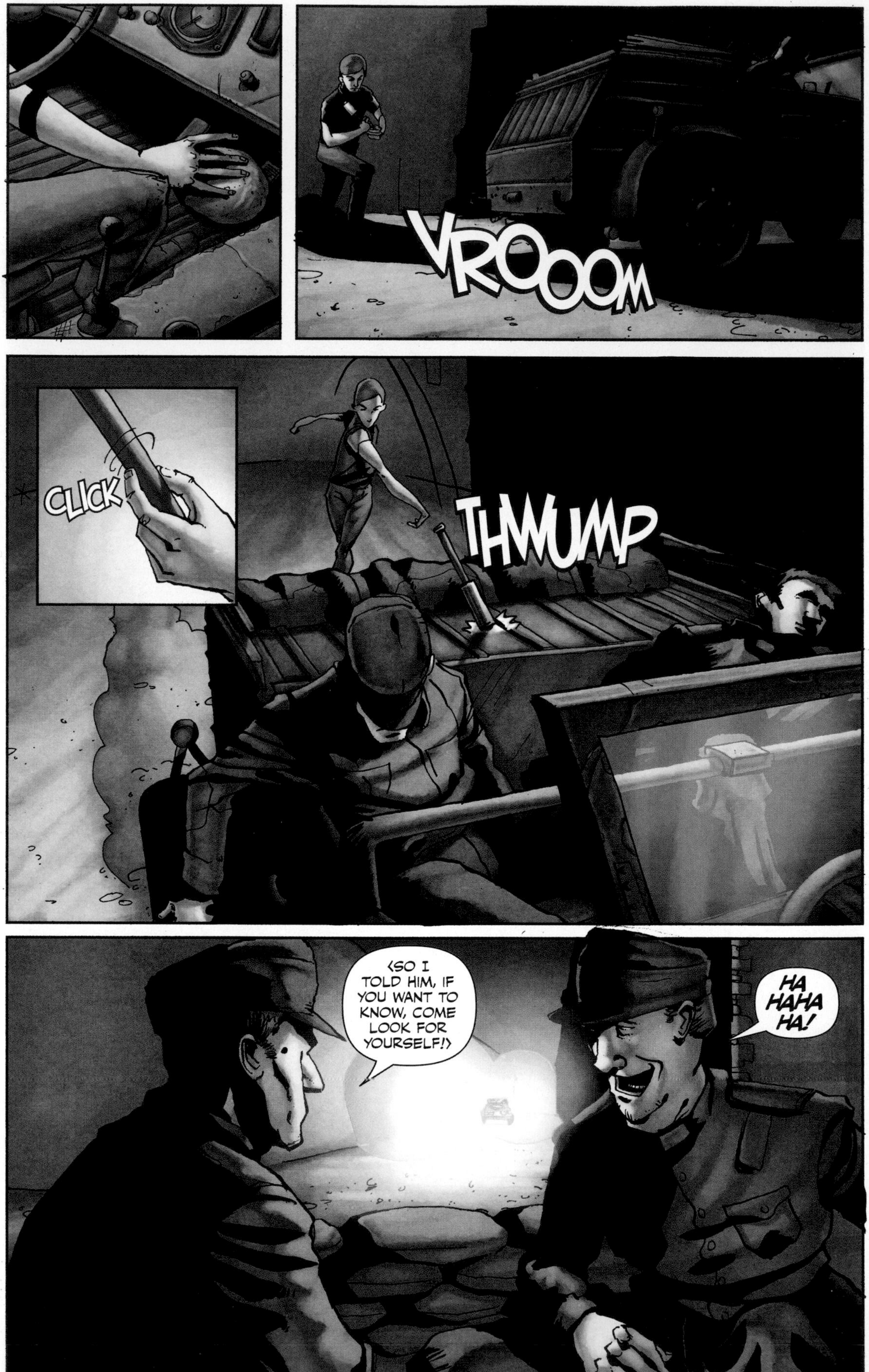
VROOOM
CLICK
THWUMP
‹SO I TOLD HIM, IF YOU WANT TO KNOW, COME LOOK FOR YOURSELF!›
HA HAHAHA HA!

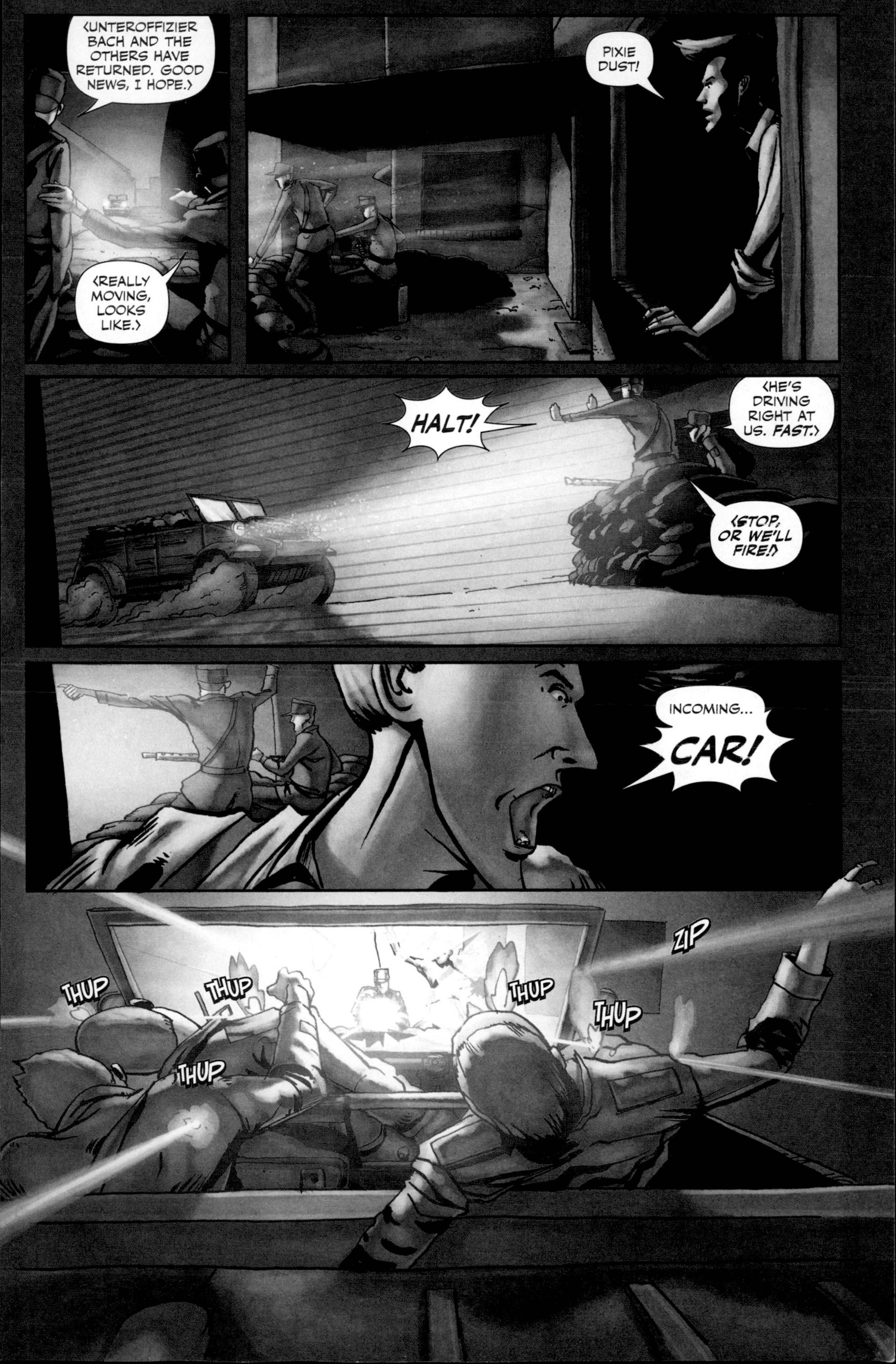

‹UNTEROFFIZIER BACH AND THE OTHERS HAVE RETURNED. GOOD NEWS, I HOPE.›
‹REALLY MOVING, LOOKS LIKE.›
PIXIE DUST!
HALT!
‹HE'S DRIVING RIGHT AT US. FAST.›
‹STOP, OR WE'LL FIRE!›
INCOMING...
CAR!
ZIP
THUP
THUP
THUP
THUP
THUP

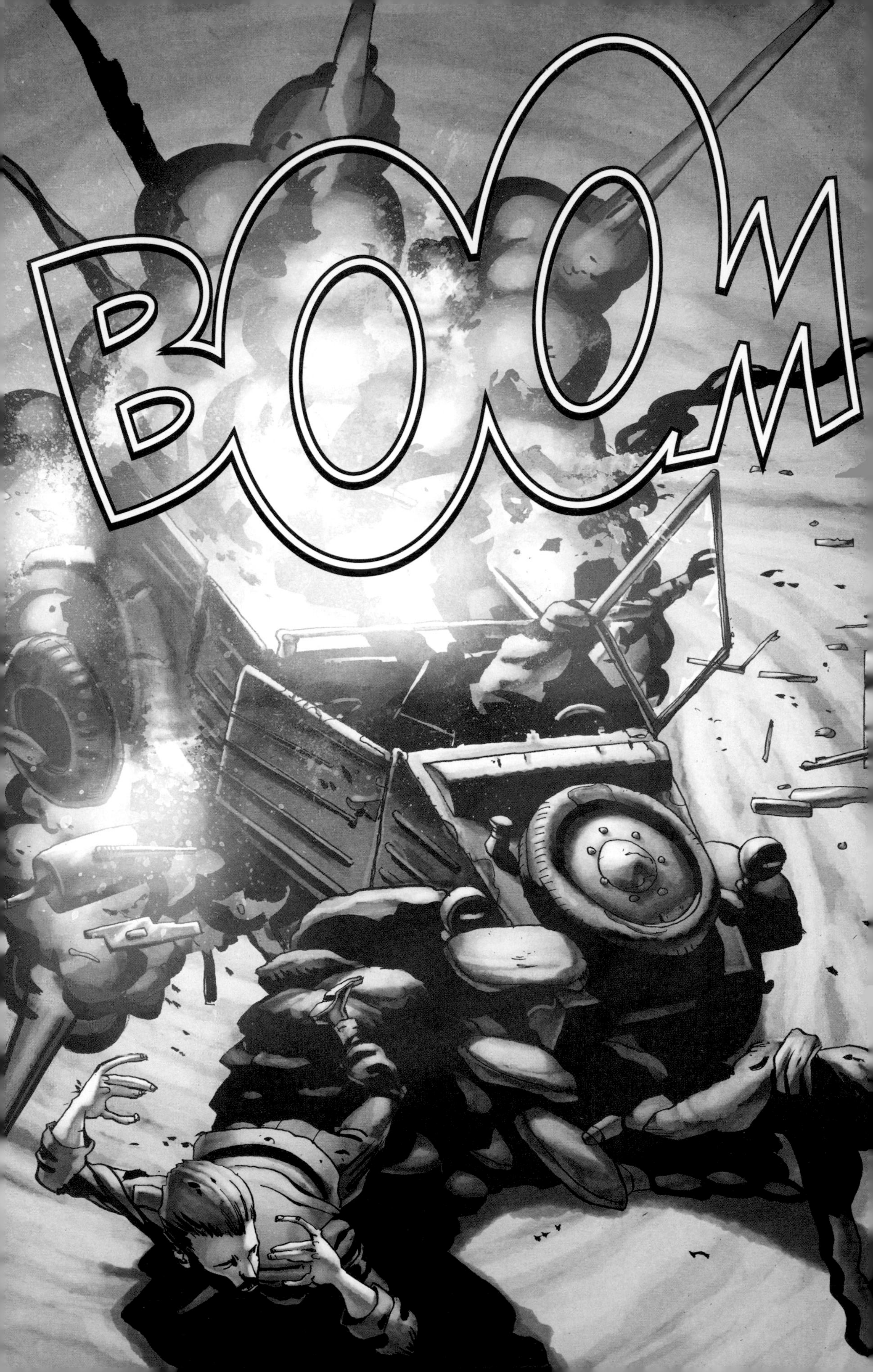
BOOM

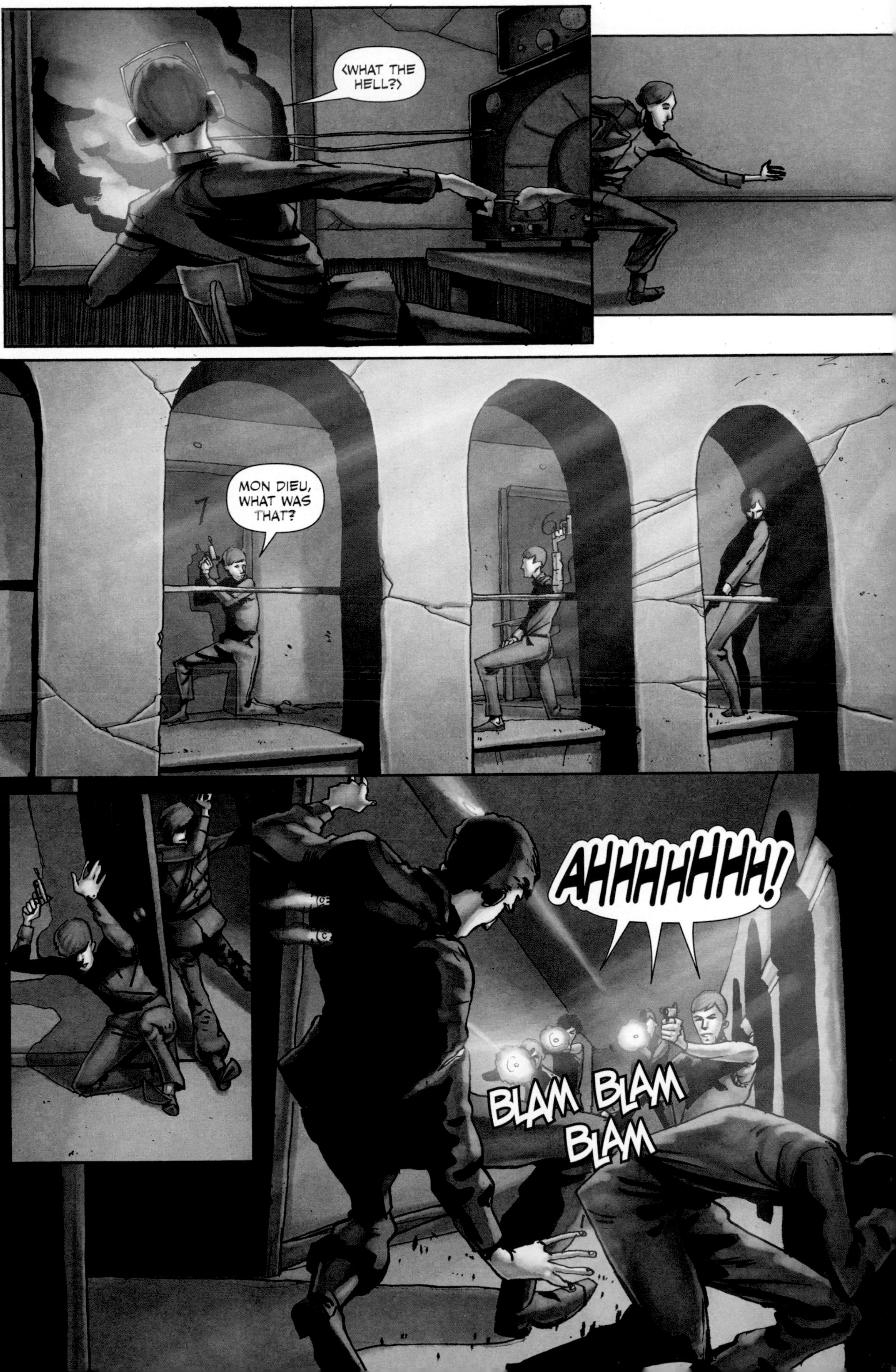

<WHAT THE HELL?>
MON DIEU, WHAT WAS THAT?
AHHHHHHH!
BLAM BLAM BLAM

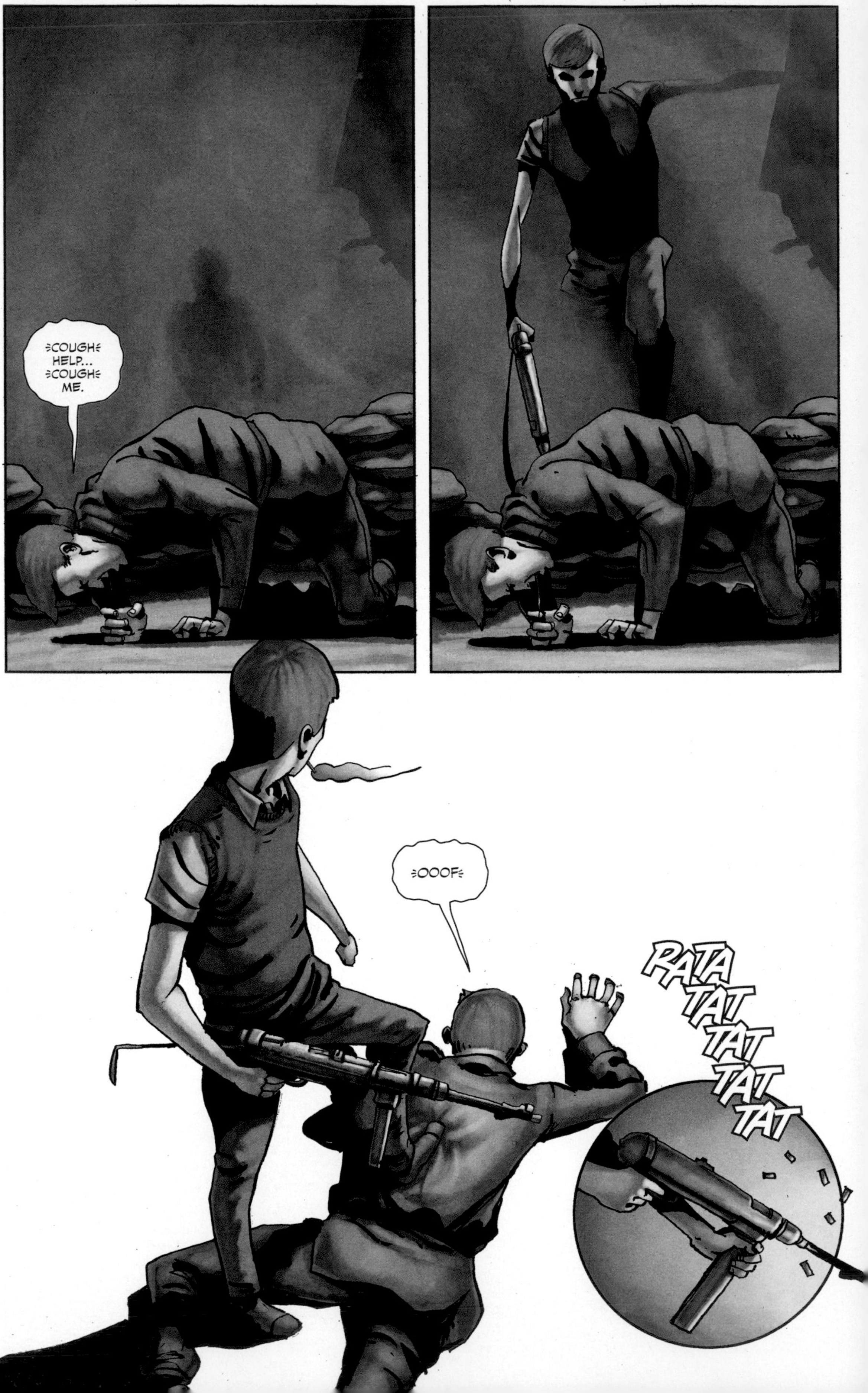

COUGH HELP... COUGH ME.
OOOF
RATA TAT TAT TAT TAT

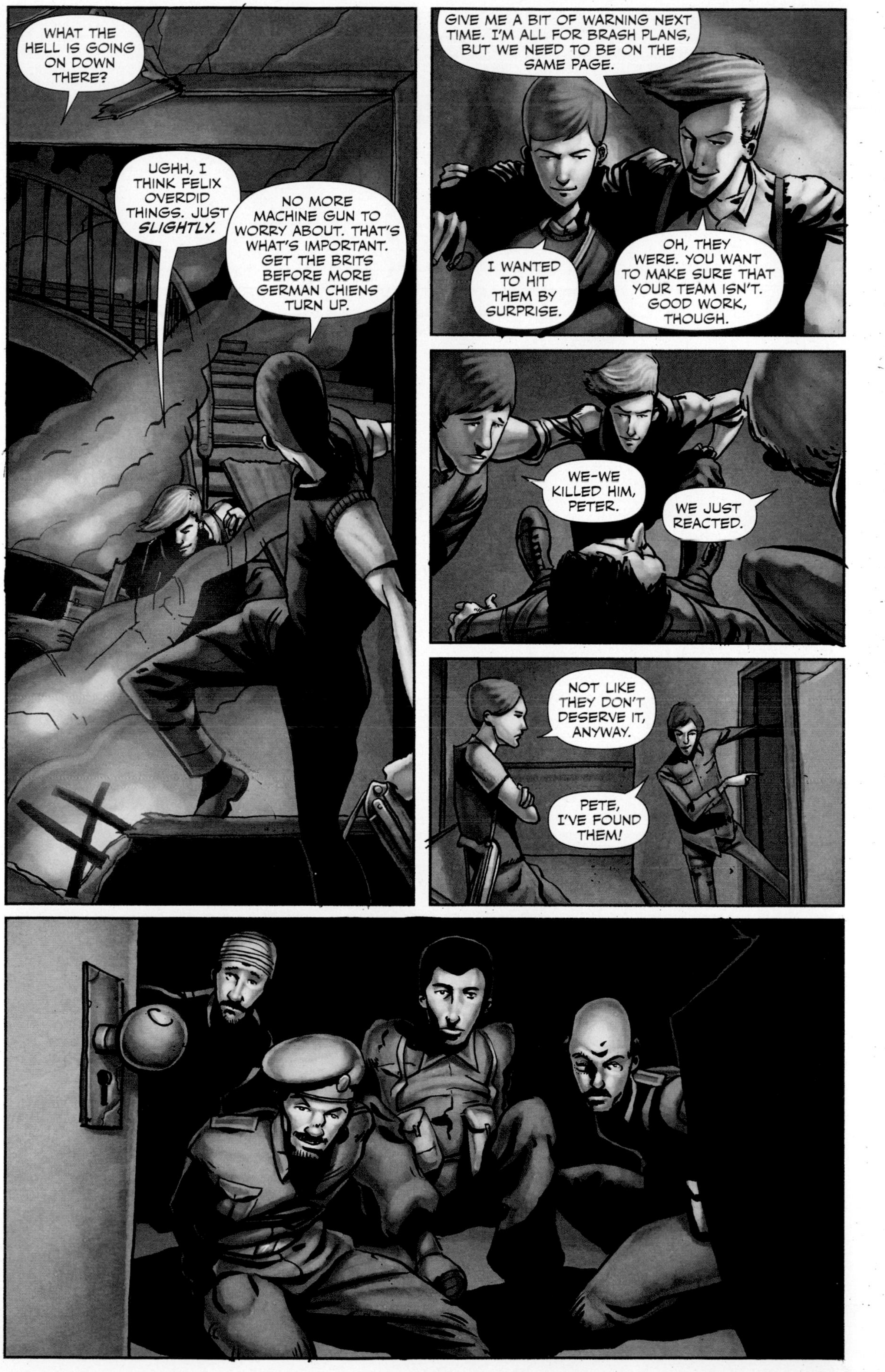
WHAT THE HELL IS GOING ON DOWN THERE?
UGHH, I THINK FELIX OVERDID THINGS. JUST *SLIGHTLY.*
NO MORE MACHINE GUN TO WORRY ABOUT. THAT'S WHAT'S IMPORTANT. GET THE BRITS BEFORE MORE GERMAN CHIENS TURN UP.
GIVE ME A BIT OF WARNING NEXT TIME. I'M ALL FOR BRASH PLANS, BUT WE NEED TO BE ON THE SAME PAGE.
I WANTED TO HIT THEM BY SURPRISE.
OH, THEY WERE. YOU WANT TO MAKE SURE THAT YOUR TEAM ISN'T. GOOD WORK, THOUGH.
WE-WE KILLED HIM, PETER.
WE JUST REACTED.
NOT LIKE THEY DON'T DESERVE IT, ANYWAY.
PETE, I'VE FOUND THEM!

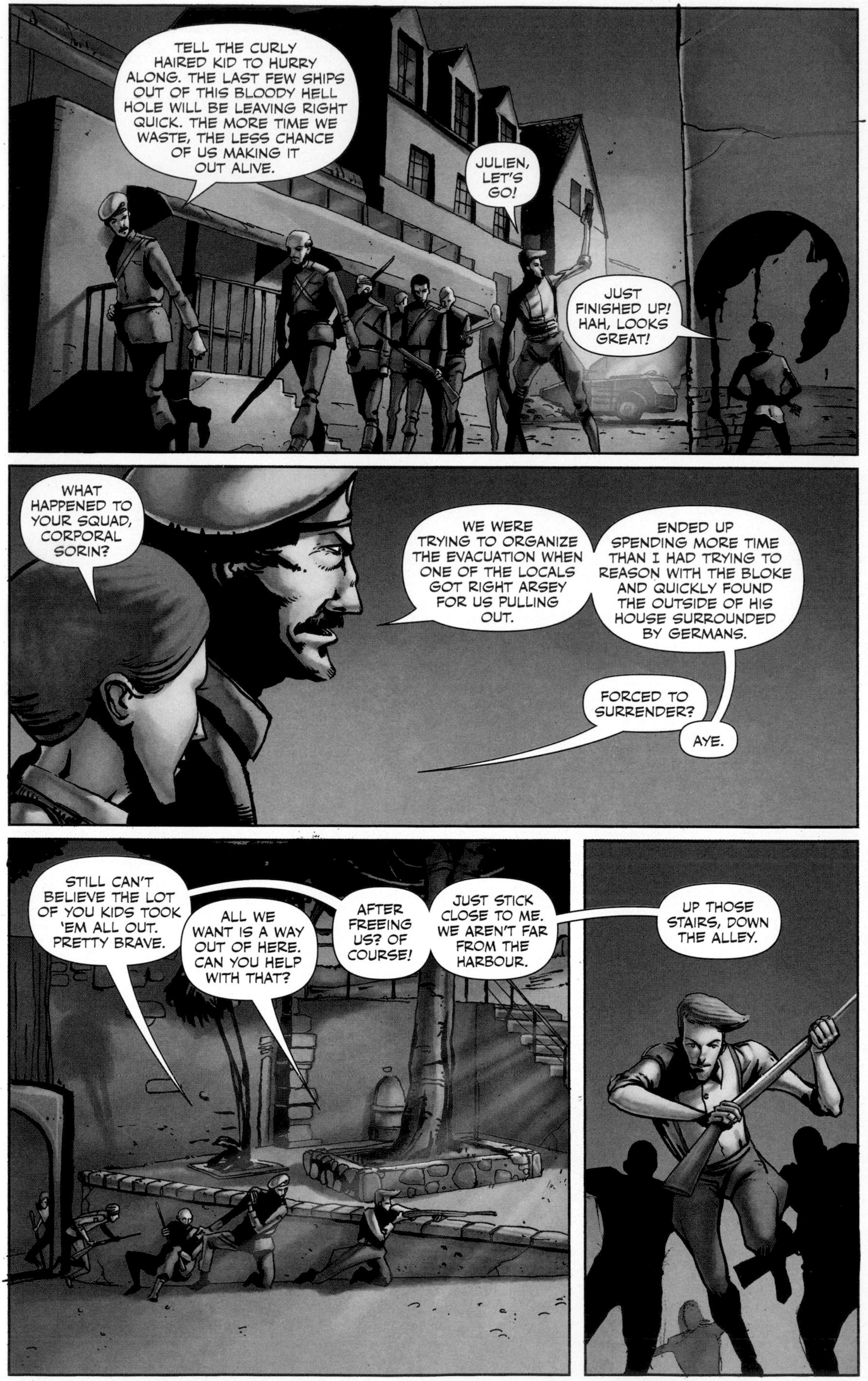
TELL THE CURLY HAIRED KID TO HURRY ALONG. THE LAST FEW SHIPS OUT OF THIS BLOODY HELL HOLE WILL BE LEAVING RIGHT QUICK. THE MORE TIME WE WASTE, THE LESS CHANCE OF US MAKING IT OUT ALIVE.
JULIEN, LET'S GO!
JUST FINISHED UP! HAH, LOOKS GREAT!
WHAT HAPPENED TO YOUR SQUAD, CORPORAL SORIN?
WE WERE TRYING TO ORGANIZE THE EVACUATION WHEN ONE OF THE LOCALS GOT RIGHT ARSEY FOR US PULLING OUT.
ENDED UP SPENDING MORE TIME THAN I HAD TRYING TO REASON WITH THE BLOKE AND QUICKLY FOUND THE OUTSIDE OF HIS HOUSE SURROUNDED BY GERMANS.
FORCED TO SURRENDER?
AYE.
STILL CAN'T BELIEVE THE LOT OF YOU KIDS TOOK 'EM ALL OUT. PRETTY BRAVE.
ALL WE WANT IS A WAY OUT OF HERE. CAN YOU HELP WITH THAT?
AFTER FREEING US? OF COURSE!
JUST STICK CLOSE TO ME. WE AREN'T FAR FROM THE HARBOUR.
UP THOSE STAIRS, DOWN THE ALLEY.

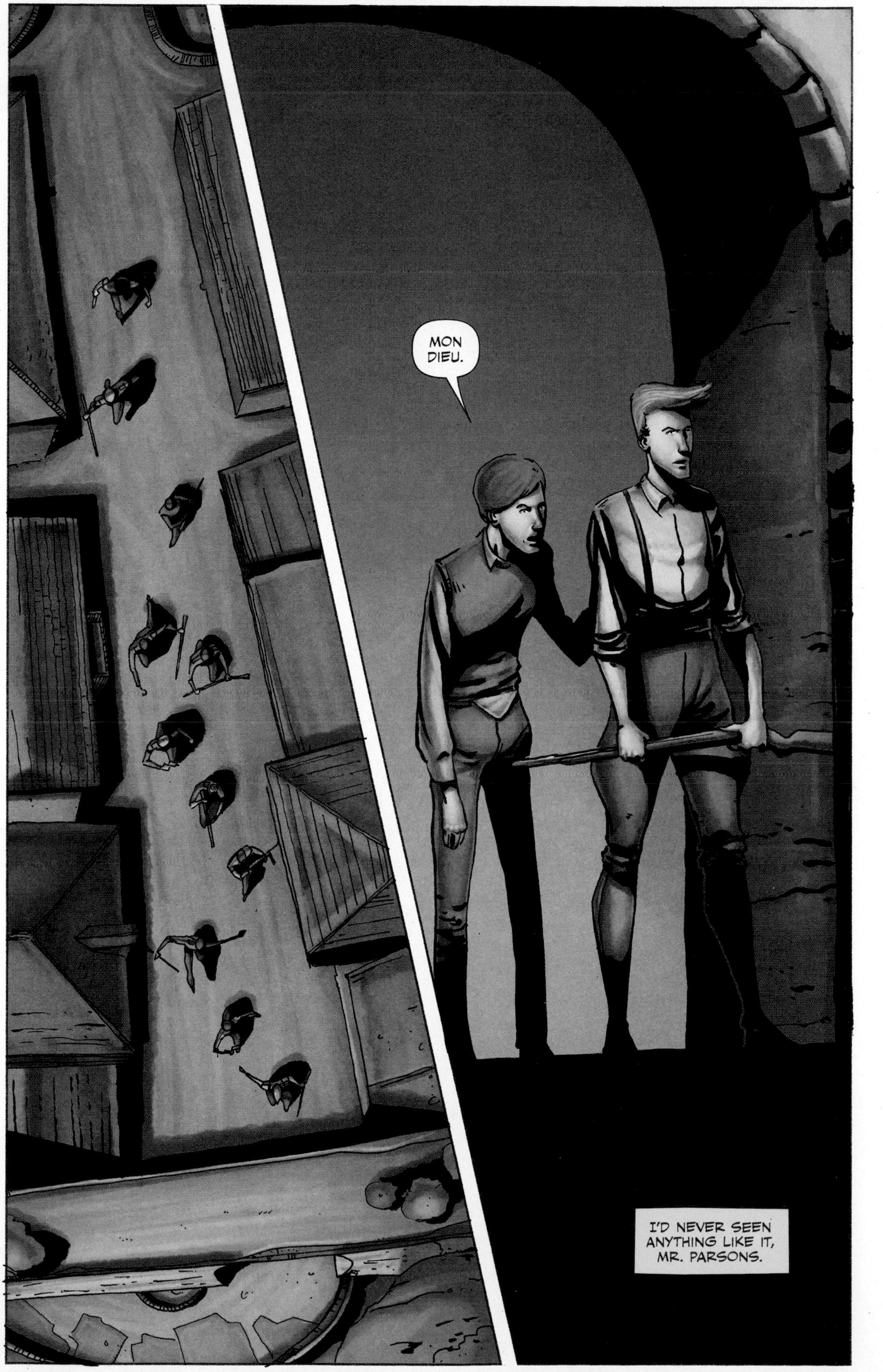
MON DIEU.
I'D NEVER SEEN ANYTHING LIKE IT, MR. PARSONS.

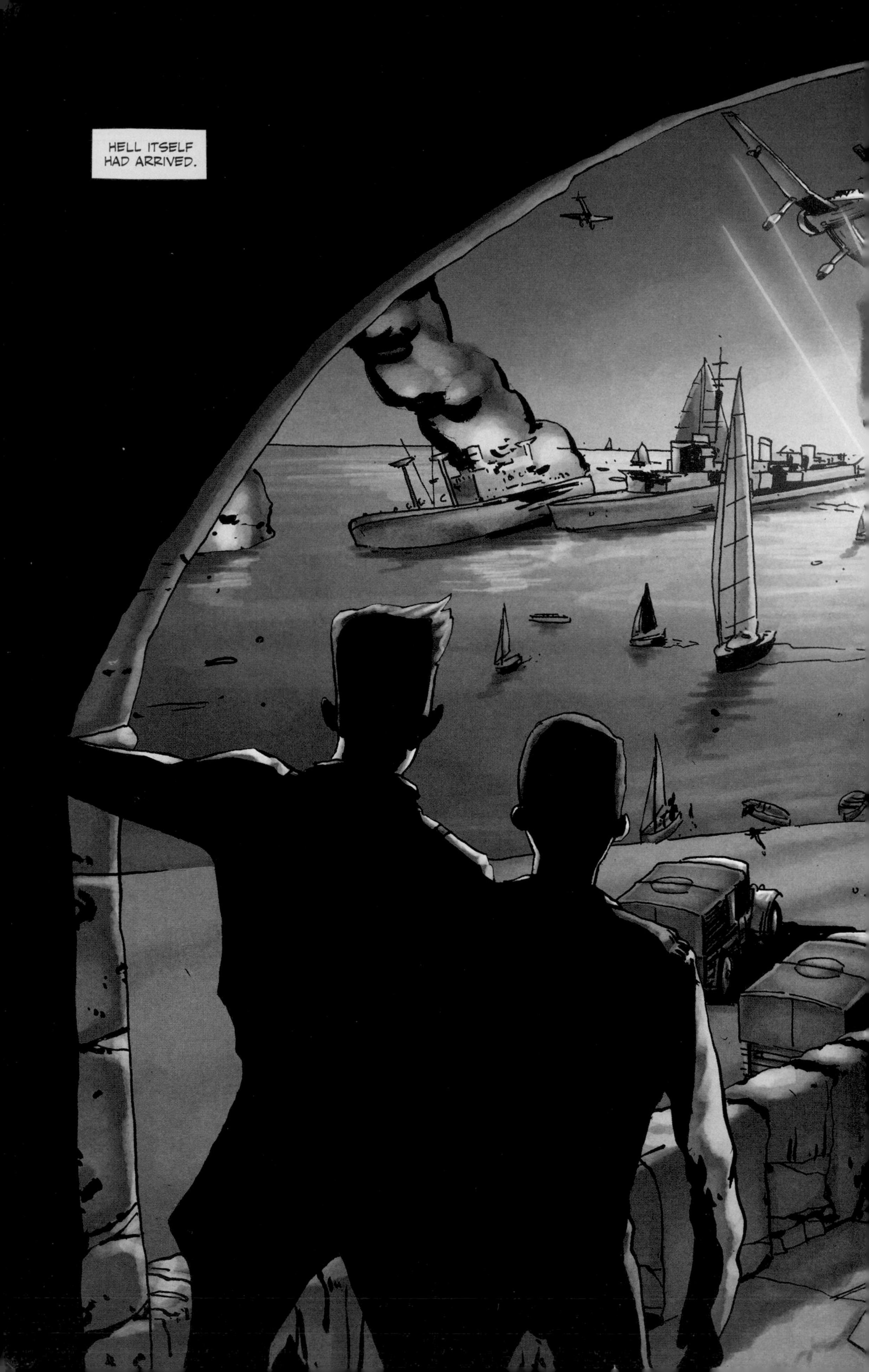
HELL ITSELF
HAD ARRIVED.

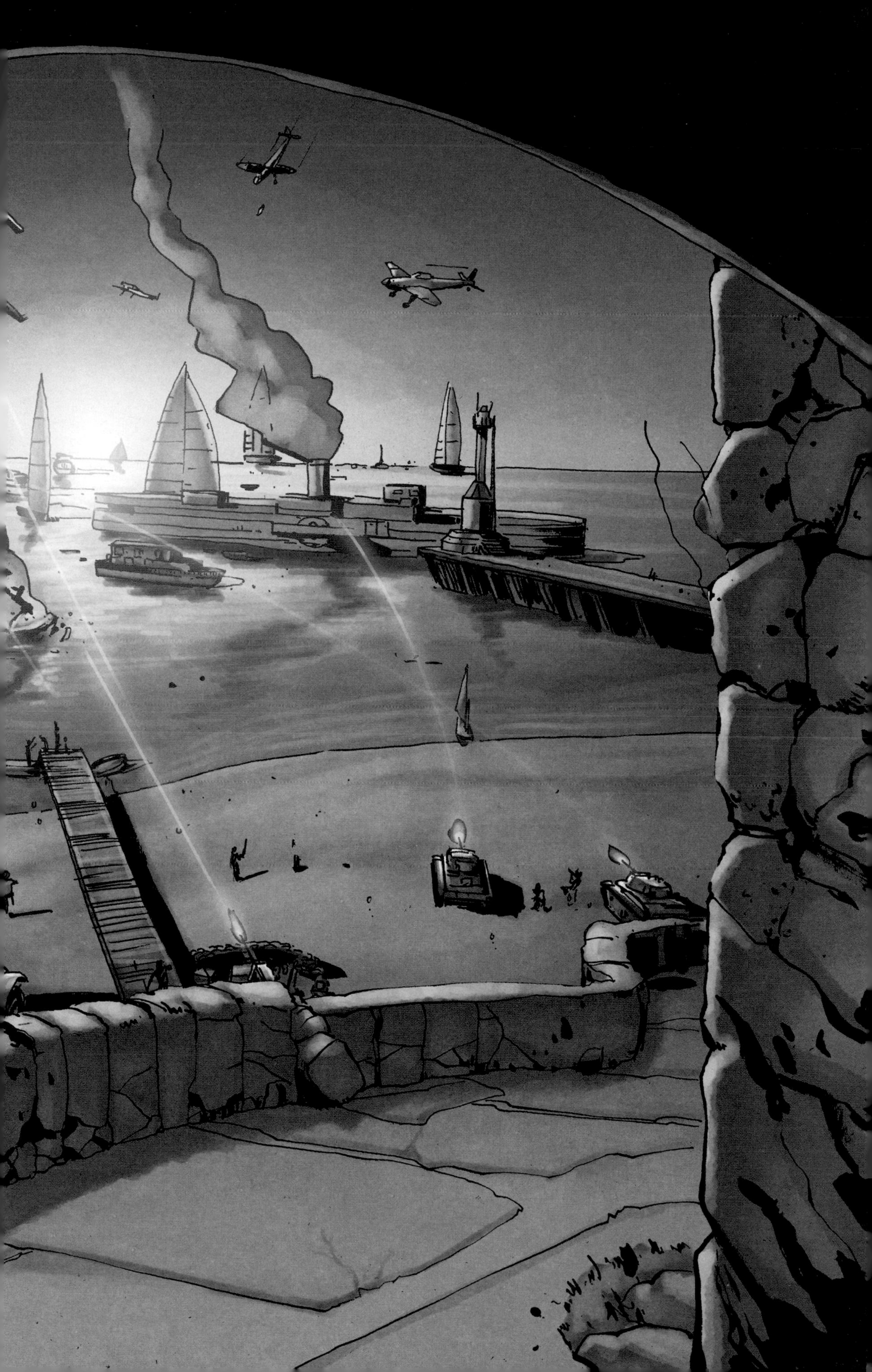

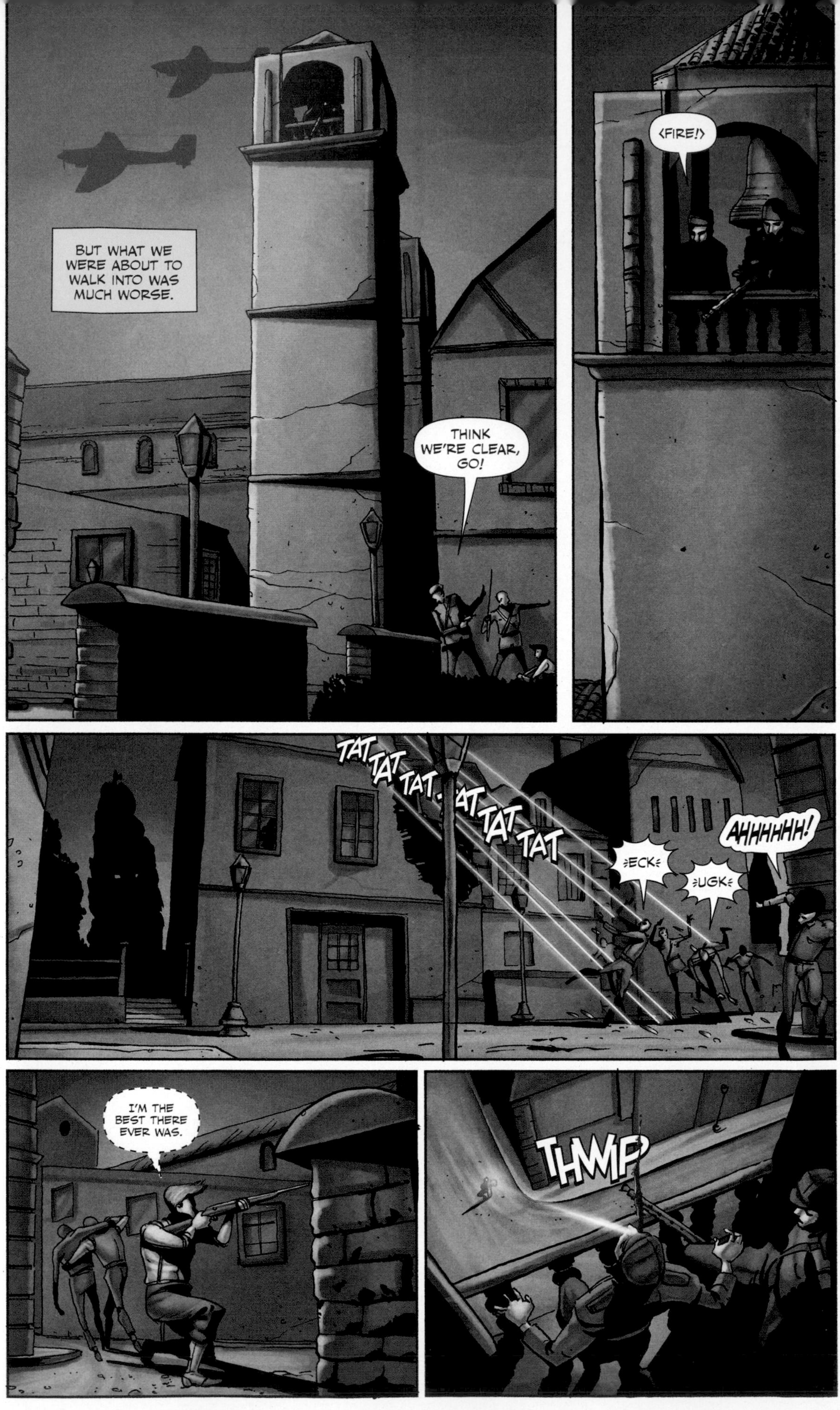
BUT WHAT WE WERE ABOUT TO WALK INTO WAS MUCH WORSE.
THINK WE'RE CLEAR, GO!
‹FIRE!›
TAT TAT TAT TAT TAT TAT TAT
ECK
UGK
AHHHHHH!
I'M THE BEST THERE EVER WAS.
THWIP

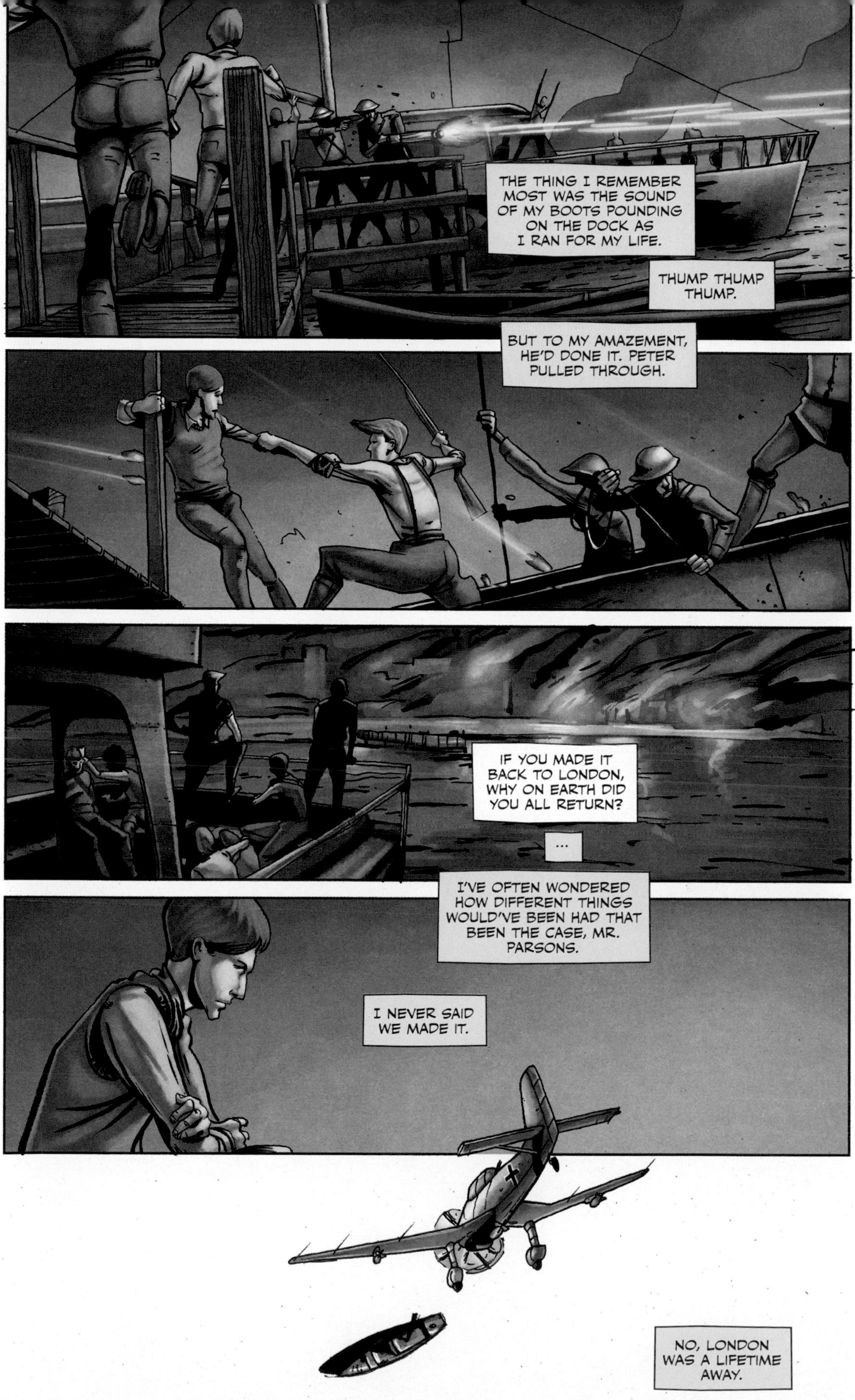
THE THING I REMEMBER MOST WAS THE SOUND OF MY BOOTS POUNDING ON THE DOCK AS I RAN FOR MY LIFE.
THUMP THUMP THUMP.
BUT TO MY AMAZEMENT, HE'D DONE IT. PETER PULLED THROUGH.
IF YOU MADE IT BACK TO LONDON, WHY ON EARTH DID YOU ALL RETURN?
...
I'VE OFTEN WONDERED HOW DIFFERENT THINGS WOULD'VE BEEN HAD THAT BEEN THE CASE, MR. PARSONS.
I NEVER SAID WE MADE IT.
NO, LONDON WAS A LIFETIME AWAY.

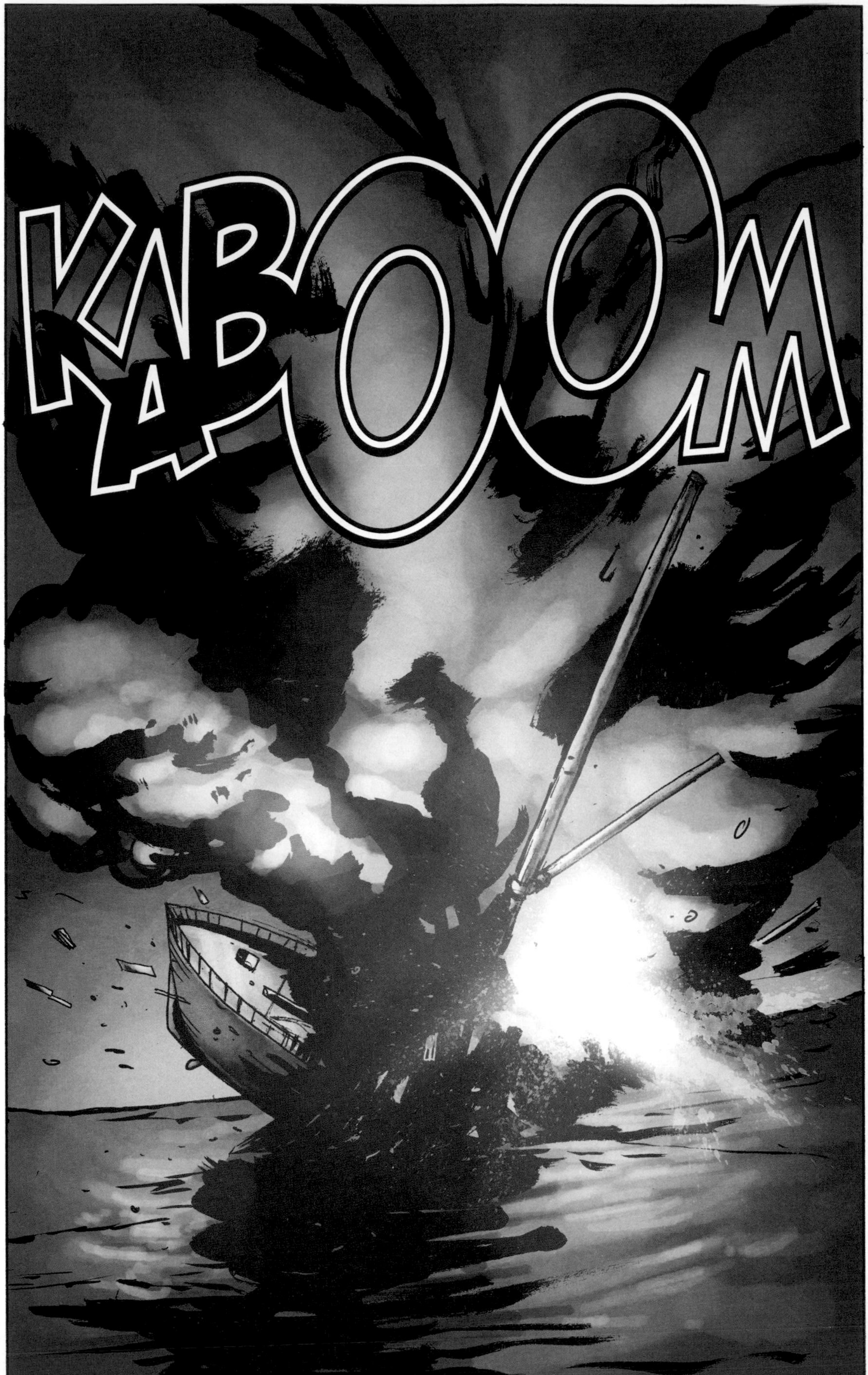
KABOOM

CHAPTER THREE

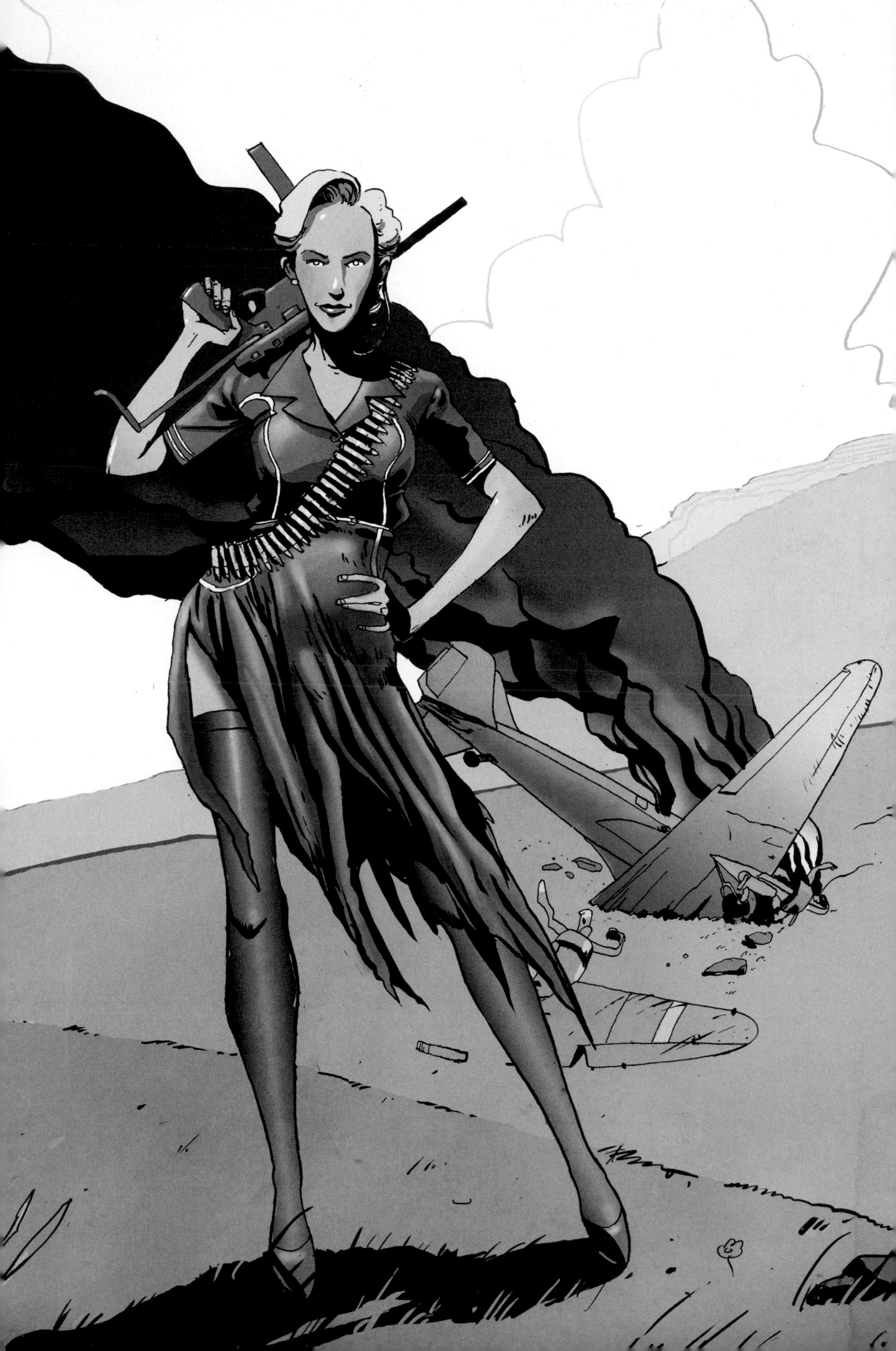

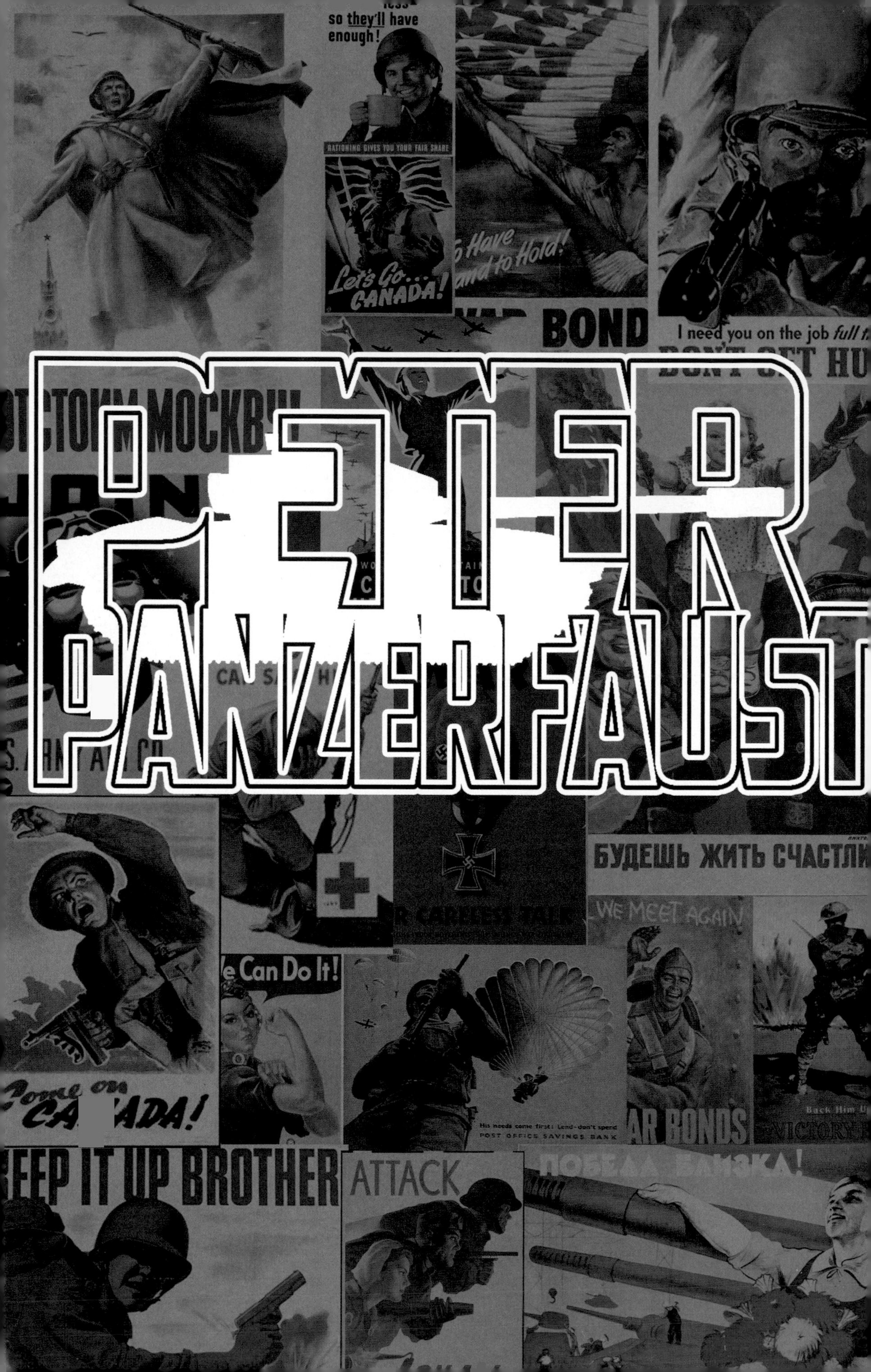
PETER
PANZERFAUST
so they'll have enough!
RATIONING GIVES YOU YOUR FAIR SHARE
Let's Go... CANADA!
BOND
WE MEET AGAIN
His needs come first: Lend–don't spend
POST OFFICE SAVINGS BANK
ATTACK

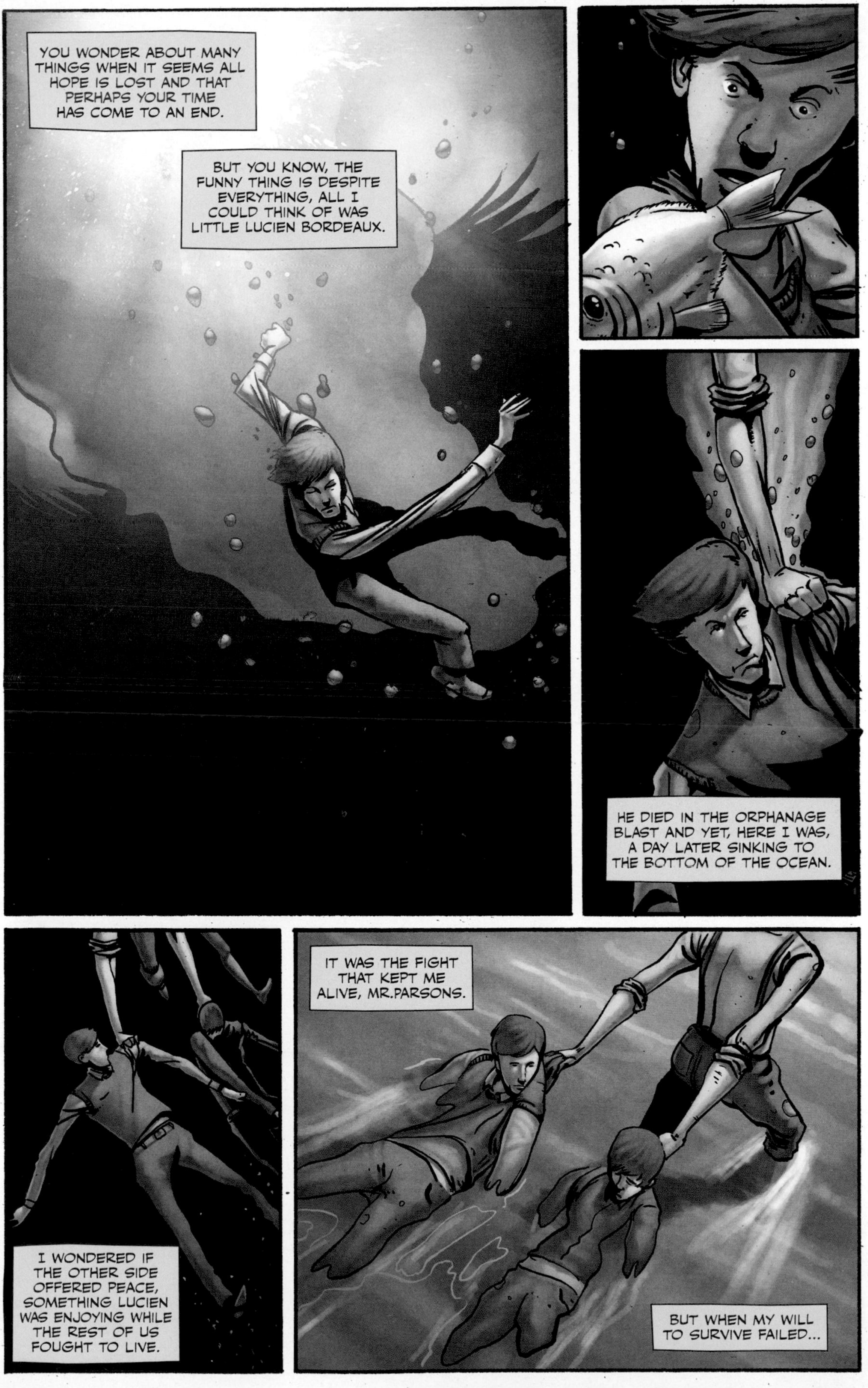
YOU WONDER ABOUT MANY THINGS WHEN IT SEEMS ALL HOPE IS LOST AND THAT PERHAPS YOUR TIME HAS COME TO AN END.
BUT YOU KNOW, THE FUNNY THING IS DESPITE EVERYTHING, ALL I COULD THINK OF WAS LITTLE LUCIEN BORDEAUX.
HE DIED IN THE ORPHANAGE BLAST AND YET, HERE I WAS, A DAY LATER SINKING TO THE BOTTOM OF THE OCEAN.
I WONDERED IF THE OTHER SIDE OFFERED PEACE, SOMETHING LUCIEN WAS ENJOYING WHILE THE REST OF US FOUGHT TO LIVE.
IT WAS THE FIGHT THAT KEPT ME ALIVE, MR.PARSONS.
BUT WHEN MY WILL TO SURVIVE FAILED...

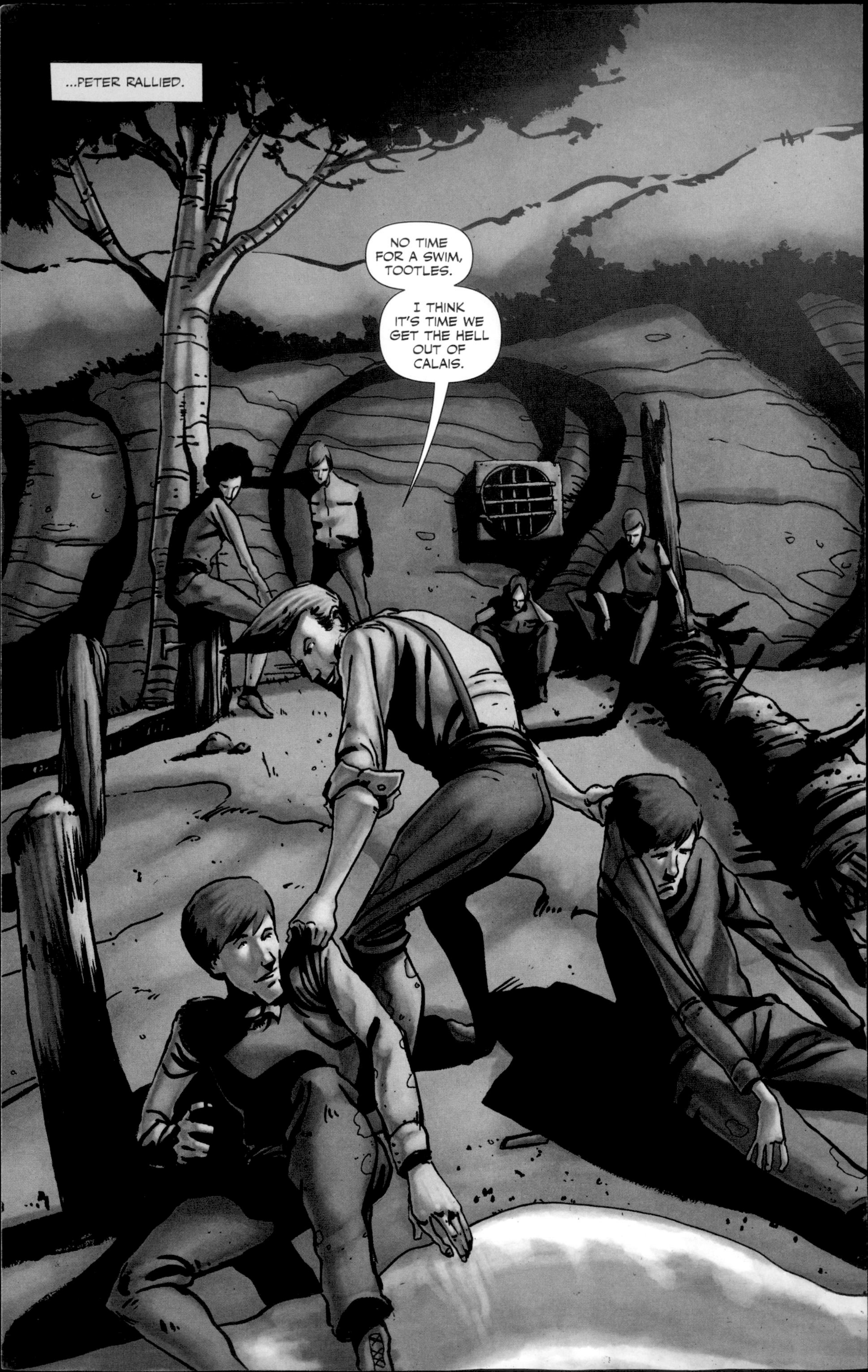
...PETER RALLIED.
NO TIME FOR A SWIM, TOOTLES.
I THINK IT'S TIME WE GET THE HELL OUT OF CALAIS.

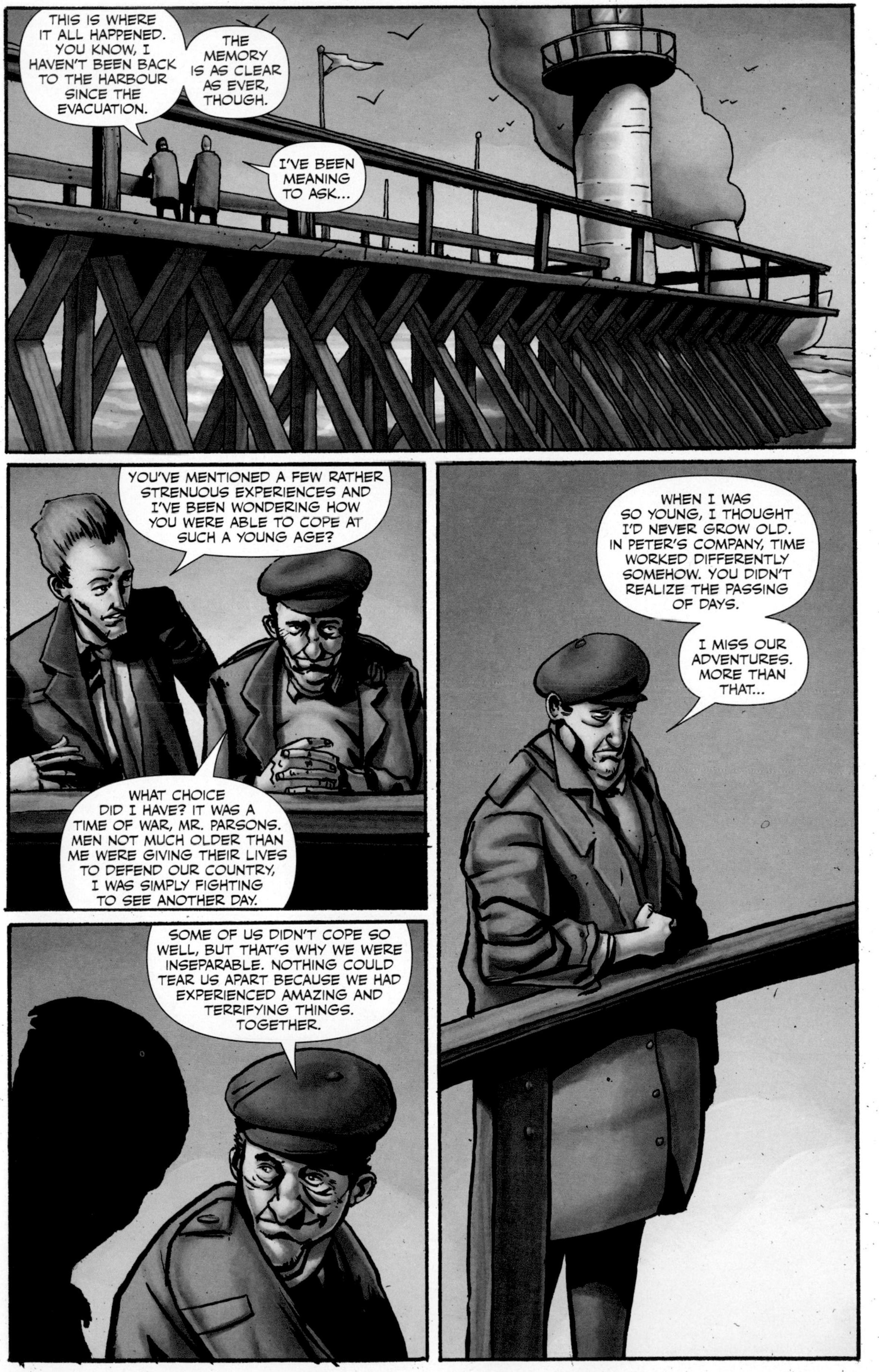
THIS IS WHERE IT ALL HAPPENED. YOU KNOW, I HAVEN'T BEEN BACK TO THE HARBOUR SINCE THE EVACUATION.
THE MEMORY IS AS CLEAR AS EVER, THOUGH.
I'VE BEEN MEANING TO ASK...
YOU'VE MENTIONED A FEW RATHER STRENUOUS EXPERIENCES AND I'VE BEEN WONDERING HOW YOU WERE ABLE TO COPE AT SUCH A YOUNG AGE?
WHAT CHOICE DID I HAVE? IT WAS A TIME OF WAR, MR. PARSONS. MEN NOT MUCH OLDER THAN ME WERE GIVING THEIR LIVES TO DEFEND OUR COUNTRY, I WAS SIMPLY FIGHTING TO SEE ANOTHER DAY.
SOME OF US DIDN'T COPE SO WELL, BUT THAT'S WHY WE WERE INSEPARABLE. NOTHING COULD TEAR US APART BECAUSE WE HAD EXPERIENCED AMAZING AND TERRIFYING THINGS. TOGETHER.
WHEN I WAS SO YOUNG, I THOUGHT I'D NEVER GROW OLD. IN PETER'S COMPANY, TIME WORKED DIFFERENTLY SOMEHOW. YOU DIDN'T REALIZE THE PASSING OF DAYS.
I MISS OUR ADVENTURES. MORE THAN THAT...

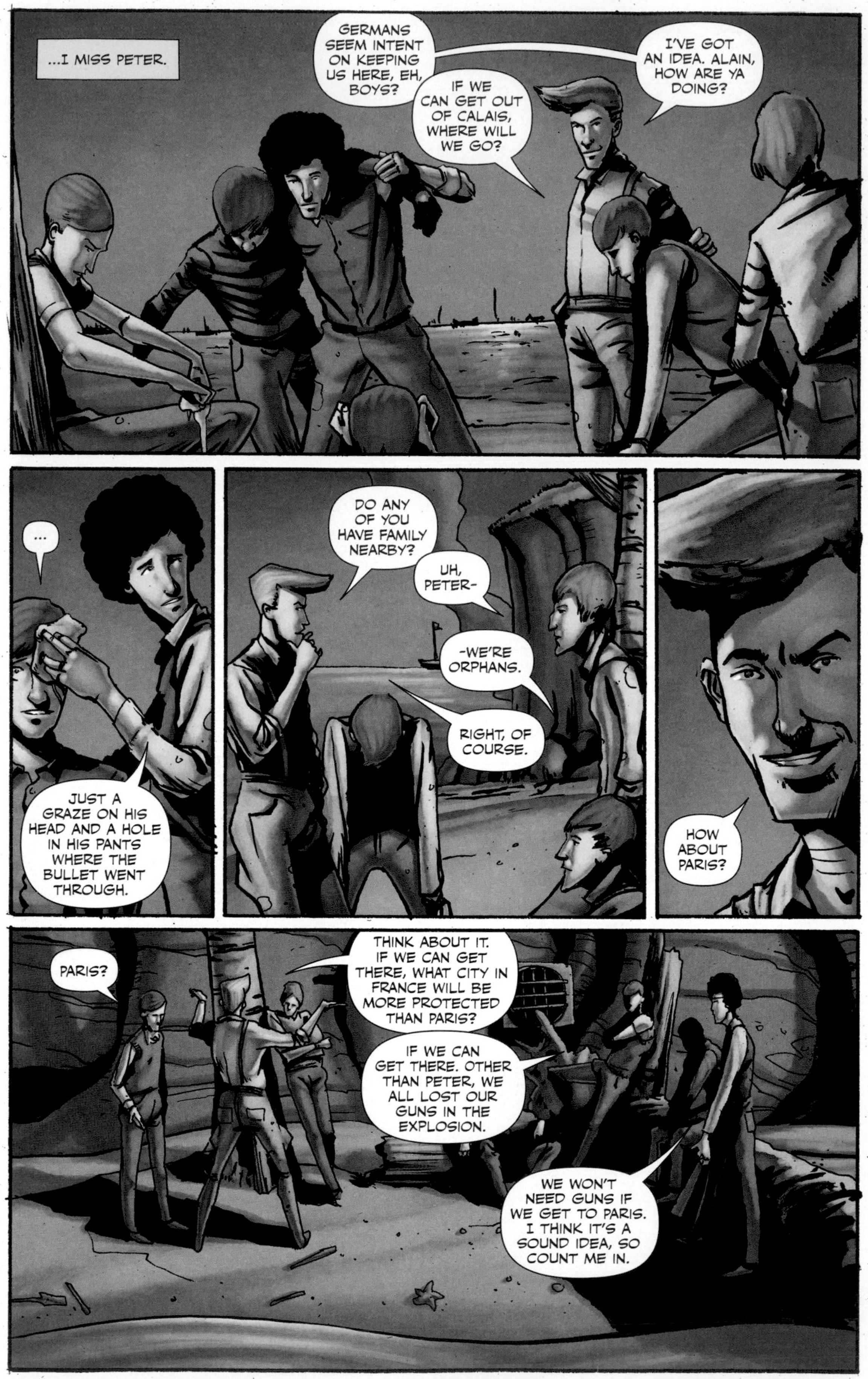
...I MISS PETER.
GERMANS SEEM INTENT ON KEEPING US HERE, EH, BOYS?
I'VE GOT AN IDEA. ALAIN, HOW ARE YA DOING?
IF WE CAN GET OUT OF CALAIS, WHERE WILL WE GO?
...
JUST A GRAZE ON HIS HEAD AND A HOLE IN HIS PANTS WHERE THE BULLET WENT THROUGH.
DO ANY OF YOU HAVE FAMILY NEARBY?
UH, PETER-
-WE'RE ORPHANS.
RIGHT, OF COURSE.
HOW ABOUT PARIS?
PARIS?
THINK ABOUT IT. IF WE CAN GET THERE, WHAT CITY IN FRANCE WILL BE MORE PROTECTED THAN PARIS?
IF WE CAN GET THERE. OTHER THAN PETER, WE ALL LOST OUR GUNS IN THE EXPLOSION.
WE WON'T NEED GUNS IF WE GET TO PARIS. I THINK IT'S A SOUND IDEA, SO COUNT ME IN.

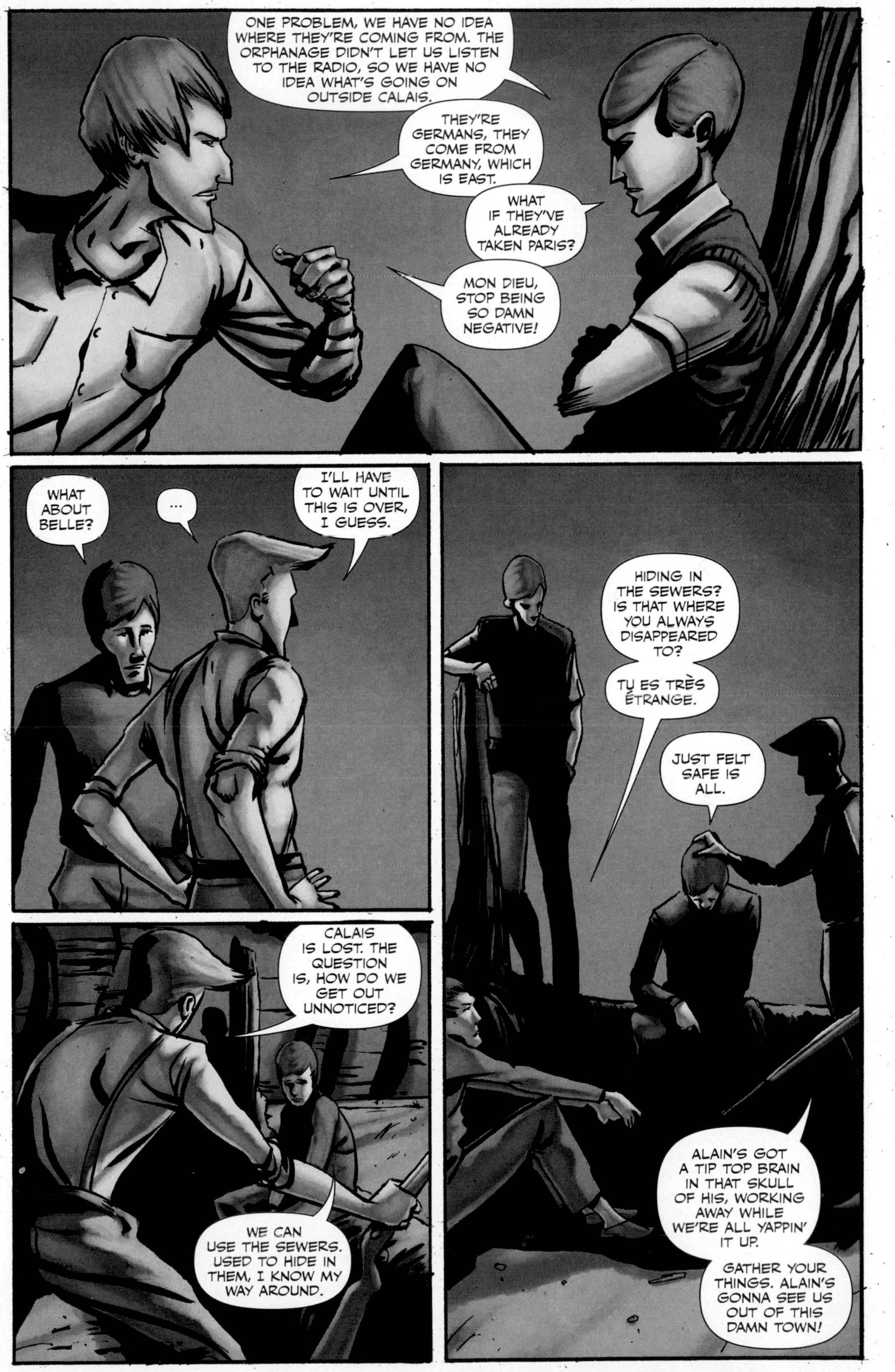
ONE PROBLEM, WE HAVE NO IDEA WHERE THEY'RE COMING FROM. THE ORPHANAGE DIDN'T LET US LISTEN TO THE RADIO, SO WE HAVE NO IDEA WHAT'S GOING ON OUTSIDE CALAIS.
THEY'RE GERMANS, THEY COME FROM GERMANY, WHICH IS EAST.
WHAT IF THEY'VE ALREADY TAKEN PARIS?
MON DIEU, STOP BEING SO DAMN NEGATIVE!
WHAT ABOUT BELLE?
...
I'LL HAVE TO WAIT UNTIL THIS IS OVER, I GUESS.
CALAIS IS LOST. THE QUESTION IS, HOW DO WE GET OUT UNNOTICED?
WE CAN USE THE SEWERS. USED TO HIDE IN THEM, I KNOW MY WAY AROUND.
HIDING IN THE SEWERS? IS THAT WHERE YOU ALWAYS DISAPPEARED TO?
TU ES TRÈS ÉTRANGE.
JUST FELT SAFE IS ALL.
ALAIN'S GOT A TIP TOP BRAIN IN THAT SKULL OF HIS, WORKING AWAY WHILE WE'RE ALL YAPPIN' IT UP.
GATHER YOUR THINGS. ALAIN'S GONNA SEE US OUT OF THIS DAMN TOWN!

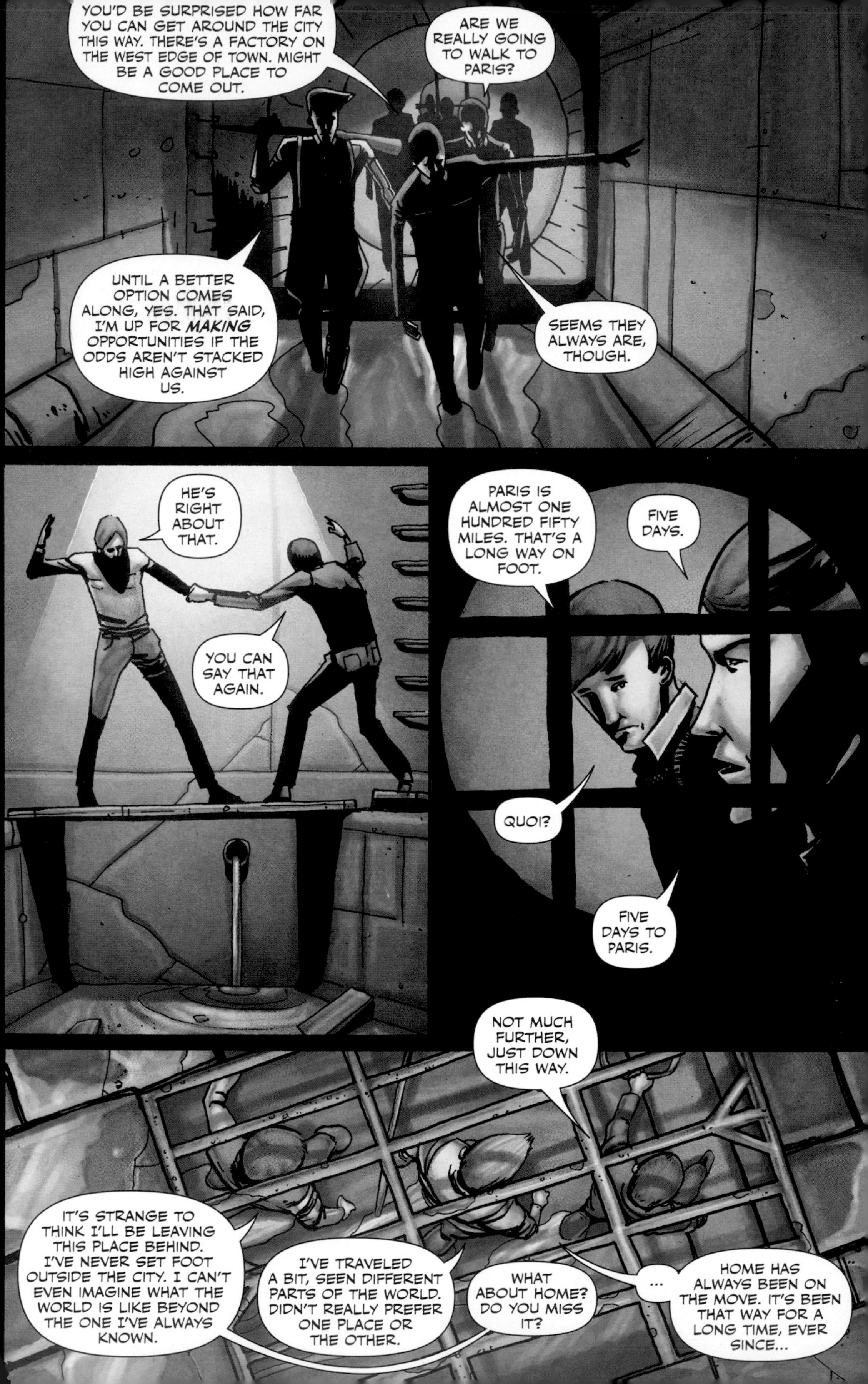
YOU'D BE SURPRISED HOW FAR YOU CAN GET AROUND THE CITY THIS WAY. THERE'S A FACTORY ON THE WEST EDGE OF TOWN. MIGHT BE A GOOD PLACE TO COME OUT.
ARE WE REALLY GOING TO WALK TO PARIS?
UNTIL A BETTER OPTION COMES ALONG, YES. THAT SAID, I'M UP FOR *MAKING* OPPORTUNITIES IF THE ODDS AREN'T STACKED HIGH AGAINST US.
SEEMS THEY ALWAYS ARE, THOUGH.
HE'S RIGHT ABOUT THAT.
YOU CAN SAY THAT AGAIN.
PARIS IS ALMOST ONE HUNDRED FIFTY MILES. THAT'S A LONG WAY ON FOOT.
FIVE DAYS.
QUOI?
FIVE DAYS TO PARIS.
NOT MUCH FURTHER, JUST DOWN THIS WAY.
IT'S STRANGE TO THINK I'LL BE LEAVING THIS PLACE BEHIND. I'VE NEVER SET FOOT OUTSIDE THE CITY. I CAN'T EVEN IMAGINE WHAT THE WORLD IS LIKE BEYOND THE ONE I'VE ALWAYS KNOWN.
I'VE TRAVELED A BIT, SEEN DIFFERENT PARTS OF THE WORLD. DIDN'T REALLY PREFER ONE PLACE OR THE OTHER.
WHAT ABOUT HOME? DO YOU MISS IT?
...
HOME HAS ALWAYS BEEN ON THE MOVE. IT'S BEEN THAT WAY FOR A LONG TIME, EVER SINCE...

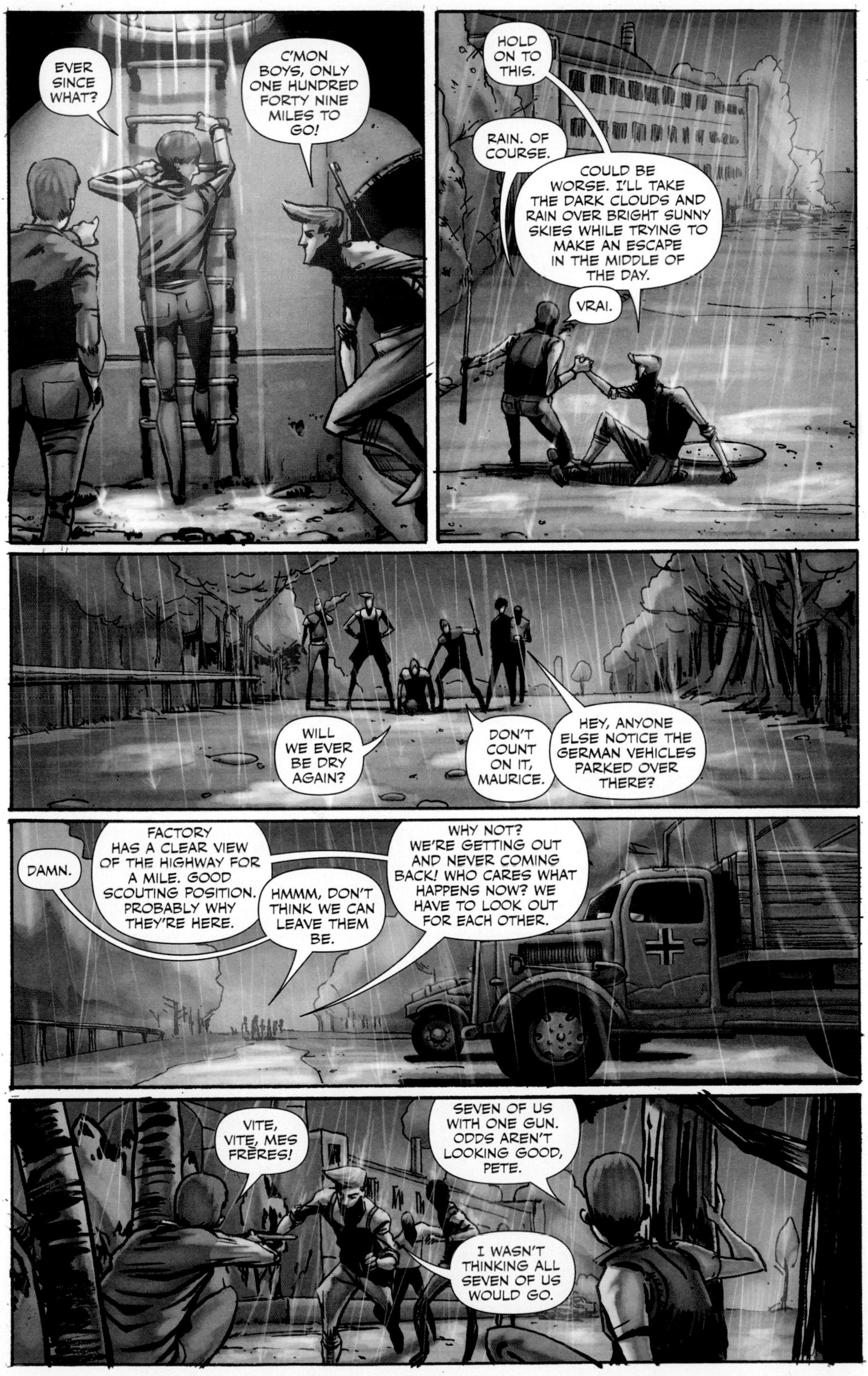
EVER SINCE WHAT?
C'MON BOYS, ONLY ONE HUNDRED FORTY NINE MILES TO GO!
HOLD ON TO THIS.
RAIN. OF COURSE.
COULD BE WORSE. I'LL TAKE THE DARK CLOUDS AND RAIN OVER BRIGHT SUNNY SKIES WHILE TRYING TO MAKE AN ESCAPE IN THE MIDDLE OF THE DAY.
VRAI.
WILL WE EVER BE DRY AGAIN?
DON'T COUNT ON IT, MAURICE.
HEY, ANYONE ELSE NOTICE THE GERMAN VEHICLES PARKED OVER THERE?
DAMN.
FACTORY HAS A CLEAR VIEW OF THE HIGHWAY FOR A MILE. GOOD SCOUTING POSITION. PROBABLY WHY THEY'RE HERE.
HMMM, DON'T THINK WE CAN LEAVE THEM BE.
WHY NOT? WE'RE GETTING OUT AND NEVER COMING BACK! WHO CARES WHAT HAPPENS NOW? WE HAVE TO LOOK OUT FOR EACH OTHER.
VITE, VITE, MES FRÈRES!
SEVEN OF US WITH ONE GUN. ODDS AREN'T LOOKING GOOD, PETE.
I WASN'T THINKING ALL SEVEN OF US WOULD GO.

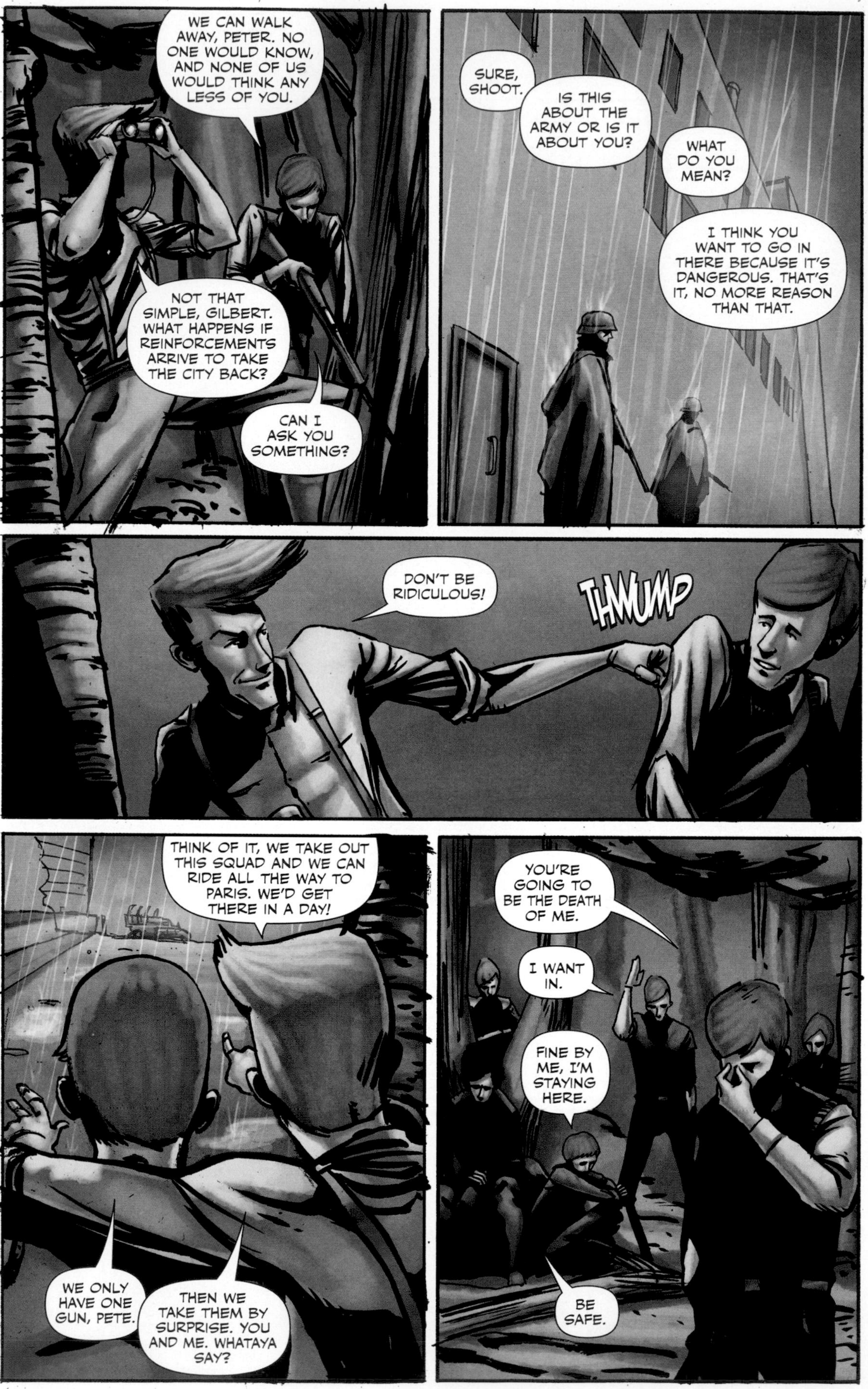
WE CAN WALK AWAY, PETER. NO ONE WOULD KNOW, AND NONE OF US WOULD THINK ANY LESS OF YOU.
NOT THAT SIMPLE, GILBERT. WHAT HAPPENS IF REINFORCEMENTS ARRIVE TO TAKE THE CITY BACK?
CAN I ASK YOU SOMETHING?
SURE, SHOOT.
IS THIS ABOUT THE ARMY OR IS IT ABOUT YOU?
WHAT DO YOU MEAN?
I THINK YOU WANT TO GO IN THERE BECAUSE IT'S DANGEROUS. THAT'S IT, NO MORE REASON THAN THAT.
DON'T BE RIDICULOUS!
THWUMP
THINK OF IT, WE TAKE OUT THIS SQUAD AND WE CAN RIDE ALL THE WAY TO PARIS. WE'D GET THERE IN A DAY!
WE ONLY HAVE ONE GUN, PETE.
THEN WE TAKE THEM BY SURPRISE. YOU AND ME. WHATAYA SAY?
YOU'RE GOING TO BE THE DEATH OF ME.
I WANT IN.
FINE BY ME, I'M STAYING HERE.
BE SAFE.

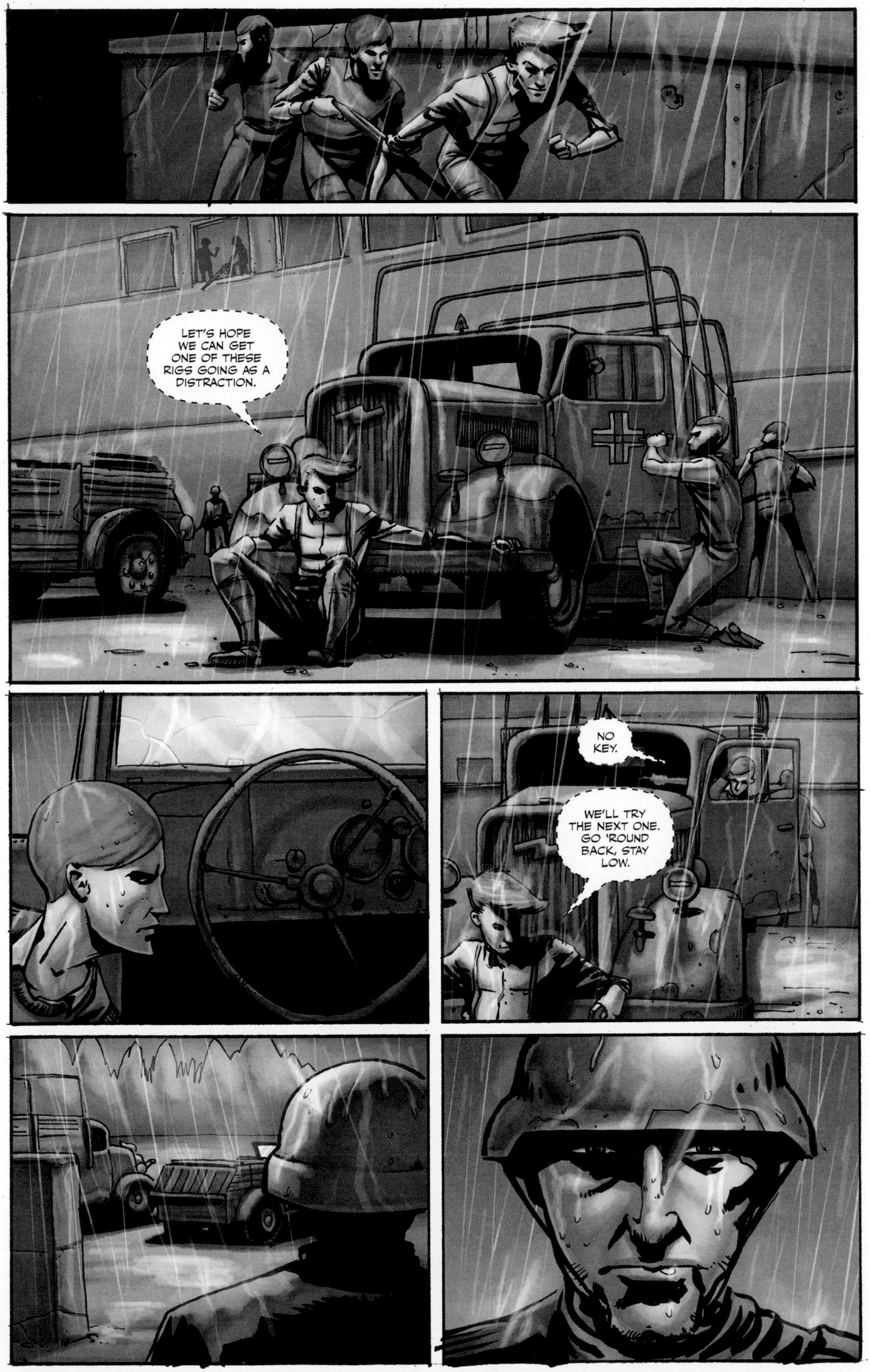
LET'S HOPE WE CAN GET ONE OF THESE RIGS GOING AS A DISTRACTION.
NO KEY.
WE'LL TRY THE NEXT ONE. GO 'ROUND BACK, STAY LOW.

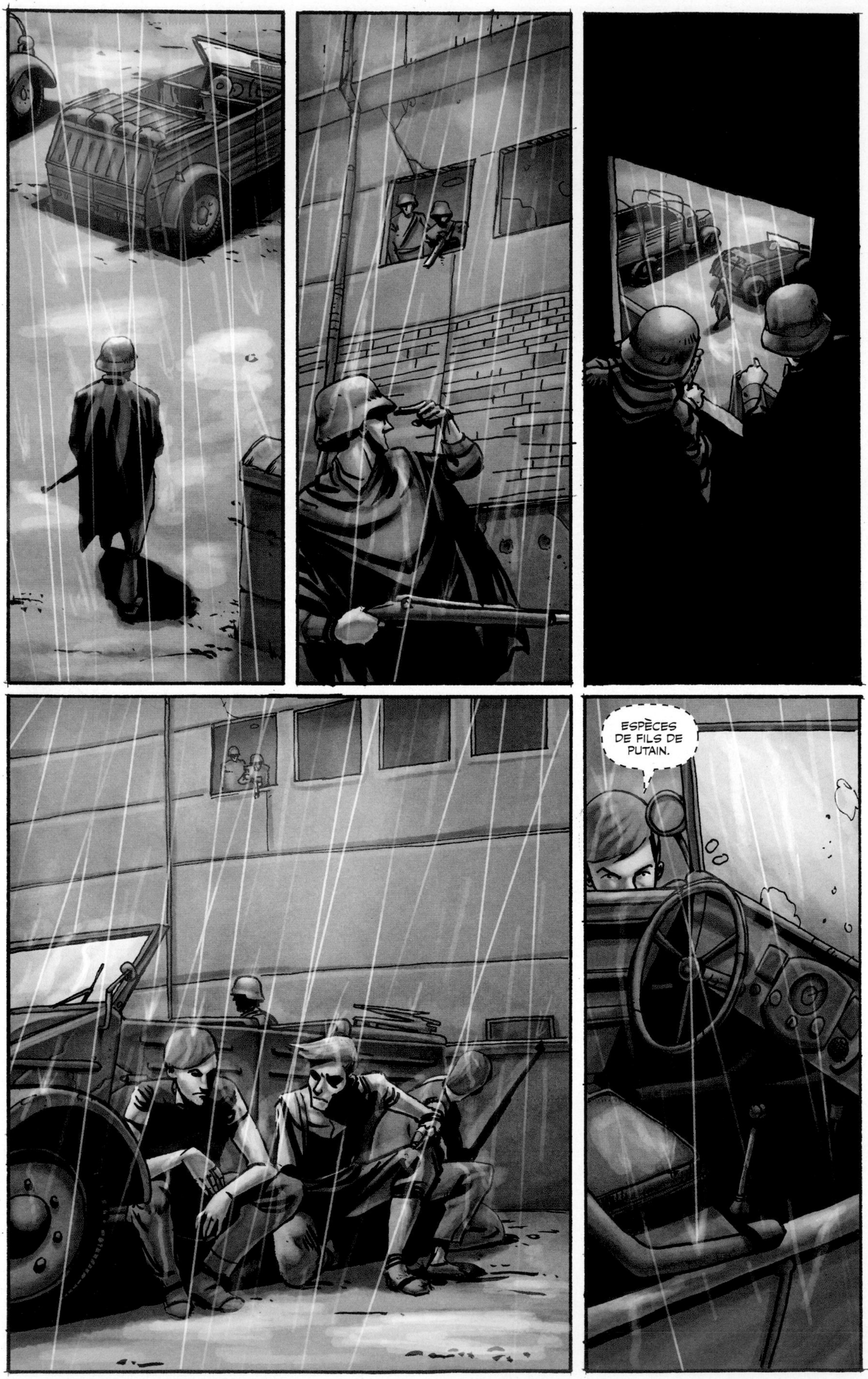
ESPÈCES DE FILS DE PUTAIN.

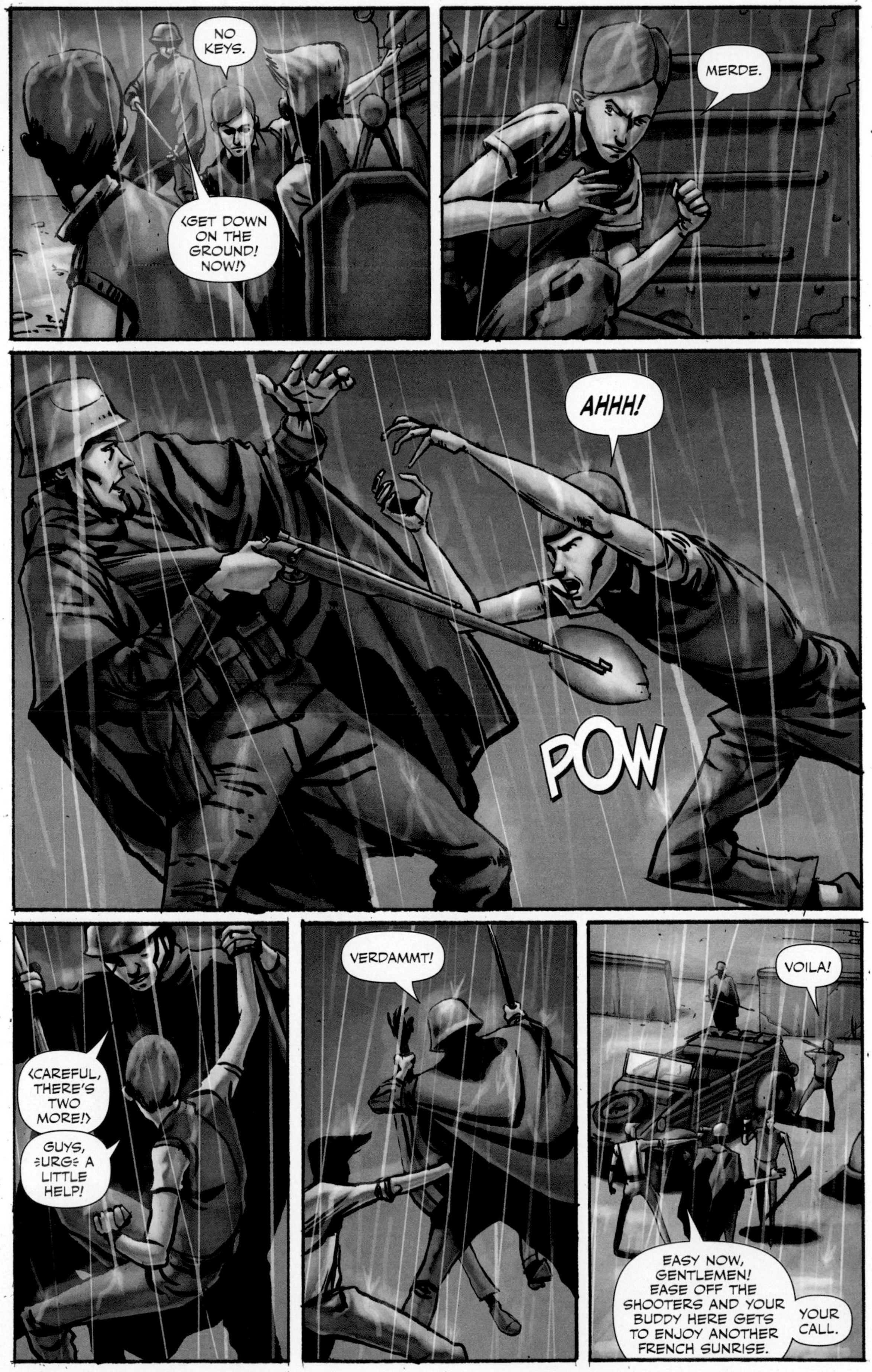
NO KEYS.
‹GET DOWN ON THE GROUND! NOW!›
MERDE.
AHHH!
POW
VERDAMMT!
‹CAREFUL, THERE'S TWO MORE!›
GUYS, ≈URG≈ A LITTLE HELP!
VOILA!
EASY NOW, GENTLEMEN! EASE OFF THE SHOOTERS AND YOUR BUDDY HERE GETS TO ENJOY ANOTHER FRENCH SUNRISE.
YOUR CALL.

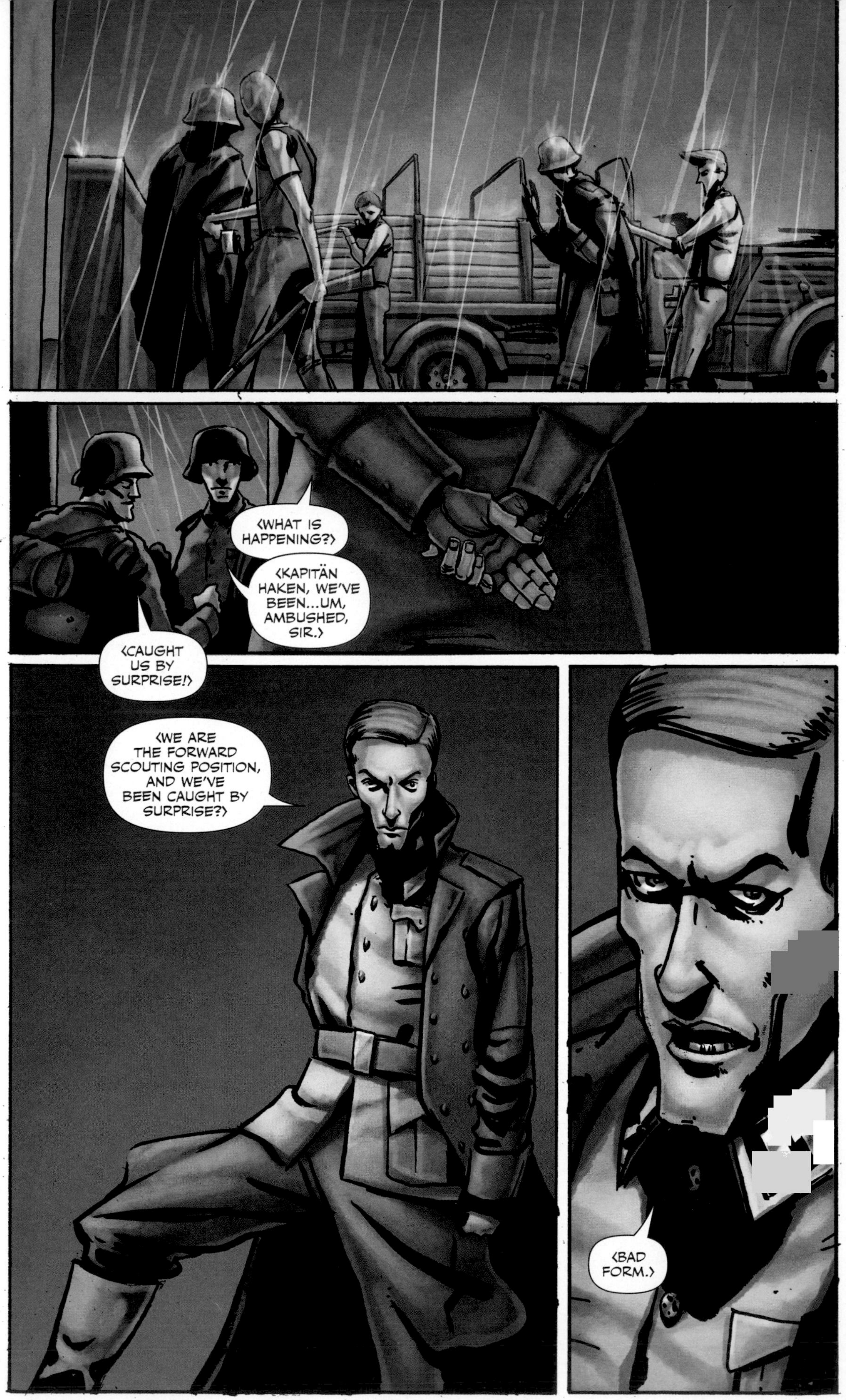

<WHAT IS HAPPENING?>
<KAPITÄN HAKEN, WE'VE BEEN...UM, AMBUSHED, SIR.>
<CAUGHT US BY SURPRISE!>
<WE ARE THE FORWARD SCOUTING POSITION, AND WE'VE BEEN CAUGHT BY SURPRISE?>
<BAD FORM.>

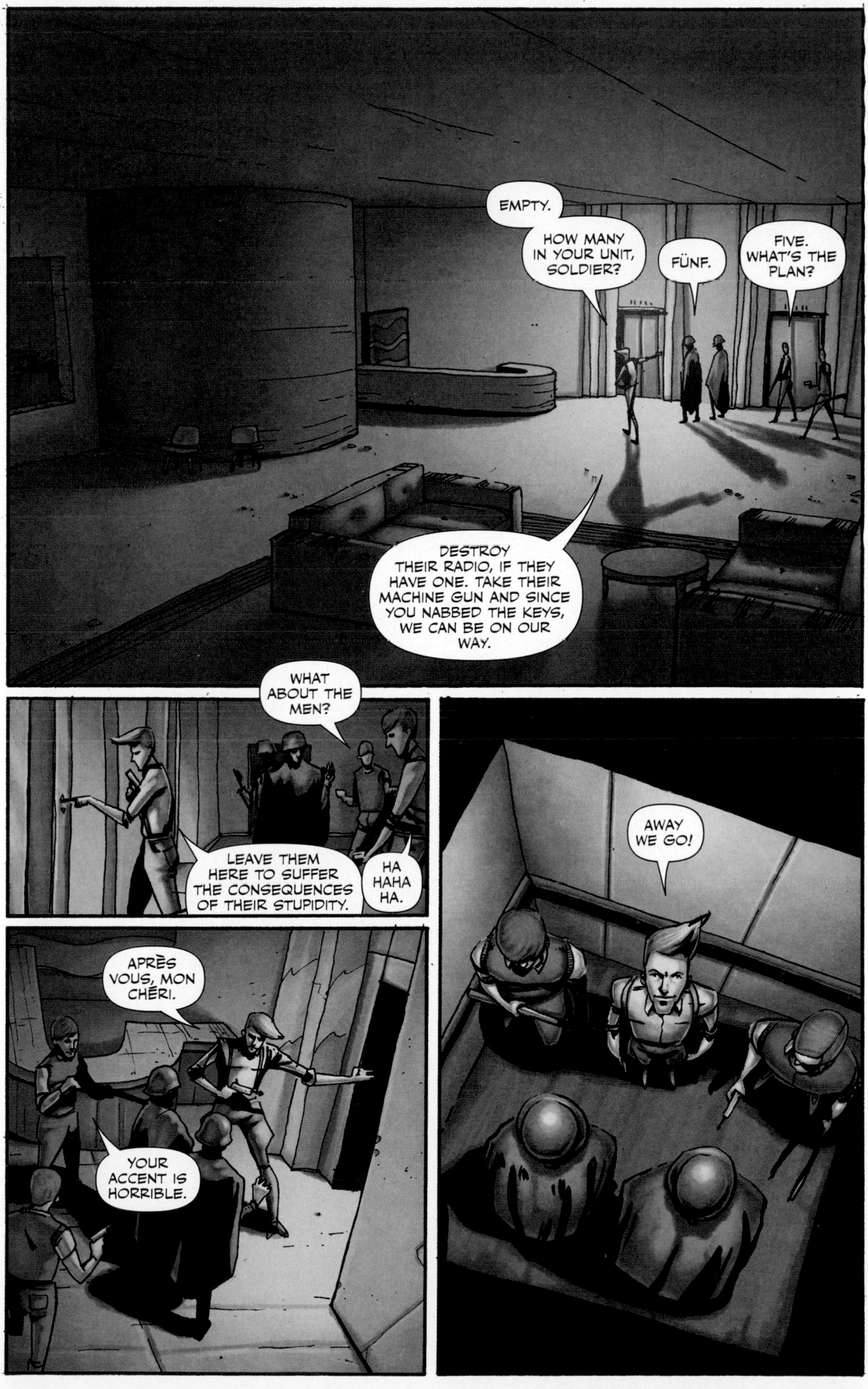
EMPTY.
HOW MANY IN YOUR UNIT, SOLDIER?
FÜNF.
FIVE. WHAT'S THE PLAN?
DESTROY THEIR RADIO, IF THEY HAVE ONE. TAKE THEIR MACHINE GUN AND SINCE YOU NABBED THE KEYS, WE CAN BE ON OUR WAY.
WHAT ABOUT THE MEN?
LEAVE THEM HERE TO SUFFER THE CONSEQUENCES OF THEIR STUPIDITY.
HA HAHA HA.
APRÈS VOUS, MON CHÉRI.
YOUR ACCENT IS HORRIBLE.
AWAY WE GO!

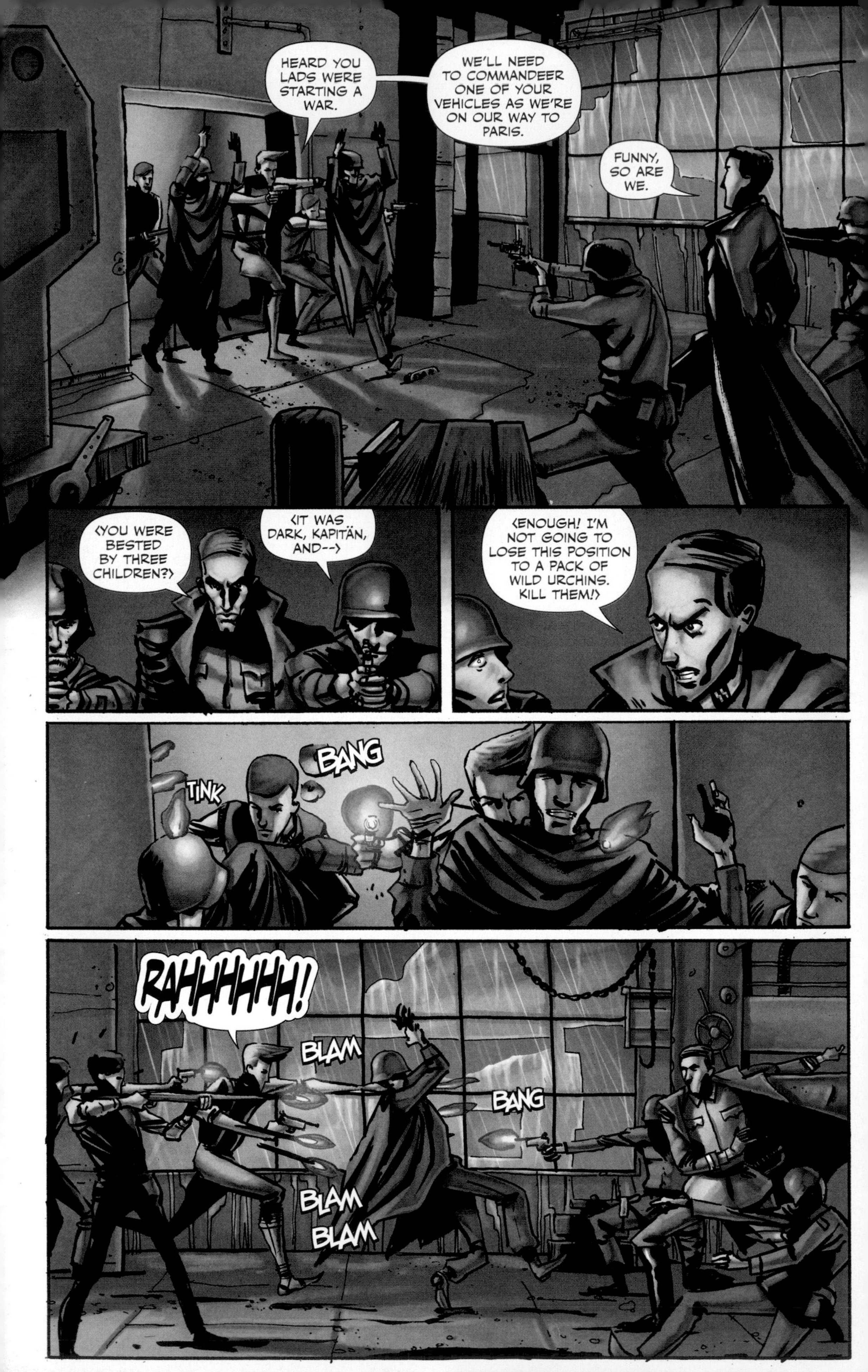
HEARD YOU LADS WERE STARTING A WAR.
WE'LL NEED TO COMMANDEER ONE OF YOUR VEHICLES AS WE'RE ON OUR WAY TO PARIS.
FUNNY, SO ARE WE.
‹YOU WERE BESTED BY THREE CHILDREN?›
‹IT WAS DARK, KAPITÄN, AND--›
‹ENOUGH! I'M NOT GOING TO LOSE THIS POSITION TO A PACK OF WILD URCHINS. KILL THEM!›
BANG
TINK
RAHHHHHH!
BLAM
BANG
BLAM
BLAM

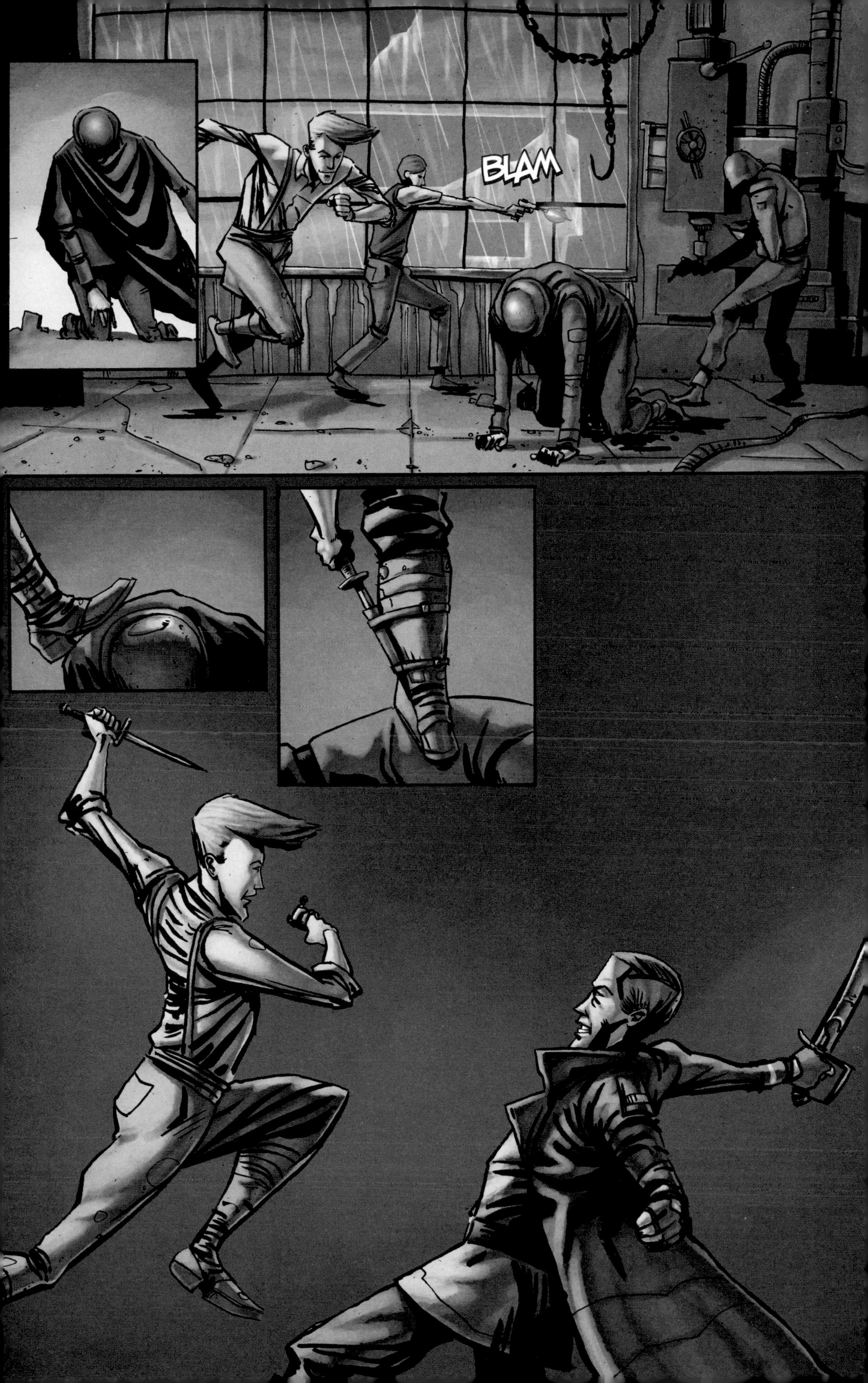
BLAM

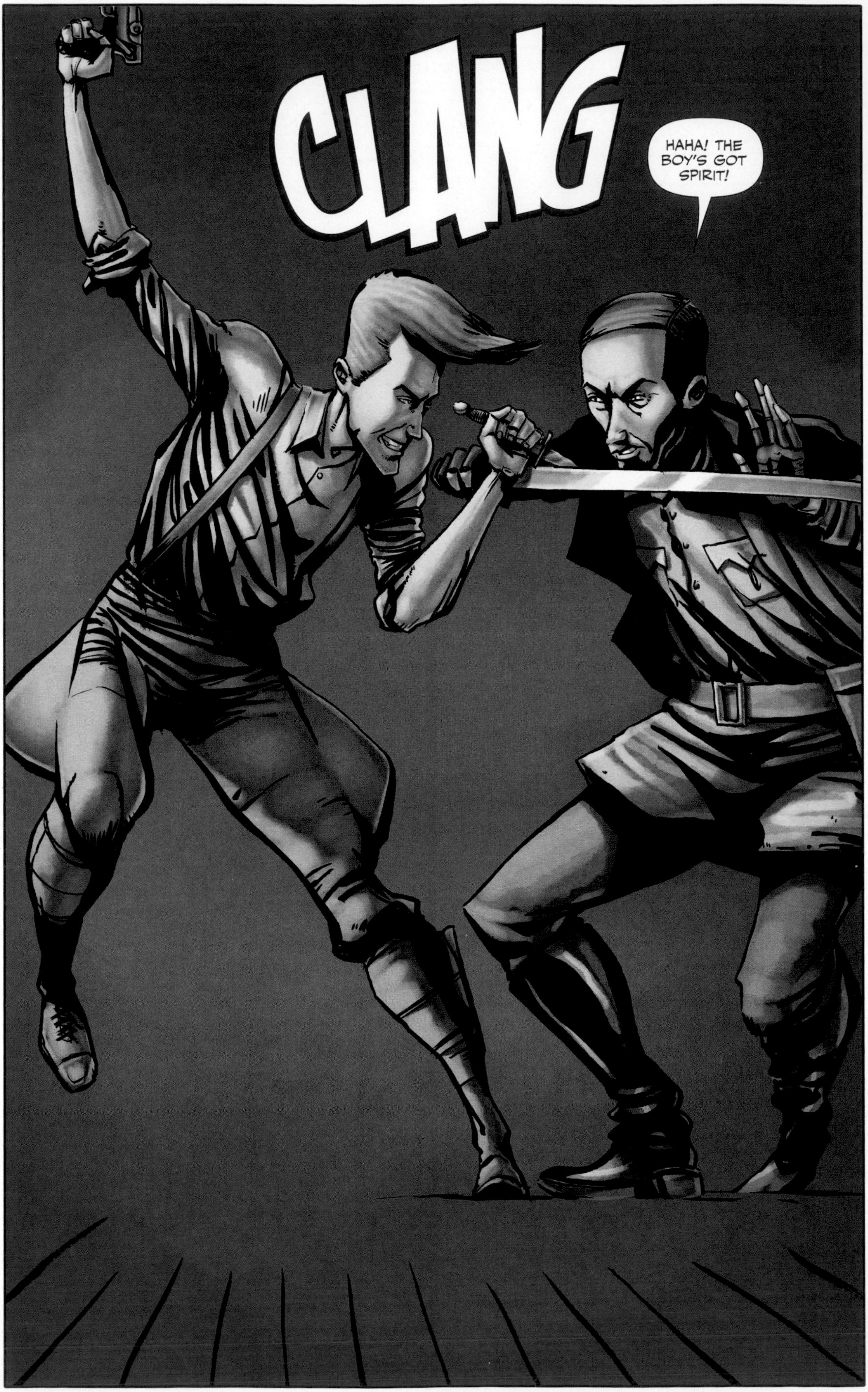
CLANG
HAHA! THE BOY'S GOT SPIRIT!

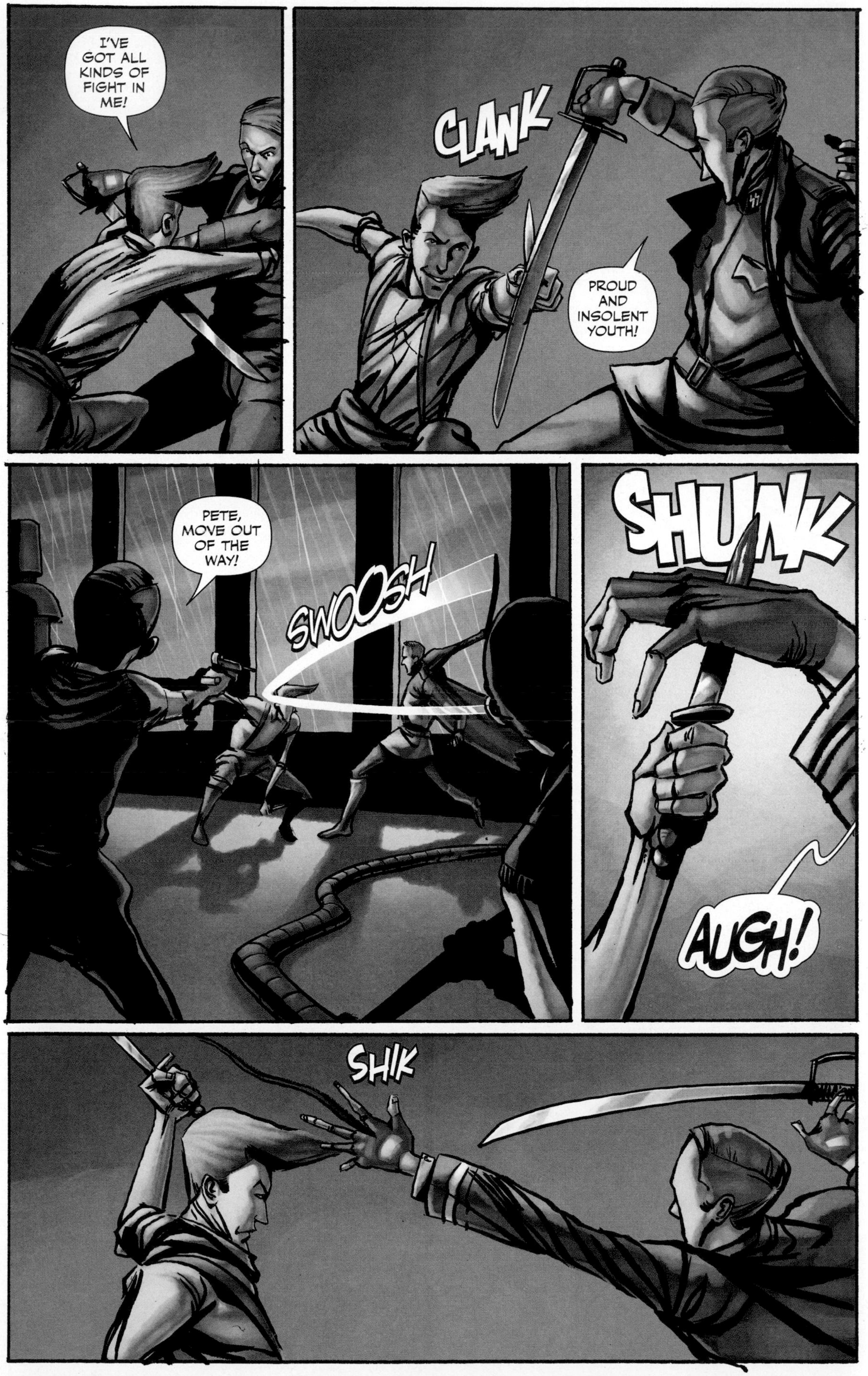
I'VE GOT ALL KINDS OF FIGHT IN ME!
CLANK
PROUD AND INSOLENT YOUTH!
PETE, MOVE OUT OF THE WAY!
SWOOSH
SHUNK
AUGH!
SHIK

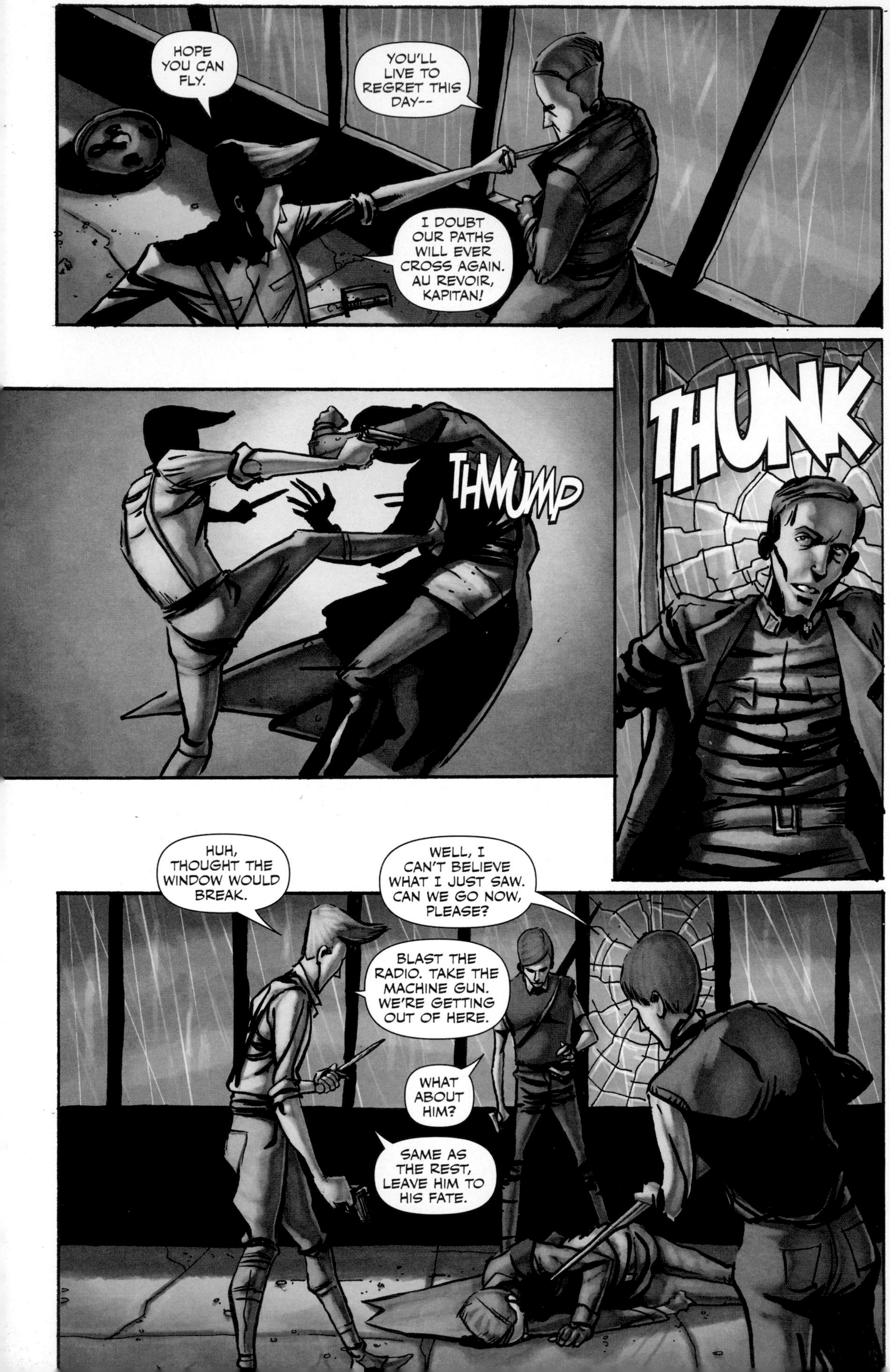
HOPE YOU CAN FLY.
YOU'LL LIVE TO REGRET THIS DAY--
I DOUBT OUR PATHS WILL EVER CROSS AGAIN. AU REVOIR, KAPITAN!
THWUMP
THUNK
HUH, THOUGHT THE WINDOW WOULD BREAK.
WELL, I CAN'T BELIEVE WHAT I JUST SAW. CAN WE GO NOW, PLEASE?
BLAST THE RADIO. TAKE THE MACHINE GUN. WE'RE GETTING OUT OF HERE.
WHAT ABOUT HIM?
SAME AS THE REST, LEAVE HIM TO HIS FATE.

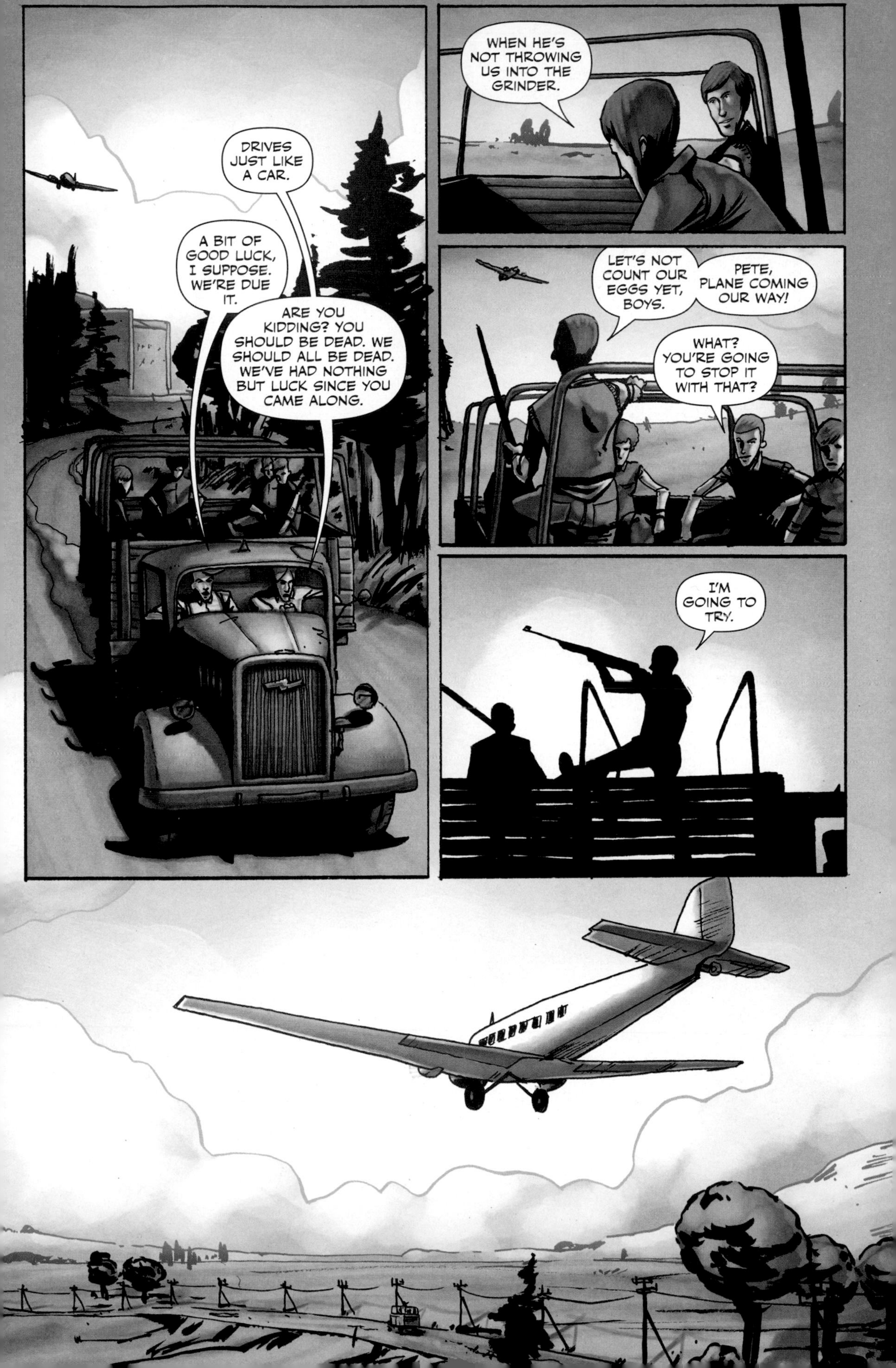
DRIVES JUST LIKE A CAR.
A BIT OF GOOD LUCK, I SUPPOSE. WE'RE DUE IT.
ARE YOU KIDDING? YOU SHOULD BE DEAD. WE SHOULD ALL BE DEAD. WE'VE HAD NOTHING BUT LUCK SINCE YOU CAME ALONG.
WHEN HE'S NOT THROWING US INTO THE GRINDER.
PETE, PLANE COMING OUR WAY!
LET'S NOT COUNT OUR EGGS YET, BOYS.
WHAT? YOU'RE GOING TO STOP IT WITH THAT?
I'M GOING TO TRY.

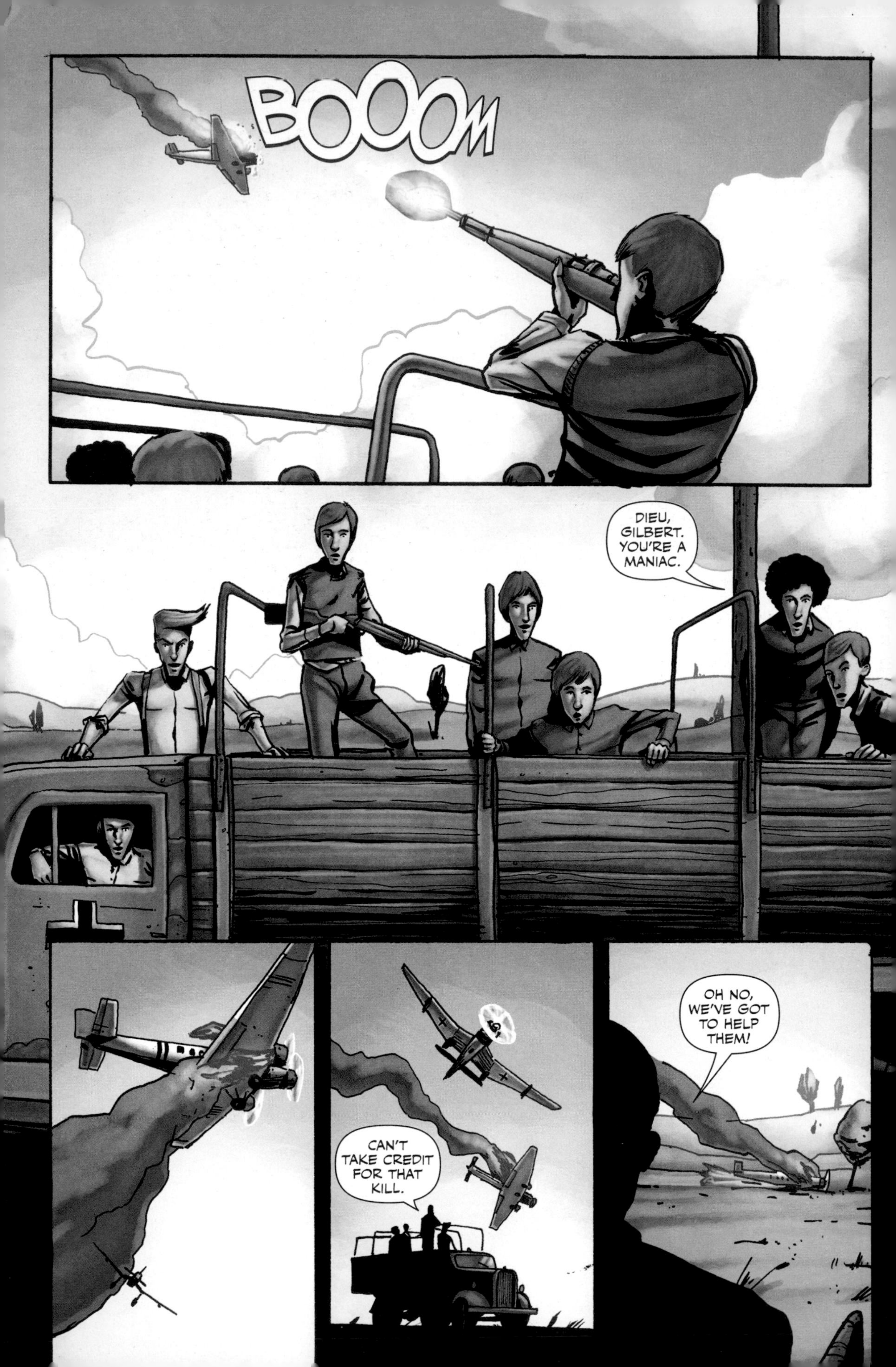
BOOOM
DIEU, GILBERT. YOU'RE A MANIAC.
CAN'T TAKE CREDIT FOR THAT KILL.
OH NO, WE'VE GOT TO HELP THEM!

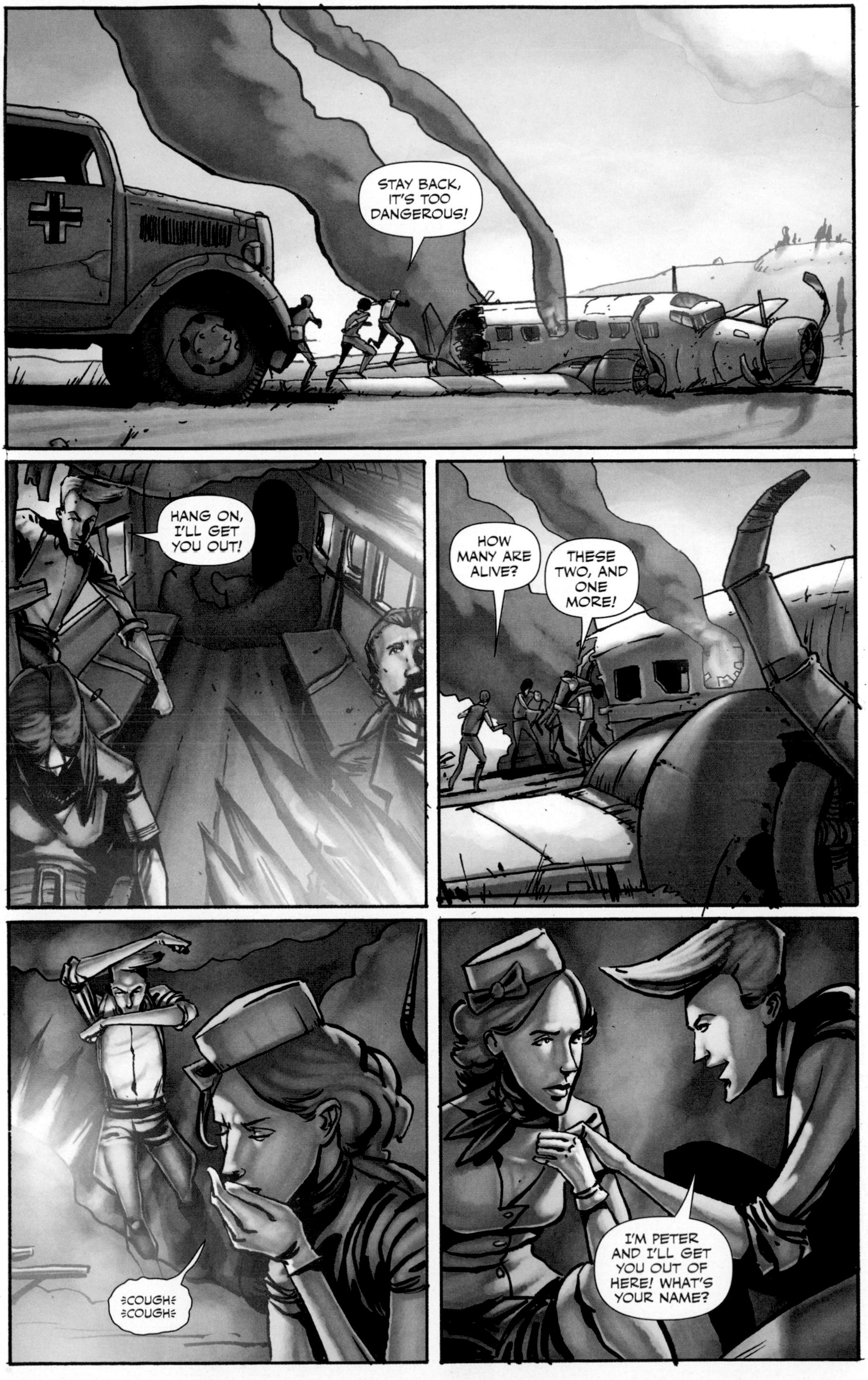
STAY BACK, IT'S TOO DANGEROUS!
HANG ON, I'LL GET YOU OUT!
HOW MANY ARE ALIVE?
THESE TWO, AND ONE MORE!
COUGH COUGH
I'M PETER AND I'LL GET YOU OUT OF HERE! WHAT'S YOUR NAME?

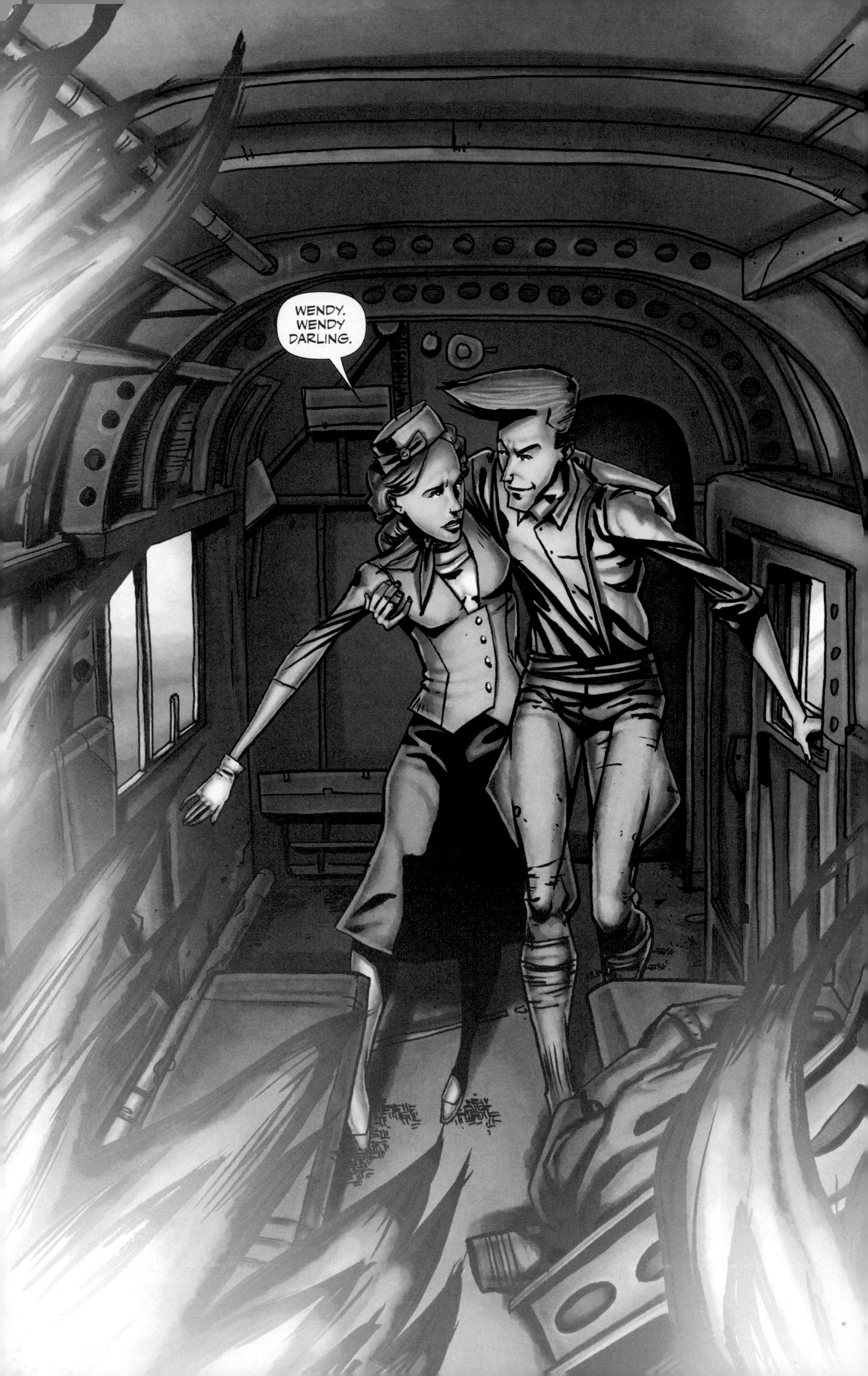
WENDY. WENDY DARLING.

CHAPTER FOUR

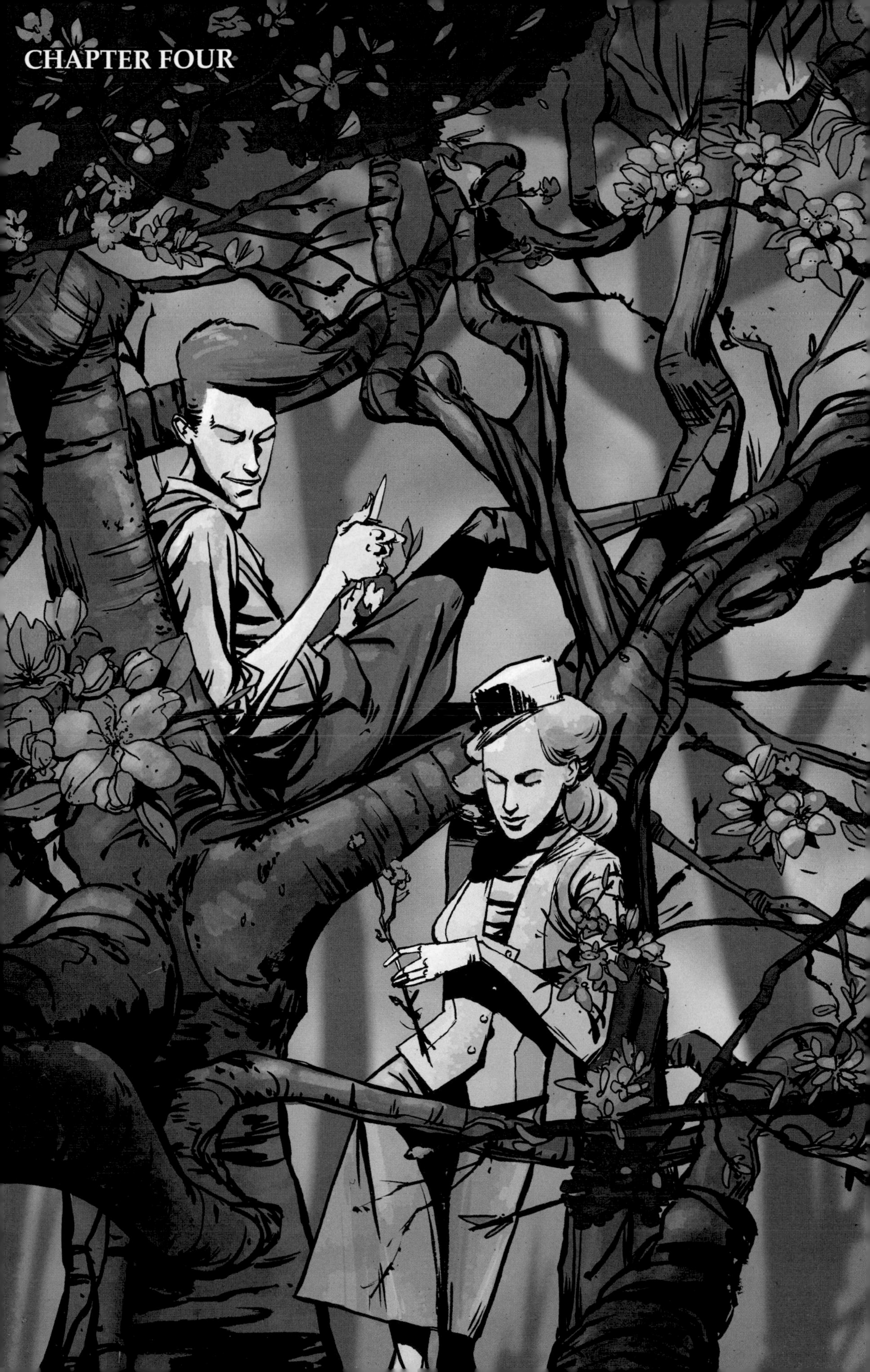

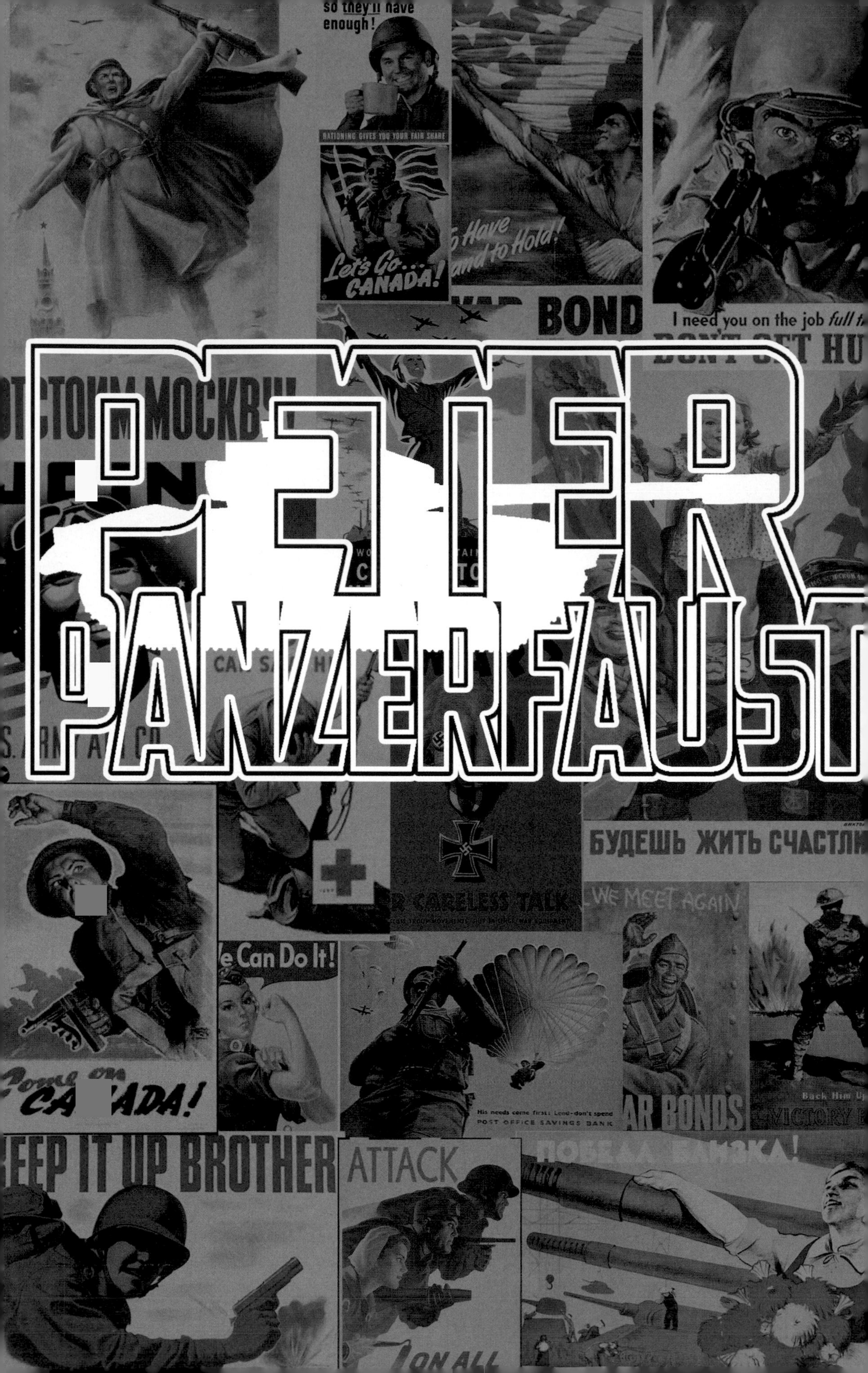
PETER
PANZERFAUST
so they'll have
enough!
RATIONING GIVES YOU YOUR FAIR SHARE
Let's Go...
CANADA!
BOND
I need you on the job
БУДЕШЬ ЖИТЬ СЧАСТЛИ
CARELESS TALK
WE MEET AGAIN
His needs come first: Lend–don't spend
POST OFFICE SAVINGS BANK
AR BONDS
Back Him Up
ATTACK
EEP IT UP BROTHER

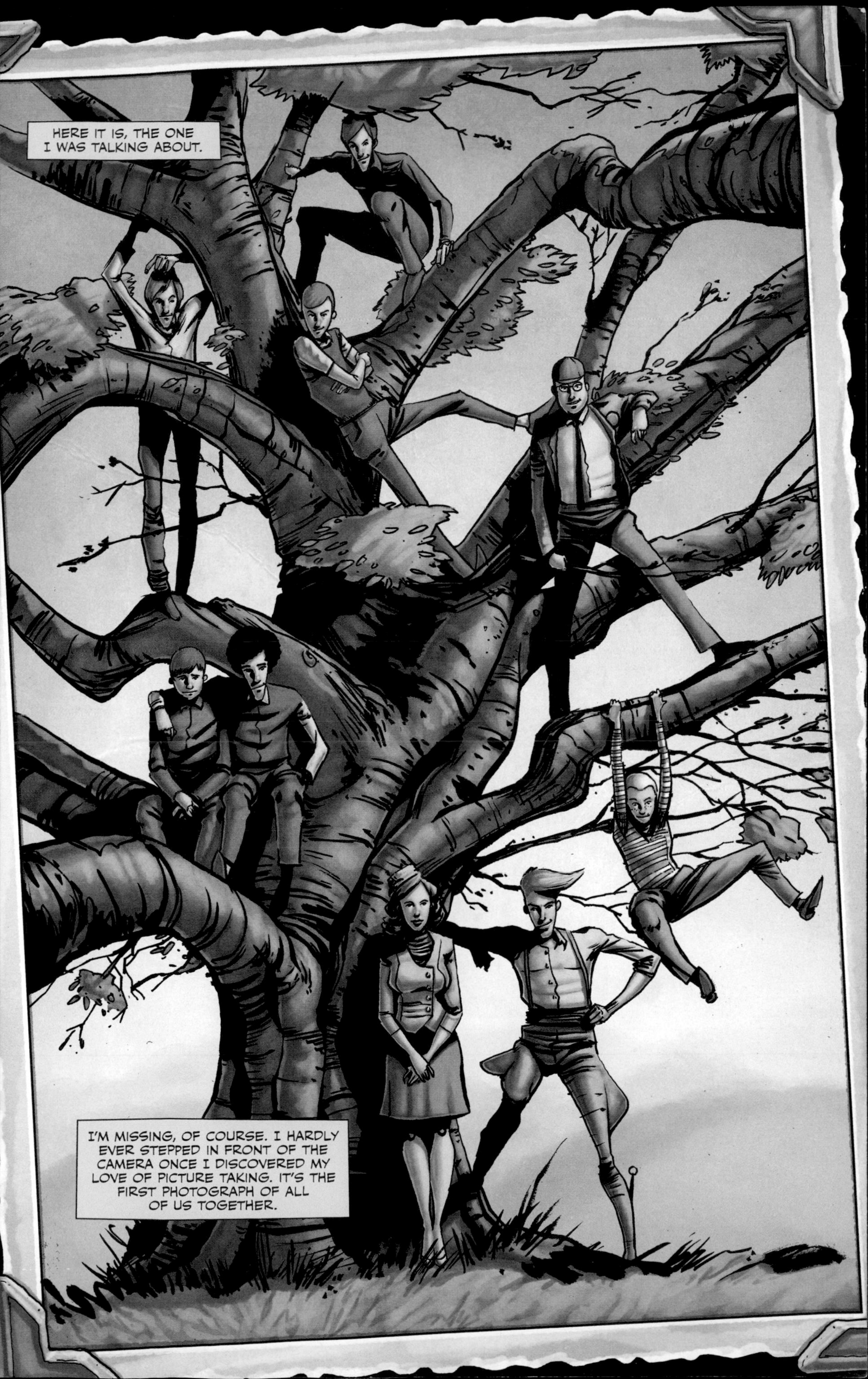
HERE IT IS, THE ONE I WAS TALKING ABOUT.
I'M MISSING, OF COURSE. I HARDLY EVER STEPPED IN FRONT OF THE CAMERA ONCE I DISCOVERED MY LOVE OF PICTURE TAKING. IT'S THE FIRST PHOTOGRAPH OF ALL OF US TOGETHER.

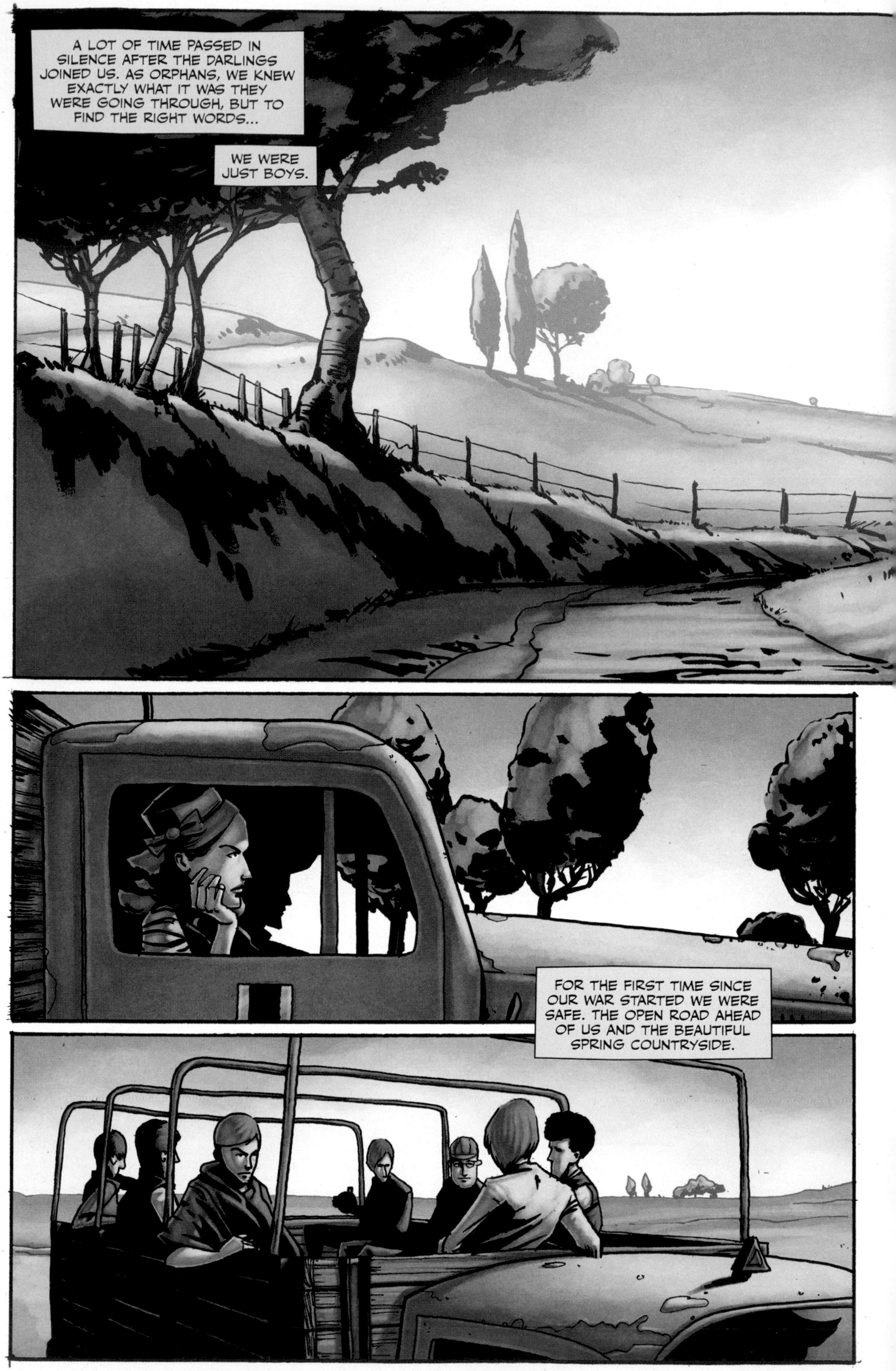
A LOT OF TIME PASSED IN SILENCE AFTER THE DARLINGS JOINED US. AS ORPHANS, WE KNEW EXACTLY WHAT IT WAS THEY WERE GOING THROUGH, BUT TO FIND THE RIGHT WORDS...
WE WERE JUST BOYS.
FOR THE FIRST TIME SINCE OUR WAR STARTED WE WERE SAFE. THE OPEN ROAD AHEAD OF US AND THE BEAUTIFUL SPRING COUNTRYSIDE.

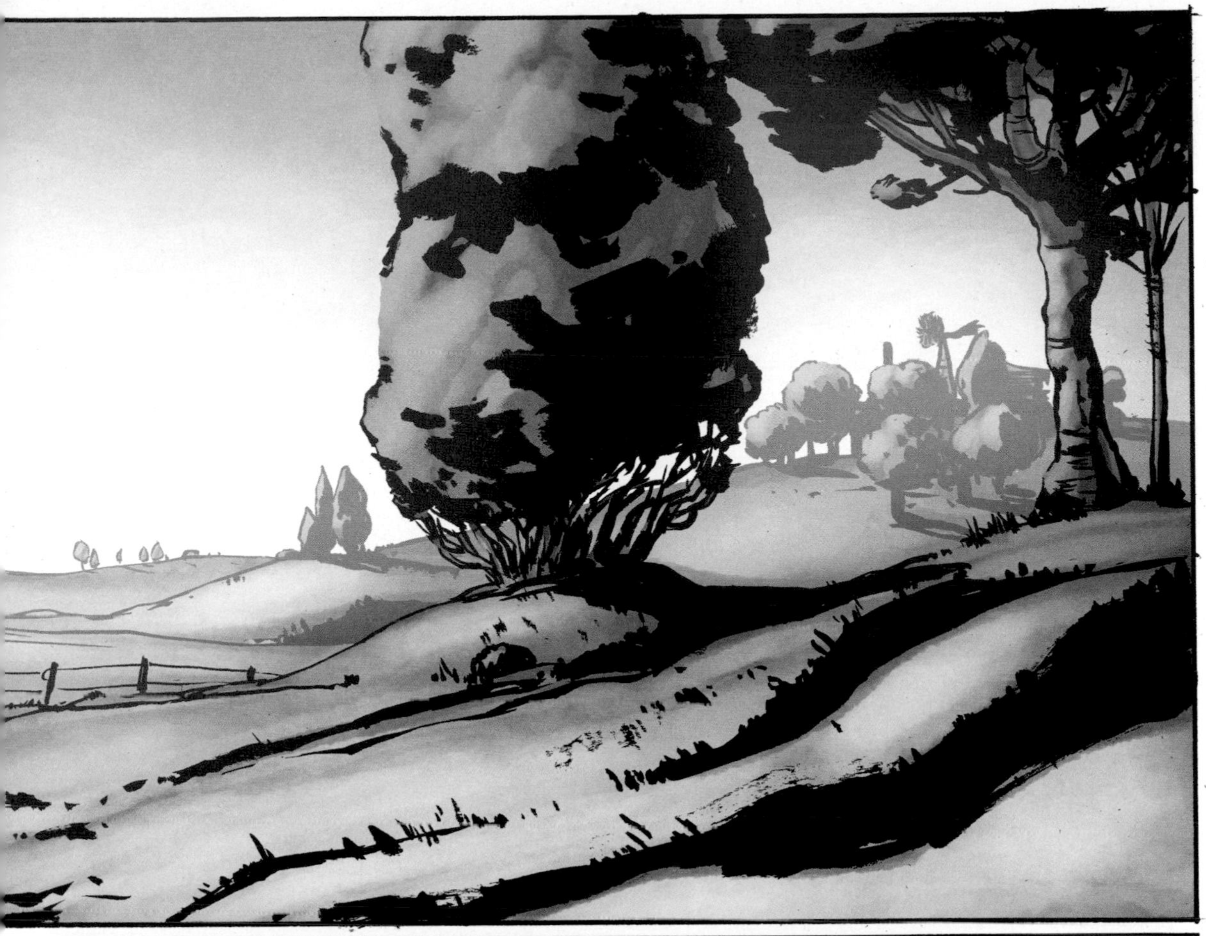

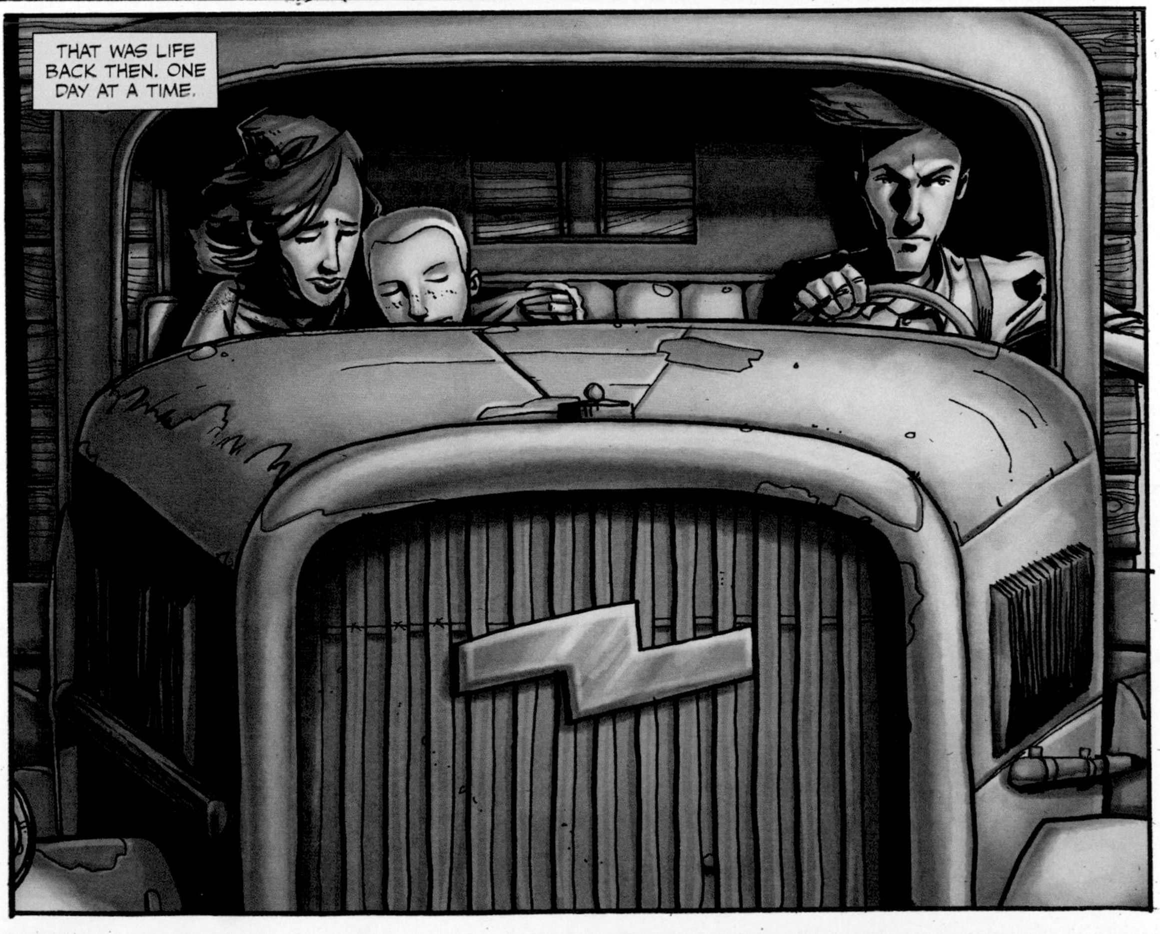
THAT WAS LIFE BACK THEN. ONE DAY AT A TIME.

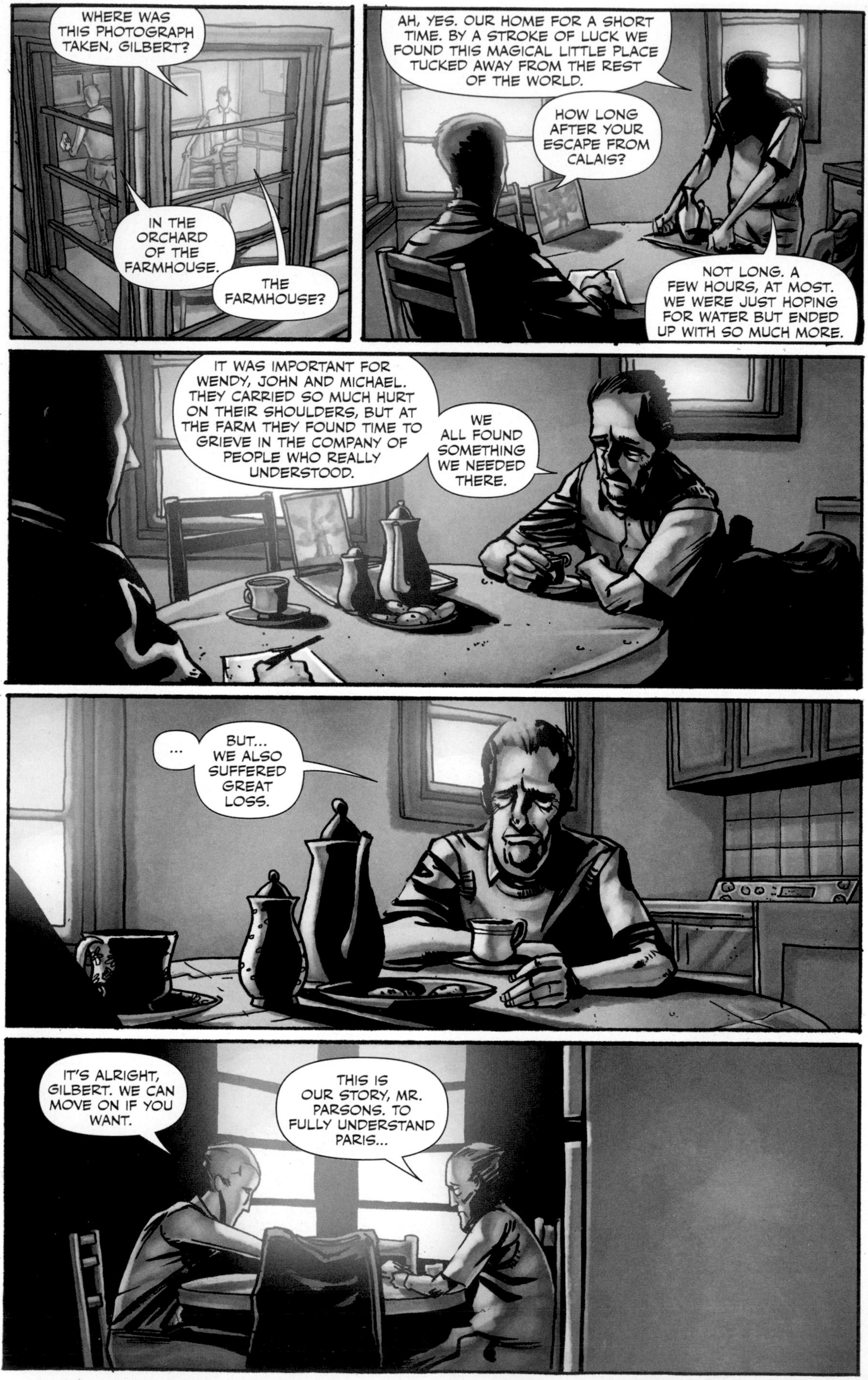
WHERE WAS THIS PHOTOGRAPH TAKEN, GILBERT?
IN THE ORCHARD OF THE FARMHOUSE.
THE FARMHOUSE?
AH, YES. OUR HOME FOR A SHORT TIME. BY A STROKE OF LUCK WE FOUND THIS MAGICAL LITTLE PLACE TUCKED AWAY FROM THE REST OF THE WORLD.
HOW LONG AFTER YOUR ESCAPE FROM CALAIS?
NOT LONG. A FEW HOURS, AT MOST. WE WERE JUST HOPING FOR WATER BUT ENDED UP WITH SO MUCH MORE.
IT WAS IMPORTANT FOR WENDY, JOHN AND MICHAEL. THEY CARRIED SO MUCH HURT ON THEIR SHOULDERS, BUT AT THE FARM THEY FOUND TIME TO GRIEVE IN THE COMPANY OF PEOPLE WHO REALLY UNDERSTOOD.
WE ALL FOUND SOMETHING WE NEEDED THERE.
...
BUT... WE ALSO SUFFERED GREAT LOSS.
IT'S ALRIGHT, GILBERT. WE CAN MOVE ON IF YOU WANT.
THIS IS OUR STORY, MR. PARSONS. TO FULLY UNDERSTAND PARIS...

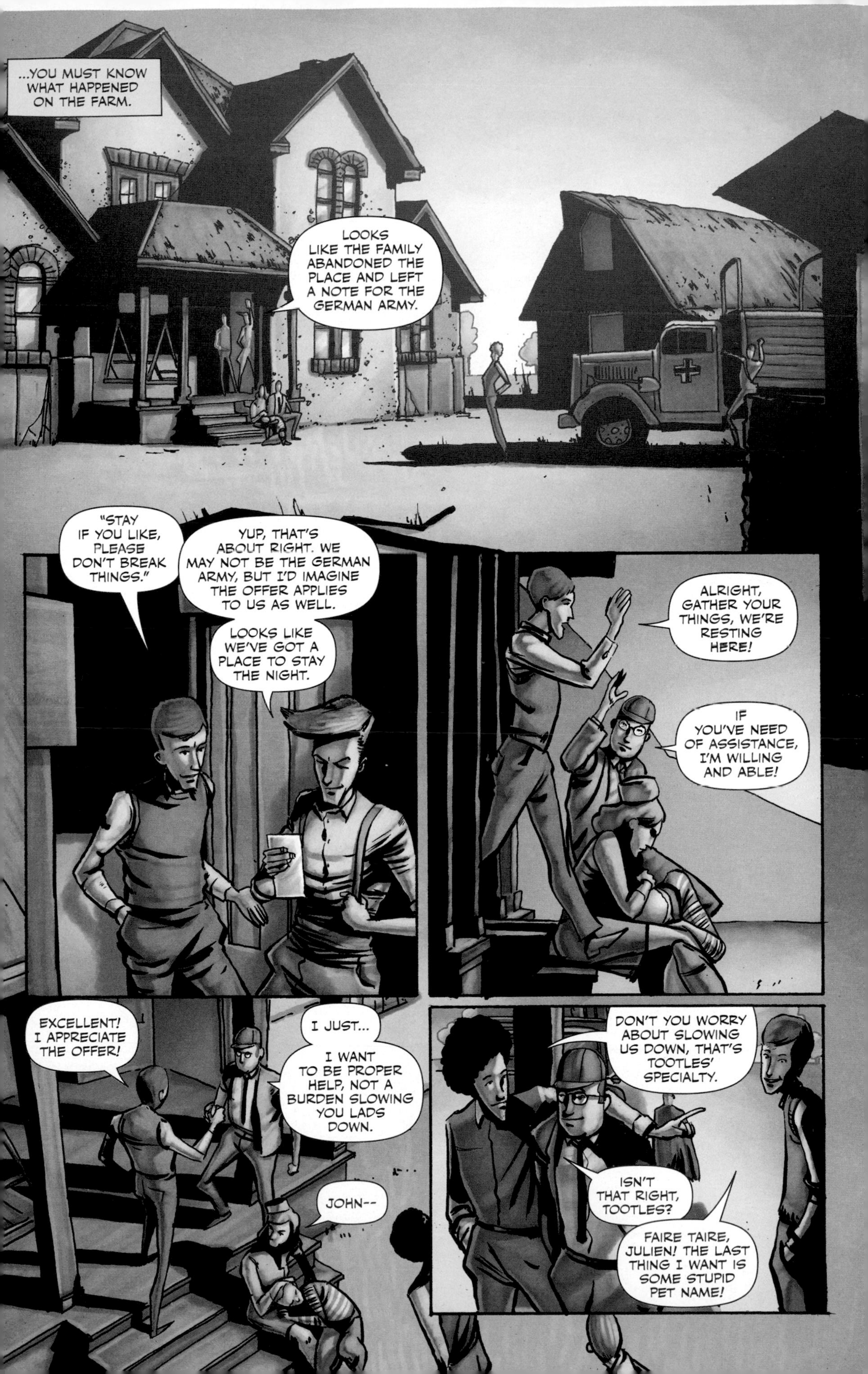
...YOU MUST KNOW WHAT HAPPENED ON THE FARM.
LOOKS LIKE THE FAMILY ABANDONED THE PLACE AND LEFT A NOTE FOR THE GERMAN ARMY.
"STAY IF YOU LIKE, PLEASE DON'T BREAK THINGS."
YUP, THAT'S ABOUT RIGHT. WE MAY NOT BE THE GERMAN ARMY, BUT I'D IMAGINE THE OFFER APPLIES TO US AS WELL.
LOOKS LIKE WE'VE GOT A PLACE TO STAY THE NIGHT.
ALRIGHT, GATHER YOUR THINGS, WE'RE RESTING HERE!
IF YOU'VE NEED OF ASSISTANCE, I'M WILLING AND ABLE!
EXCELLENT! I APPRECIATE THE OFFER!
I JUST...
I WANT TO BE PROPER HELP, NOT A BURDEN SLOWING YOU LADS DOWN.
JOHN--
DON'T YOU WORRY ABOUT SLOWING US DOWN, THAT'S TOOTLES' SPECIALTY.
ISN'T THAT RIGHT, TOOTLES?
FAIRE TAIRE, JULIEN! THE LAST THING I WANT IS SOME STUPID PET NAME!

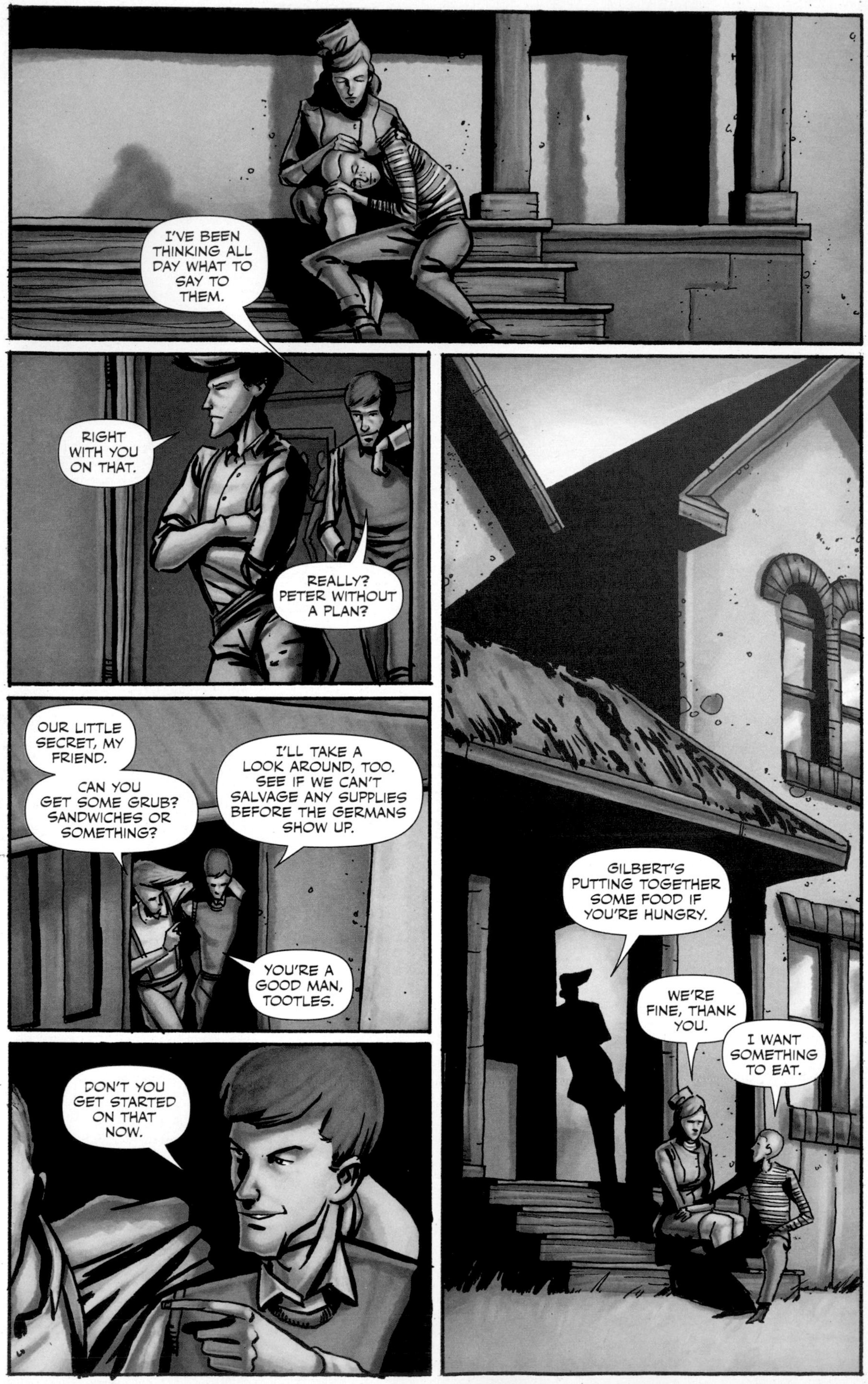
I'VE BEEN THINKING ALL DAY WHAT TO SAY TO THEM.
RIGHT WITH YOU ON THAT.
REALLY? PETER WITHOUT A PLAN?
OUR LITTLE SECRET, MY FRIEND.
CAN YOU GET SOME GRUB? SANDWICHES OR SOMETHING?
I'LL TAKE A LOOK AROUND, TOO. SEE IF WE CAN'T SALVAGE ANY SUPPLIES BEFORE THE GERMANS SHOW UP.
YOU'RE A GOOD MAN, TOOTLES.
DON'T YOU GET STARTED ON THAT NOW.
GILBERT'S PUTTING TOGETHER SOME FOOD IF YOU'RE HUNGRY.
WE'RE FINE, THANK YOU.
I WANT SOMETHING TO EAT.

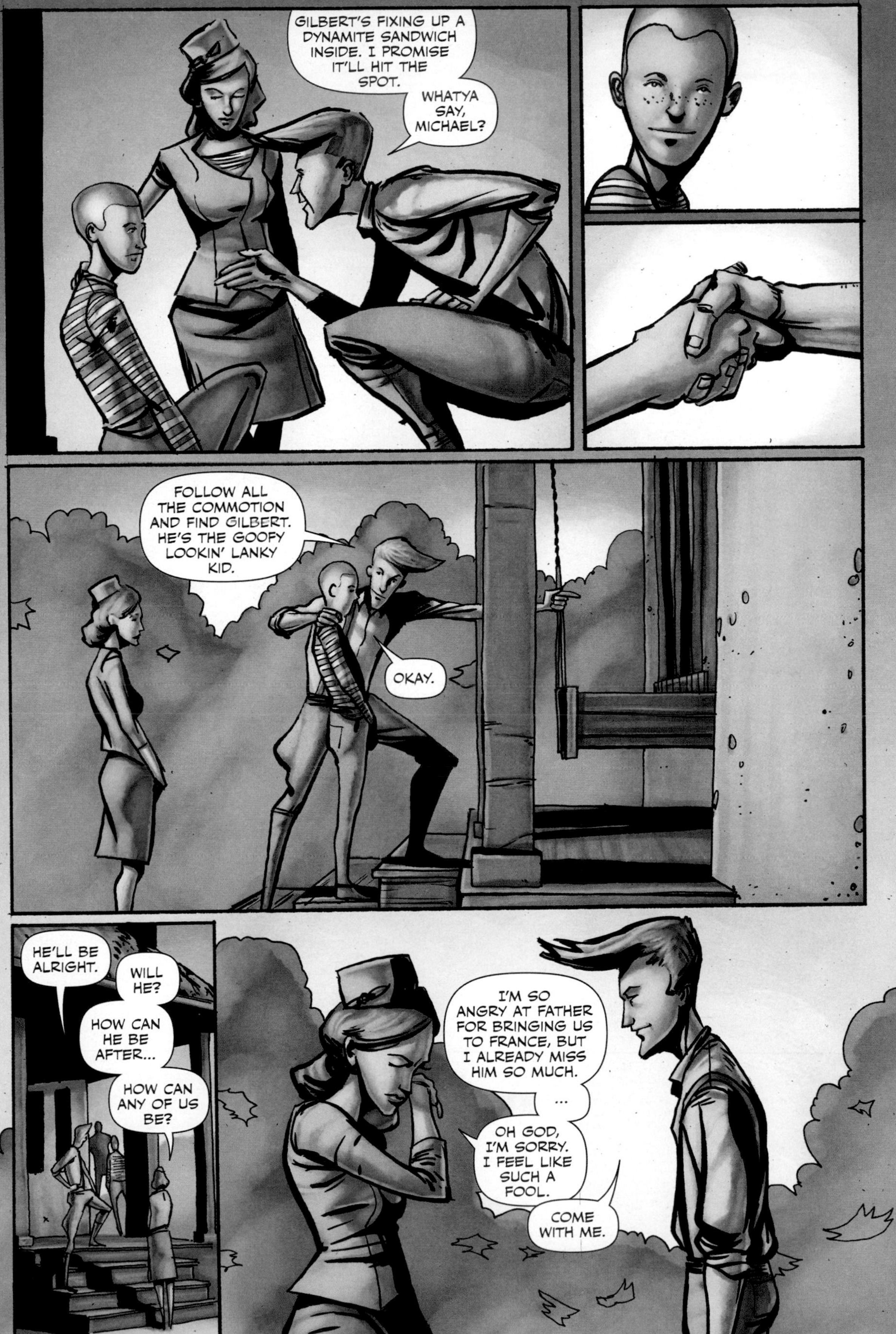
GILBERT'S FIXING UP A DYNAMITE SANDWICH INSIDE. I PROMISE IT'LL HIT THE SPOT.
WHATYA SAY, MICHAEL?
FOLLOW ALL THE COMMOTION AND FIND GILBERT. HE'S THE GOOFY LOOKIN' LANKY KID.
OKAY.
HE'LL BE ALRIGHT.
WILL HE?
HOW CAN HE BE AFTER...
HOW CAN ANY OF US BE?
I'M SO ANGRY AT FATHER FOR BRINGING US TO FRANCE, BUT I ALREADY MISS HIM SO MUCH.
...
OH GOD, I'M SORRY. I FEEL LIKE SUCH A FOOL.
COME WITH ME.

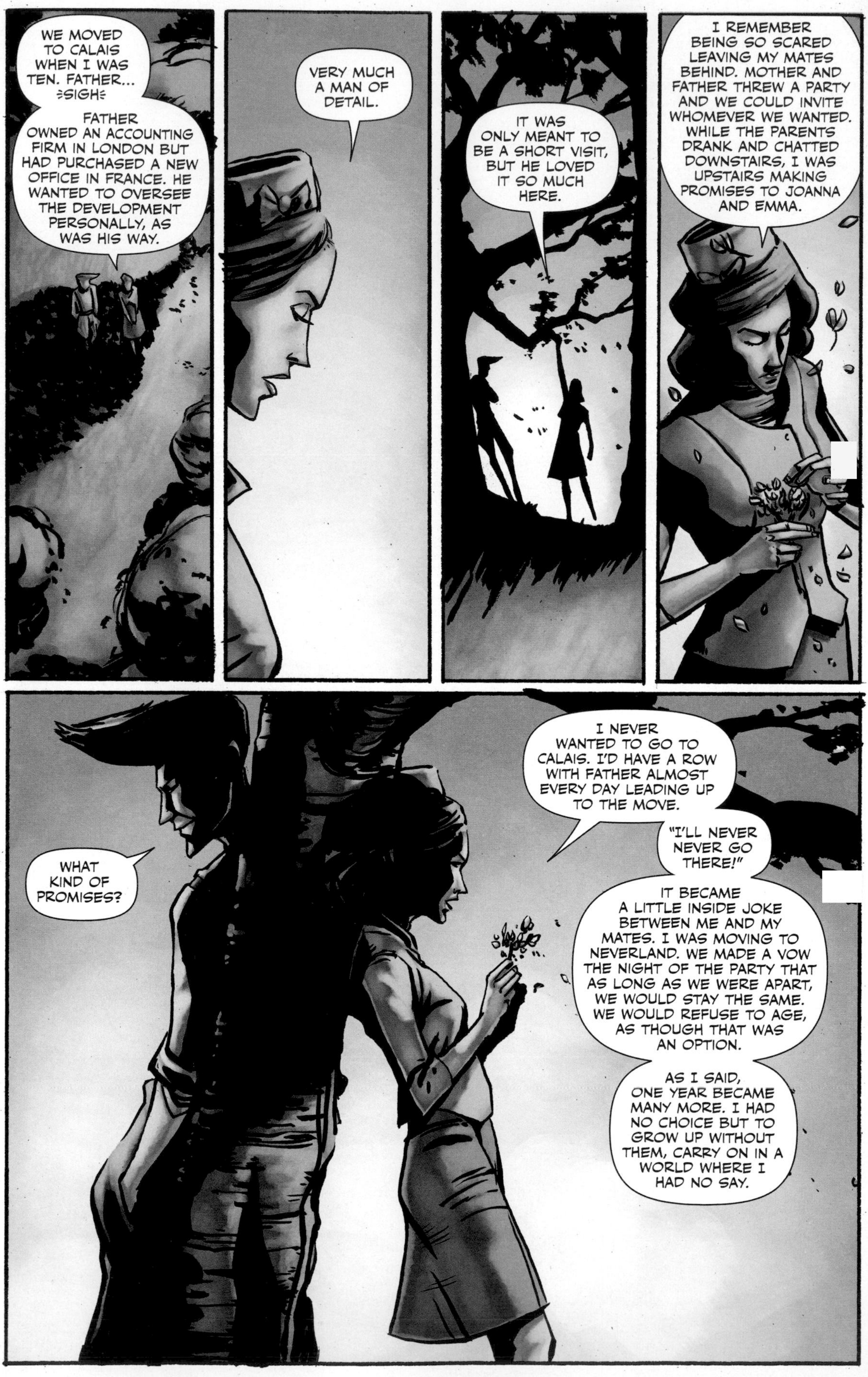
WE MOVED TO CALAIS WHEN I WAS TEN. FATHER... ≡SIGH≡
FATHER OWNED AN ACCOUNTING FIRM IN LONDON BUT HAD PURCHASED A NEW OFFICE IN FRANCE. HE WANTED TO OVERSEE THE DEVELOPMENT PERSONALLY, AS WAS HIS WAY.
VERY MUCH A MAN OF DETAIL.
IT WAS ONLY MEANT TO BE A SHORT VISIT, BUT HE LOVED IT SO MUCH HERE.
I REMEMBER BEING SO SCARED LEAVING MY MATES BEHIND. MOTHER AND FATHER THREW A PARTY AND WE COULD INVITE WHOMEVER WE WANTED. WHILE THE PARENTS DRANK AND CHATTED DOWNSTAIRS, I WAS UPSTAIRS MAKING PROMISES TO JOANNA AND EMMA.
WHAT KIND OF PROMISES?
I NEVER WANTED TO GO TO CALAIS. I'D HAVE A ROW WITH FATHER ALMOST EVERY DAY LEADING UP TO THE MOVE.
"I'LL NEVER NEVER GO THERE!"
IT BECAME A LITTLE INSIDE JOKE BETWEEN ME AND MY MATES. I WAS MOVING TO NEVERLAND. WE MADE A VOW THE NIGHT OF THE PARTY THAT AS LONG AS WE WERE APART, WE WOULD STAY THE SAME. WE WOULD REFUSE TO AGE, AS THOUGH THAT WAS AN OPTION.
AS I SAID, ONE YEAR BECAME MANY MORE. I HAD NO CHOICE BUT TO GROW UP WITHOUT THEM, CARRY ON IN A WORLD WHERE I HAD NO SAY.

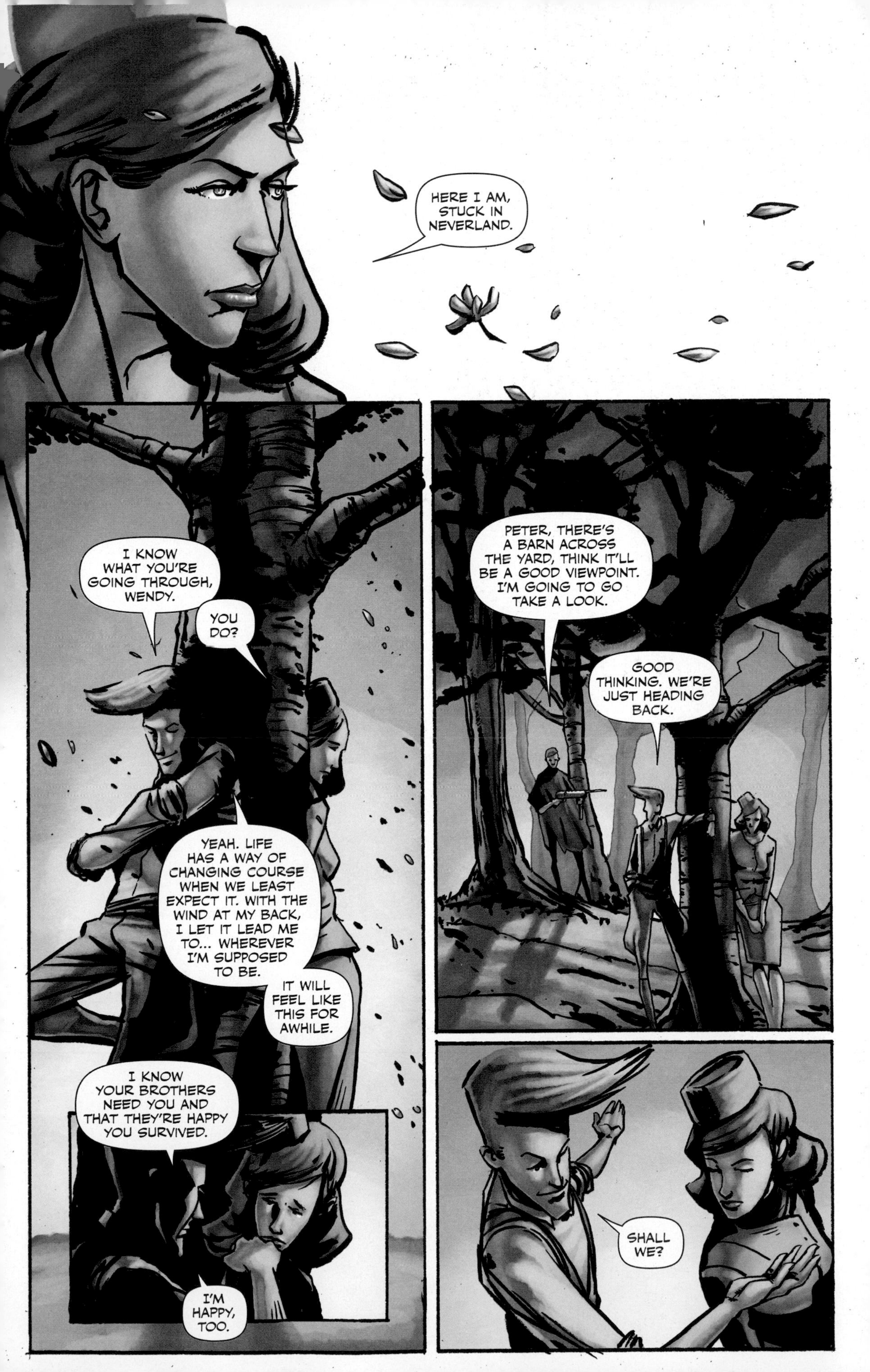
HERE I AM, STUCK IN NEVERLAND.
I KNOW WHAT YOU'RE GOING THROUGH, WENDY.
YOU DO?
YEAH. LIFE HAS A WAY OF CHANGING COURSE WHEN WE LEAST EXPECT IT. WITH THE WIND AT MY BACK, I LET IT LEAD ME TO... WHEREVER I'M SUPPOSED TO BE.
IT WILL FEEL LIKE THIS FOR AWHILE.
I KNOW YOUR BROTHERS NEED YOU AND THAT THEY'RE HAPPY YOU SURVIVED.
I'M HAPPY, TOO.
PETER, THERE'S A BARN ACROSS THE YARD, THINK IT'LL BE A GOOD VIEWPOINT. I'M GOING TO GO TAKE A LOOK.
GOOD THINKING. WE'RE JUST HEADING BACK.
SHALL WE?

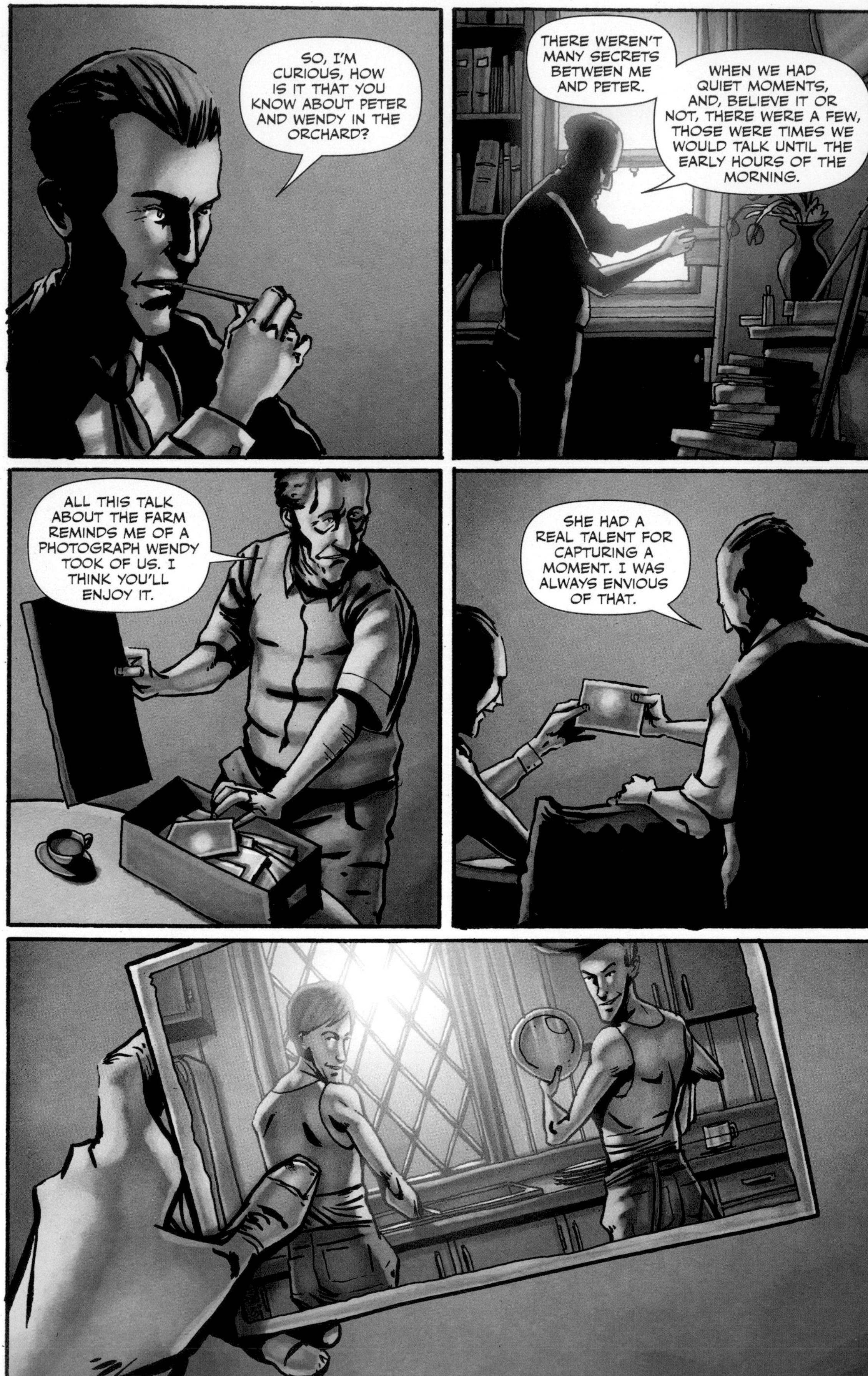
SO, I'M CURIOUS, HOW IS IT THAT YOU KNOW ABOUT PETER AND WENDY IN THE ORCHARD?
THERE WEREN'T MANY SECRETS BETWEEN ME AND PETER.
WHEN WE HAD QUIET MOMENTS, AND, BELIEVE IT OR NOT, THERE WERE A FEW, THOSE WERE TIMES WE WOULD TALK UNTIL THE EARLY HOURS OF THE MORNING.
ALL THIS TALK ABOUT THE FARM REMINDS ME OF A PHOTOGRAPH WENDY TOOK OF US. I THINK YOU'LL ENJOY IT.
SHE HAD A REAL TALENT FOR CAPTURING A MOMENT. I WAS ALWAYS ENVIOUS OF THAT.

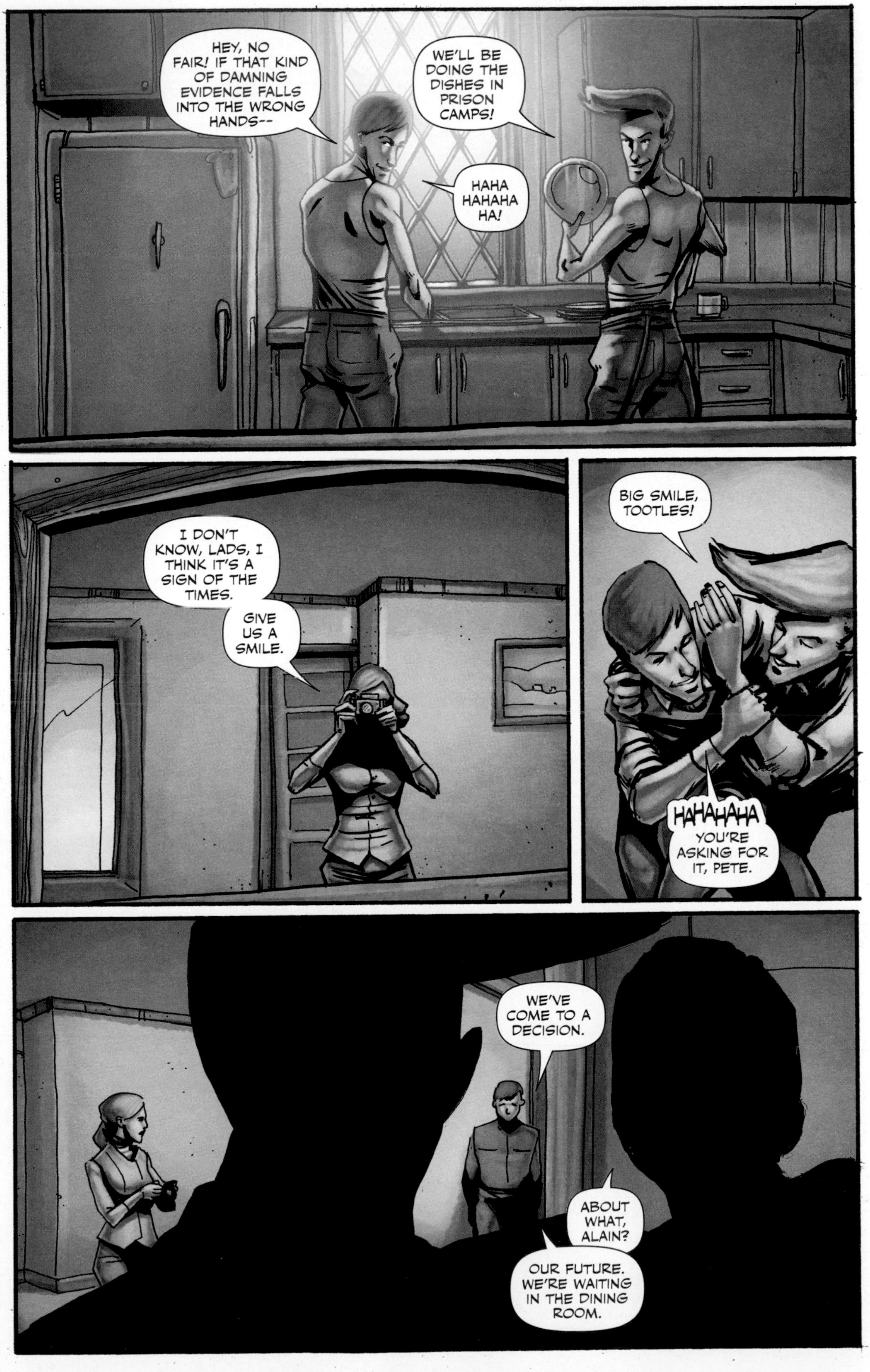
HEY, NO FAIR! IF THAT KIND OF DAMNING EVIDENCE FALLS INTO THE WRONG HANDS--
WE'LL BE DOING THE DISHES IN PRISON CAMPS!
HAHA HAHAHA HA!
I DON'T KNOW, LADS, I THINK IT'S A SIGN OF THE TIMES.
GIVE US A SMILE.
BIG SMILE, TOOTLES!
HAHAHAHA
YOU'RE ASKING FOR IT, PETE.
WE'VE COME TO A DECISION.
ABOUT WHAT, ALAIN?
OUR FUTURE. WE'RE WAITING IN THE DINING ROOM.

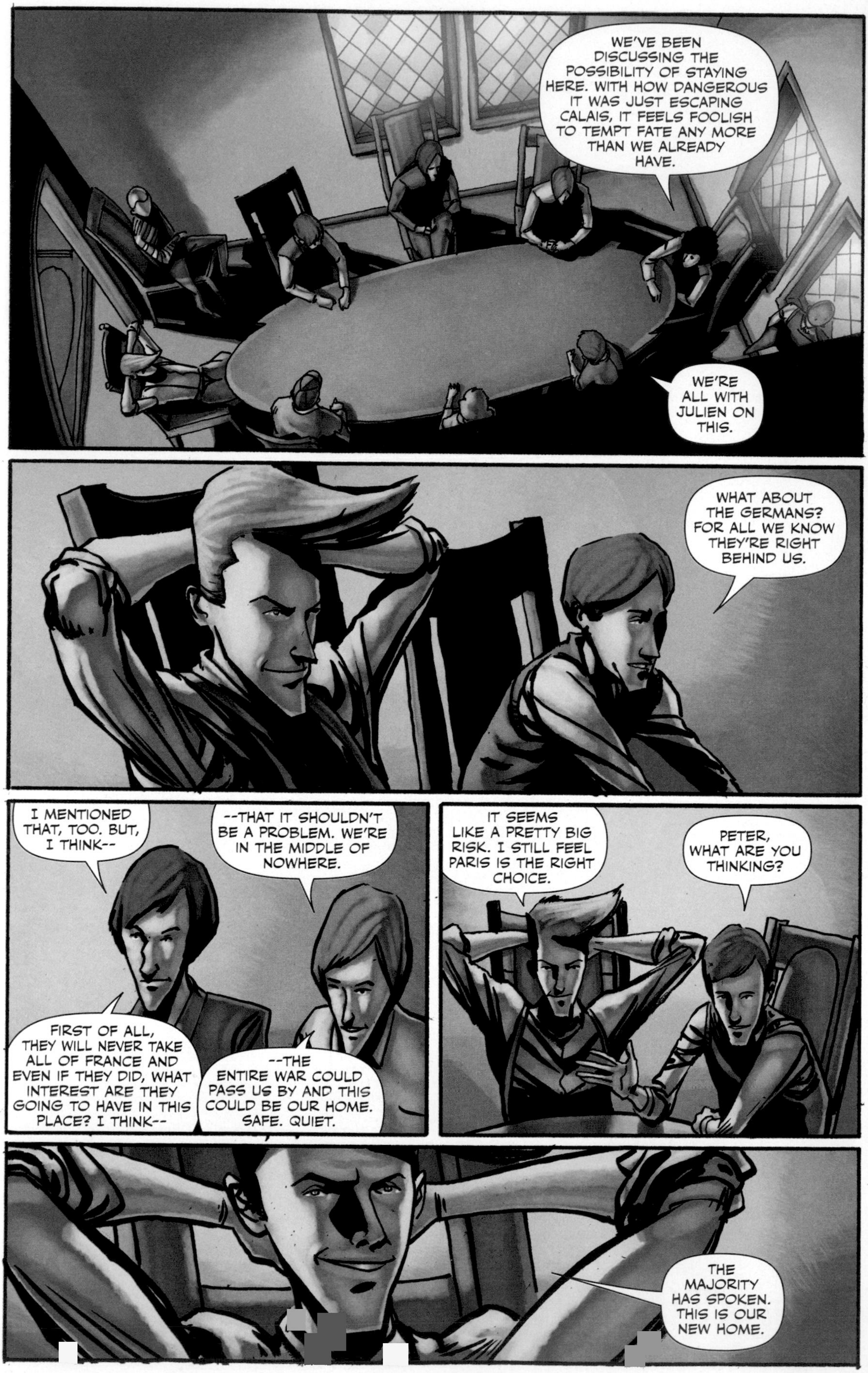
WE'VE BEEN DISCUSSING THE POSSIBILITY OF STAYING HERE. WITH HOW DANGEROUS IT WAS JUST ESCAPING CALAIS, IT FEELS FOOLISH TO TEMPT FATE ANY MORE THAN WE ALREADY HAVE.
WE'RE ALL WITH JULIEN ON THIS.
WHAT ABOUT THE GERMANS? FOR ALL WE KNOW THEY'RE RIGHT BEHIND US.
I MENTIONED THAT, TOO. BUT, I THINK--
--THAT IT SHOULDN'T BE A PROBLEM. WE'RE IN THE MIDDLE OF NOWHERE.
FIRST OF ALL, THEY WILL NEVER TAKE ALL OF FRANCE AND EVEN IF THEY DID, WHAT INTEREST ARE THEY GOING TO HAVE IN THIS PLACE? I THINK--
--THE ENTIRE WAR COULD PASS US BY AND THIS COULD BE OUR HOME. SAFE. QUIET.
IT SEEMS LIKE A PRETTY BIG RISK. I STILL FEEL PARIS IS THE RIGHT CHOICE.
PETER, WHAT ARE YOU THINKING?
THE MAJORITY HAS SPOKEN. THIS IS OUR NEW HOME.

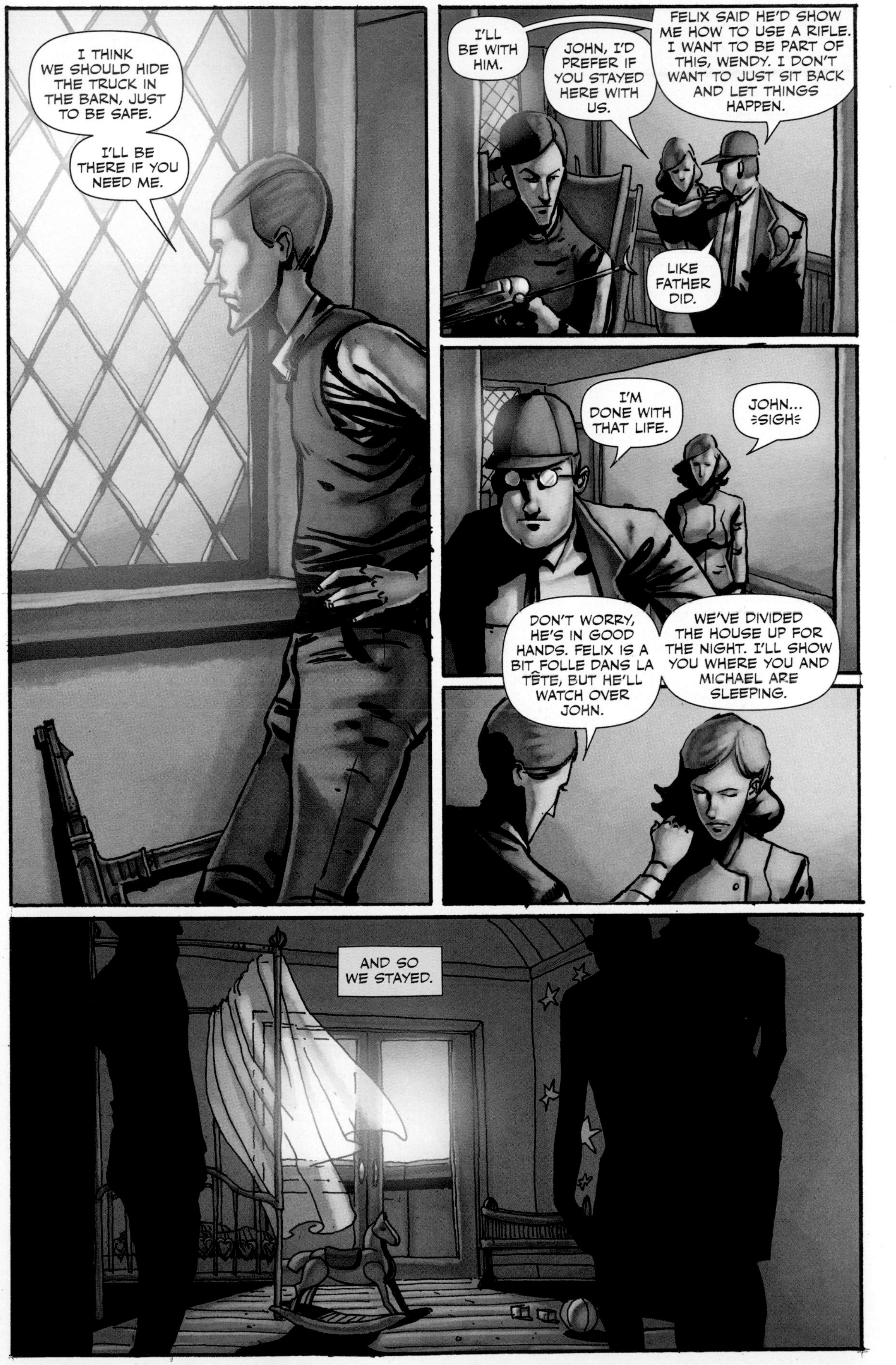
I THINK WE SHOULD HIDE THE TRUCK IN THE BARN, JUST TO BE SAFE.
I'LL BE THERE IF YOU NEED ME.
I'LL BE WITH HIM.
JOHN, I'D PREFER IF YOU STAYED HERE WITH US.
FELIX SAID HE'D SHOW ME HOW TO USE A RIFLE. I WANT TO BE PART OF THIS, WENDY. I DON'T WANT TO JUST SIT BACK AND LET THINGS HAPPEN.
LIKE FATHER DID.
I'M DONE WITH THAT LIFE.
JOHN... ≈SIGH≈
DON'T WORRY, HE'S IN GOOD HANDS. FELIX IS A BIT FOLLE DANS LA TÊTE, BUT HE'LL WATCH OVER JOHN.
WE'VE DIVIDED THE HOUSE UP FOR THE NIGHT. I'LL SHOW YOU WHERE YOU AND MICHAEL ARE SLEEPING.
AND SO WE STAYED.

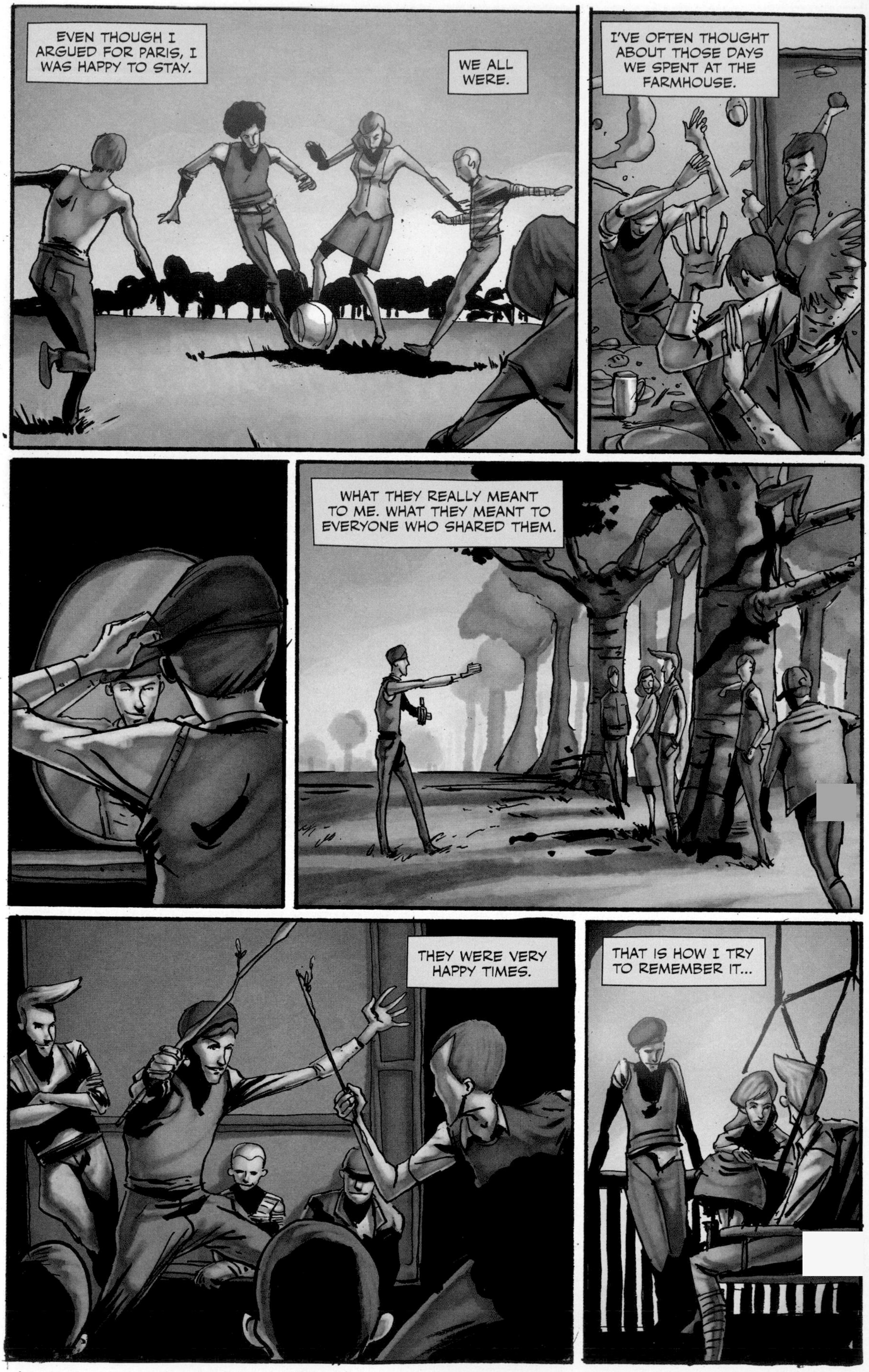
EVEN THOUGH I ARGUED FOR PARIS, I WAS HAPPY TO STAY.
WE ALL WERE.
I'VE OFTEN THOUGHT ABOUT THOSE DAYS WE SPENT AT THE FARMHOUSE.
WHAT THEY REALLY MEANT TO ME. WHAT THEY MEANT TO EVERYONE WHO SHARED THEM.
THEY WERE VERY HAPPY TIMES.
THAT IS HOW I TRY TO REMEMBER IT...

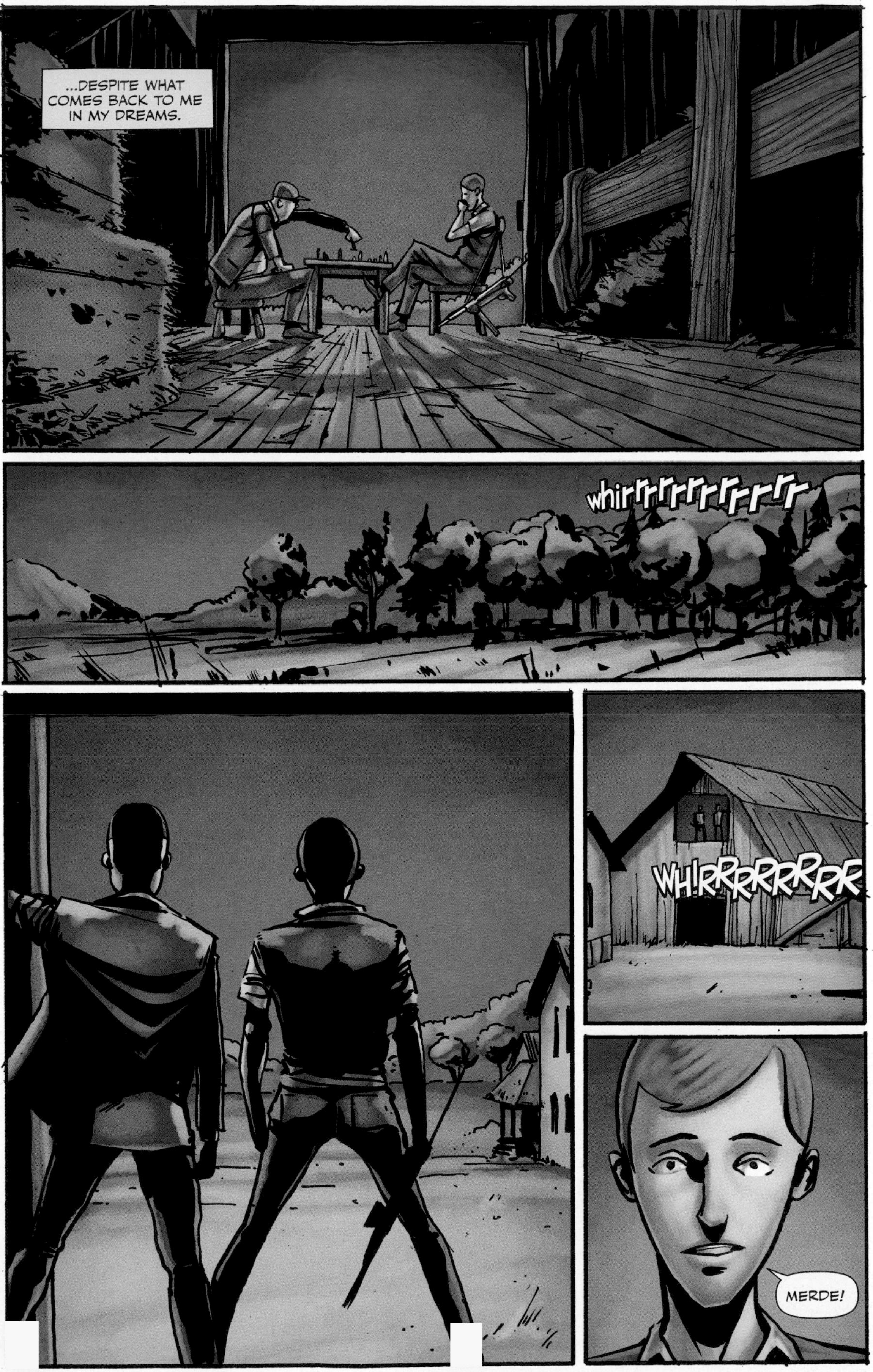
...DESPITE WHAT COMES BACK TO ME IN MY DREAMS.
whirrrrrrrrrrr
WHIRRRRRRRR
MERDE!

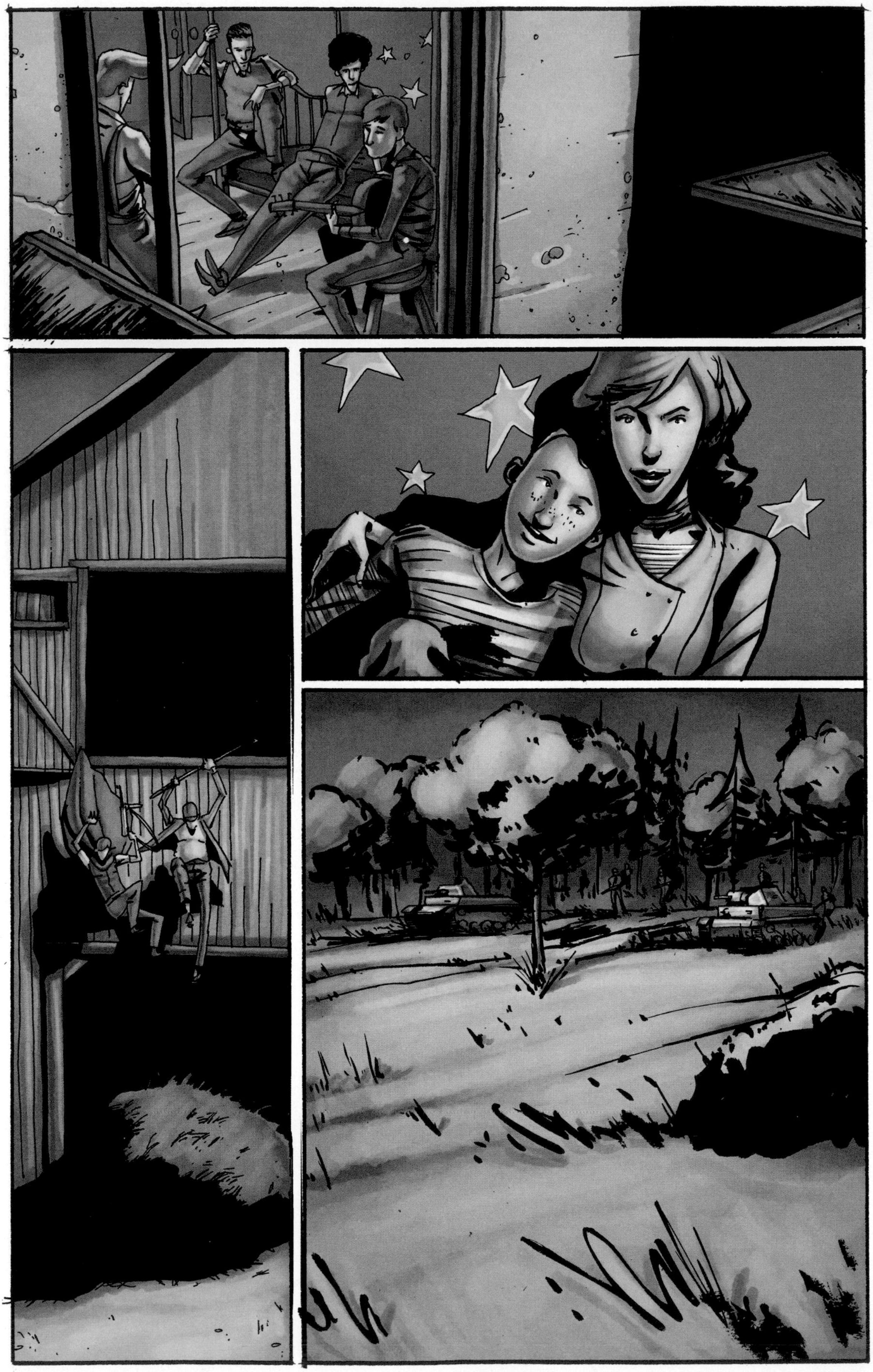

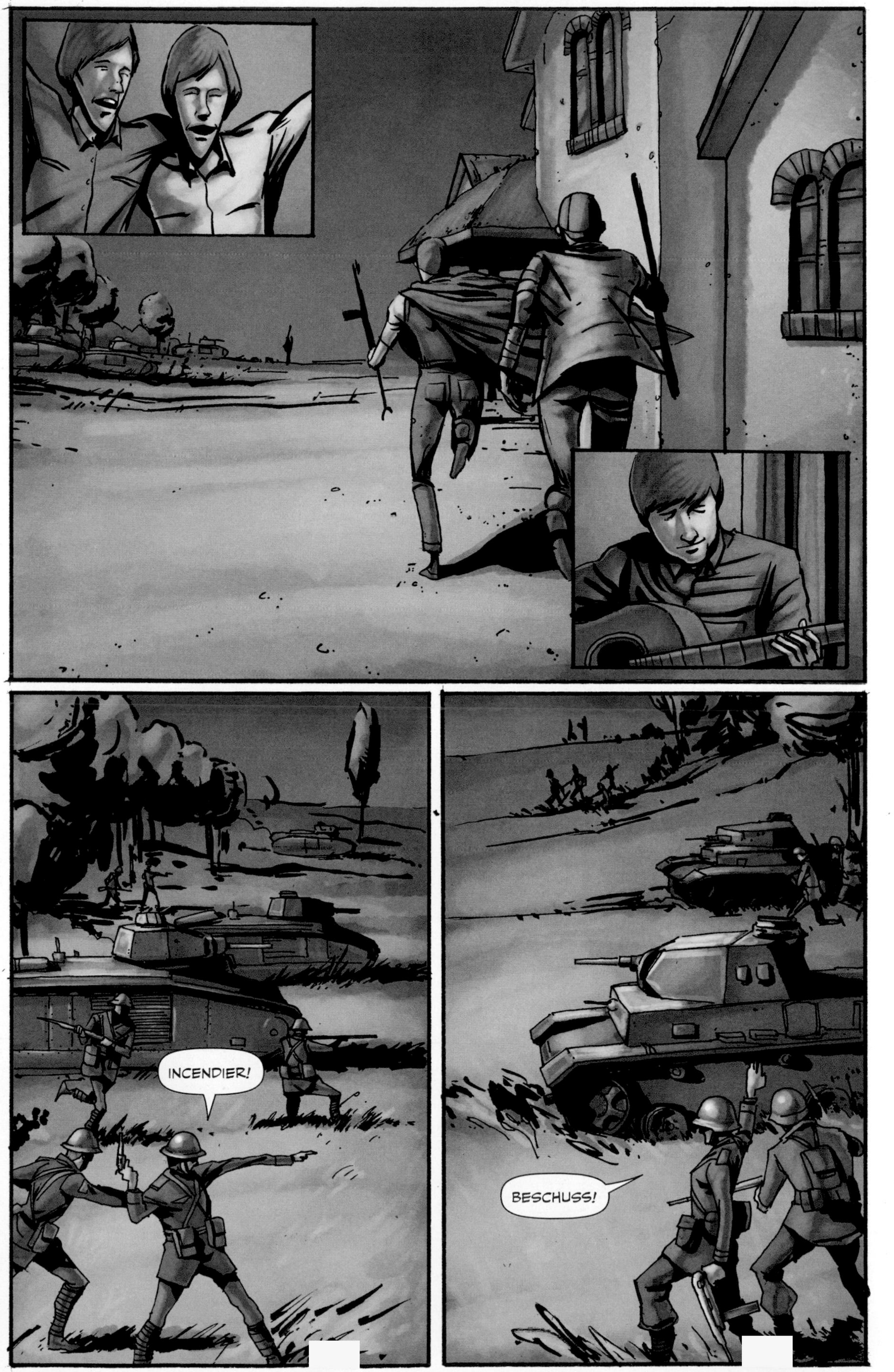
INCENDIER!
BESCHUSS!

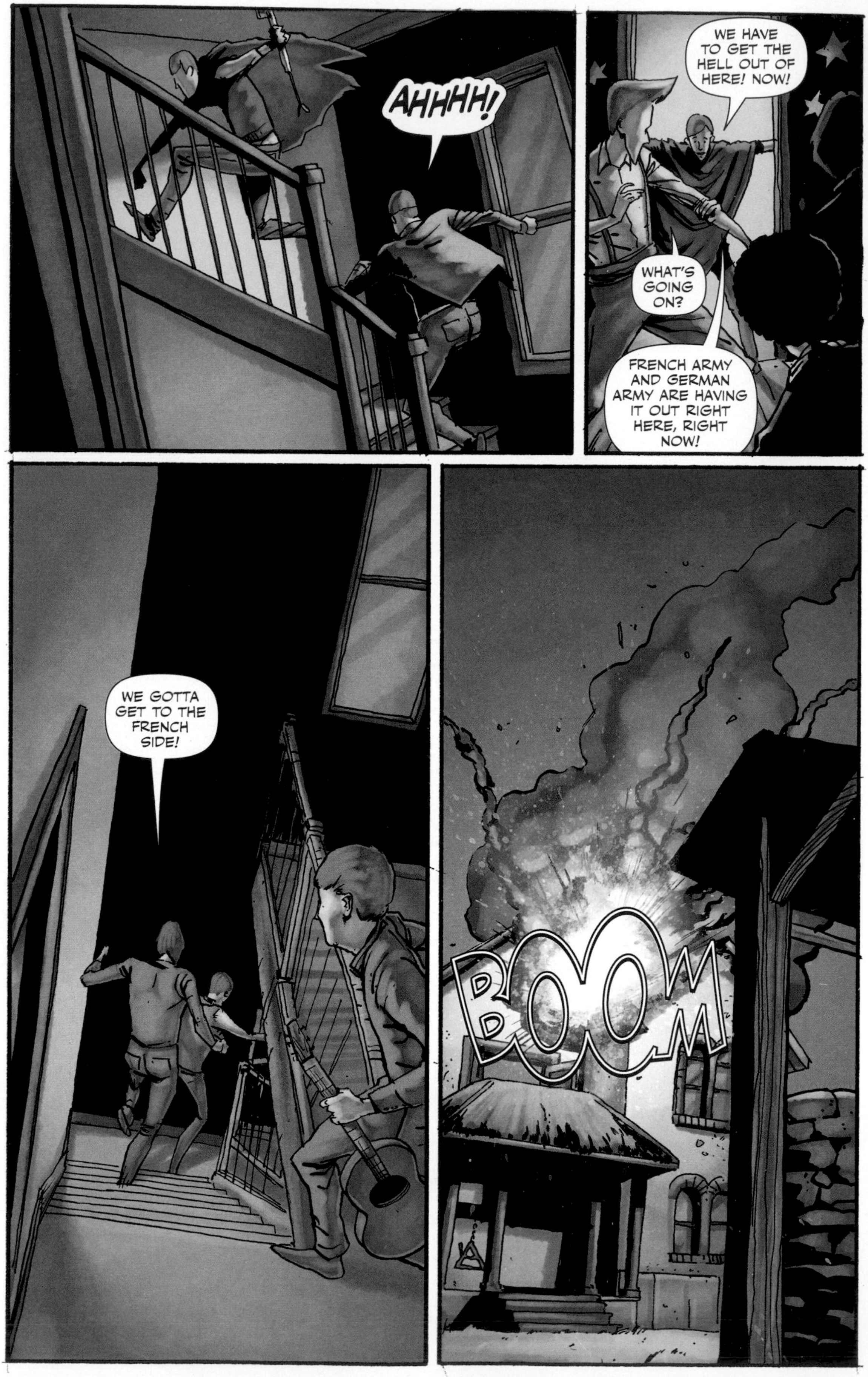
AHHHH!
WE HAVE TO GET THE HELL OUT OF HERE! NOW!
WHAT'S GOING ON?
FRENCH ARMY AND GERMAN ARMY ARE HAVING IT OUT RIGHT HERE, RIGHT NOW!
WE GOTTA GET TO THE FRENCH SIDE!
BOOOM

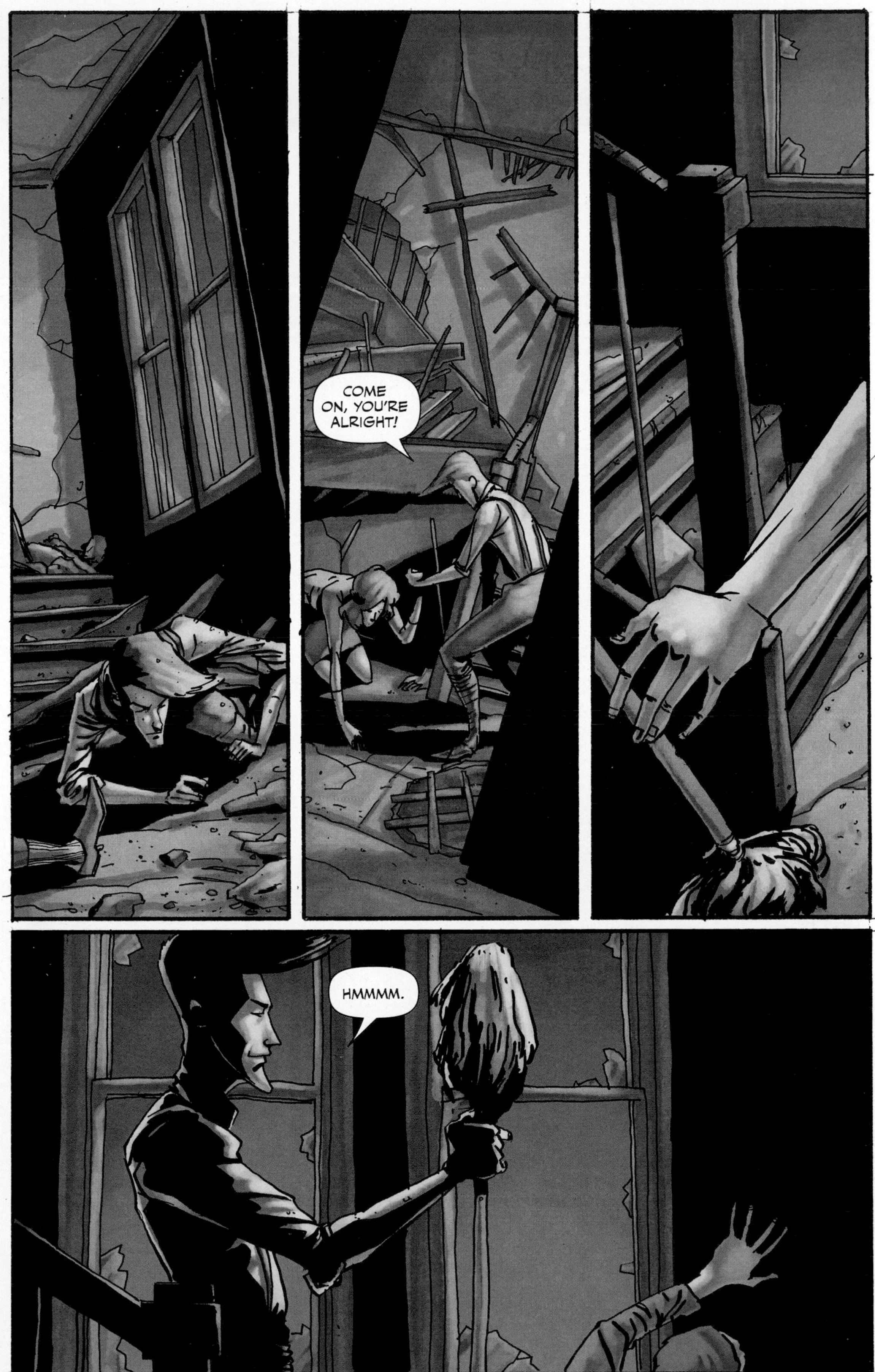
COME ON, YOU'RE ALRIGHT!
HMMMM.

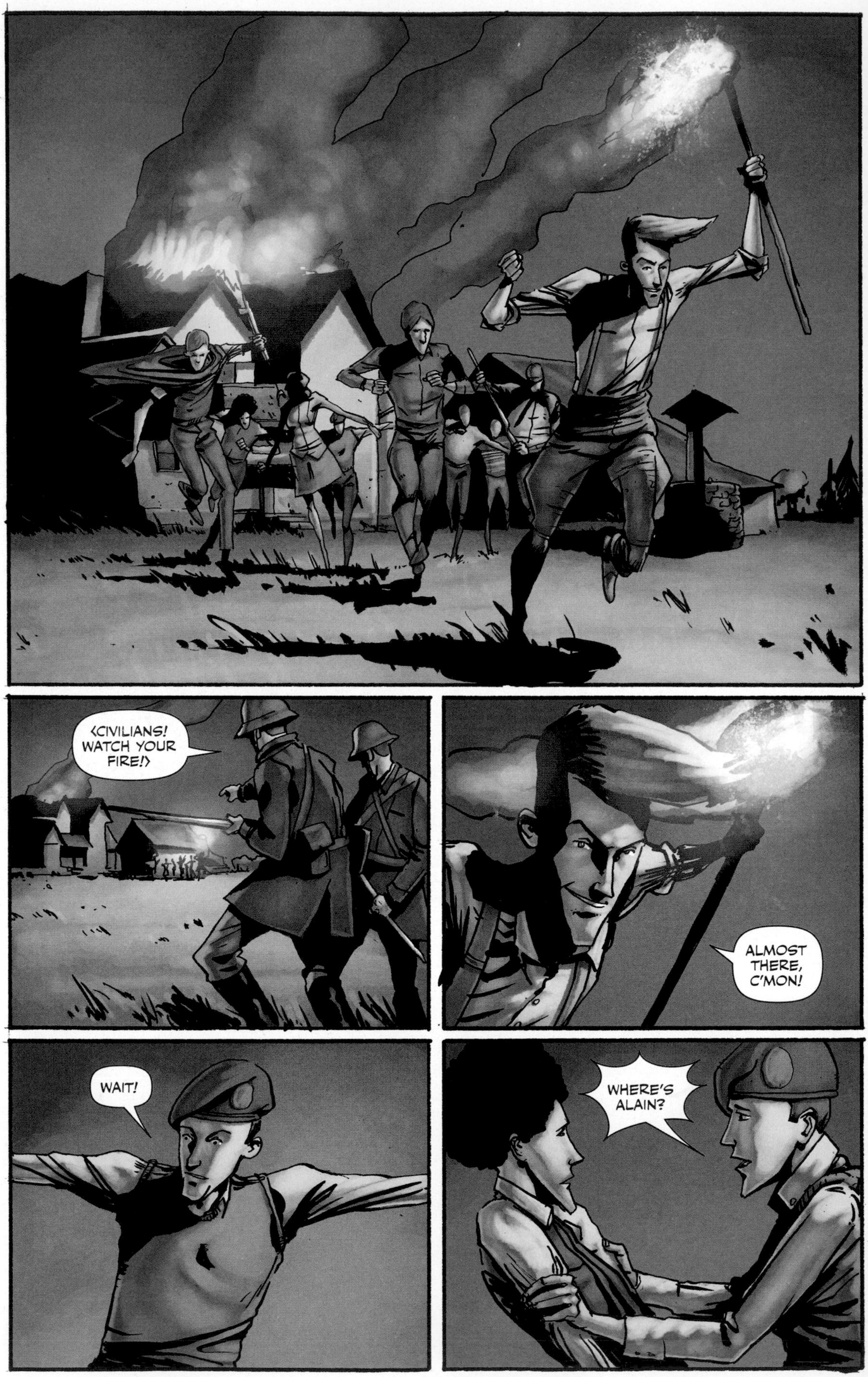
<CIVILIANS! WATCH YOUR FIRE!>
ALMOST THERE, C'MON!
WAIT!
WHERE'S ALAIN?

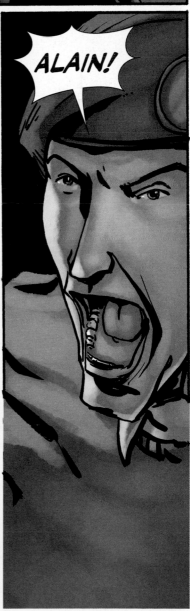

ALAIN!

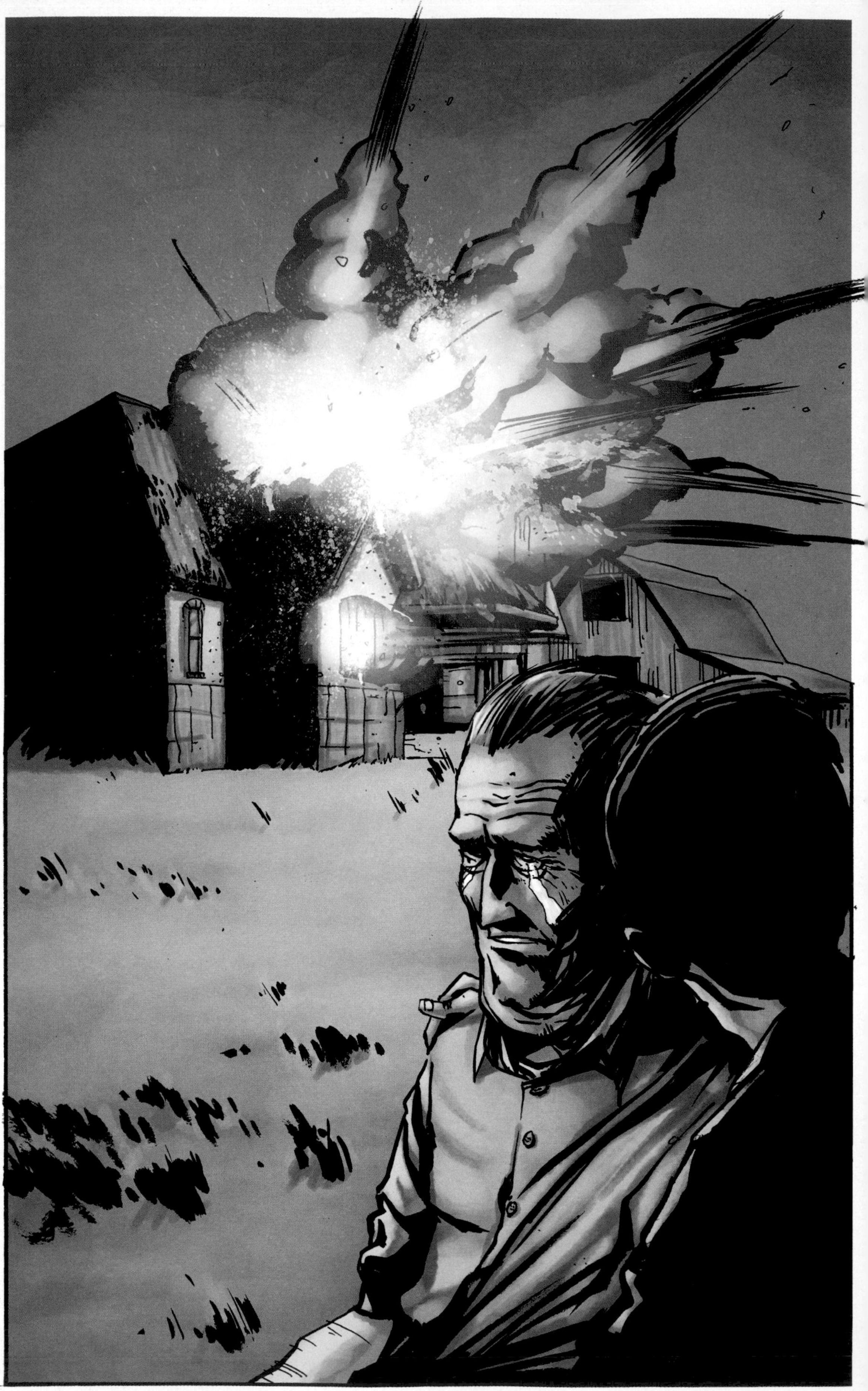

CHAPTER FIVE

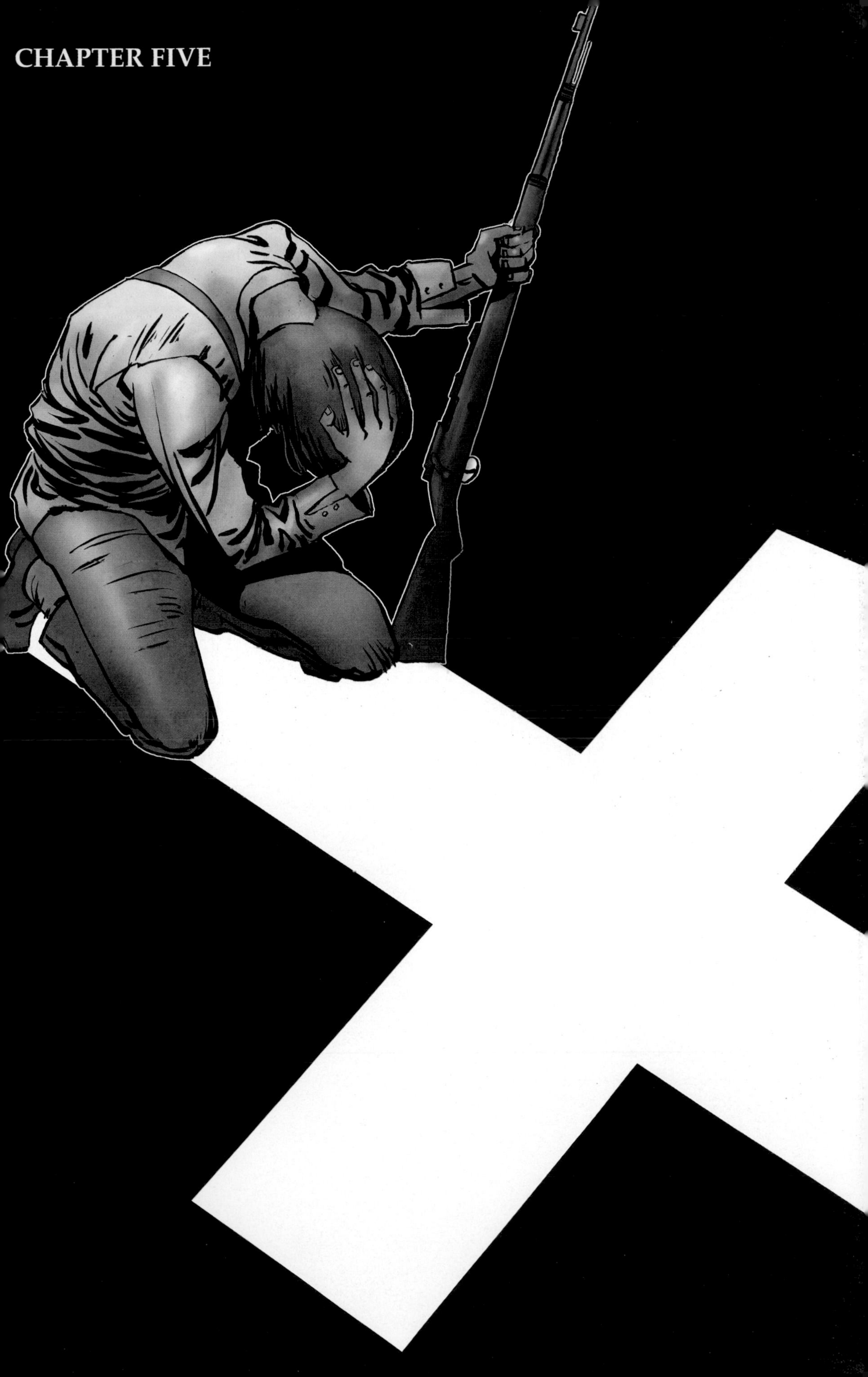

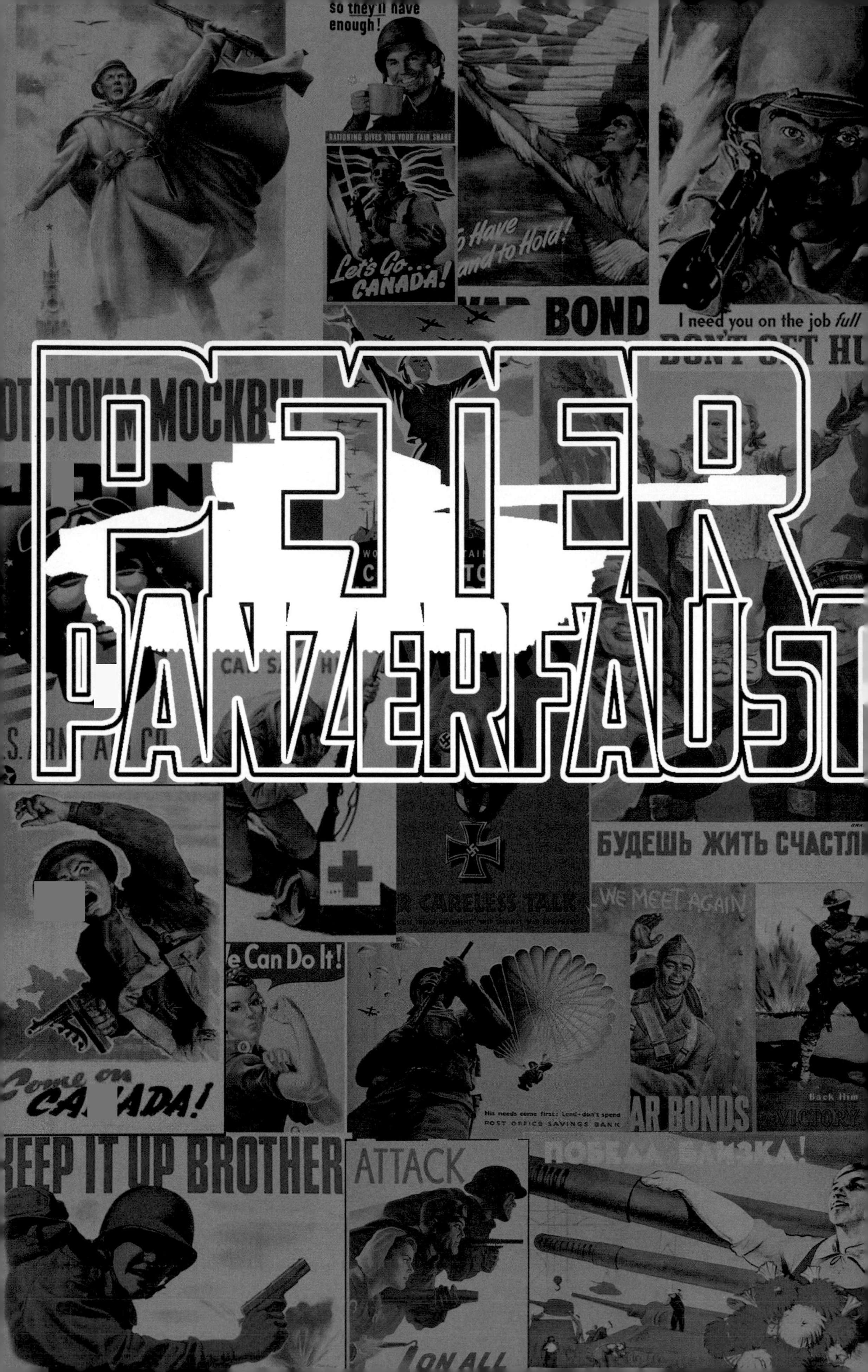

so they'll have
enough!
RATIONING GIVES YOU YOUR FAIR SHARE
Let's Go...
CANADA!
and to Hold!
BOND
I need you on the job full
PETER
PANZERFAUST
БУДЕШЬ ЖИТЬ СЧАСТЛ
CARELESS TALK
WE MEET AGAIN
e Can Do It!
His needs come first: Lend—don't spend
POST OFFICE SAVINGS BANK
AR BONDS
Back Him
VICTORY
EEP IT UP BROTHER
ATTACK

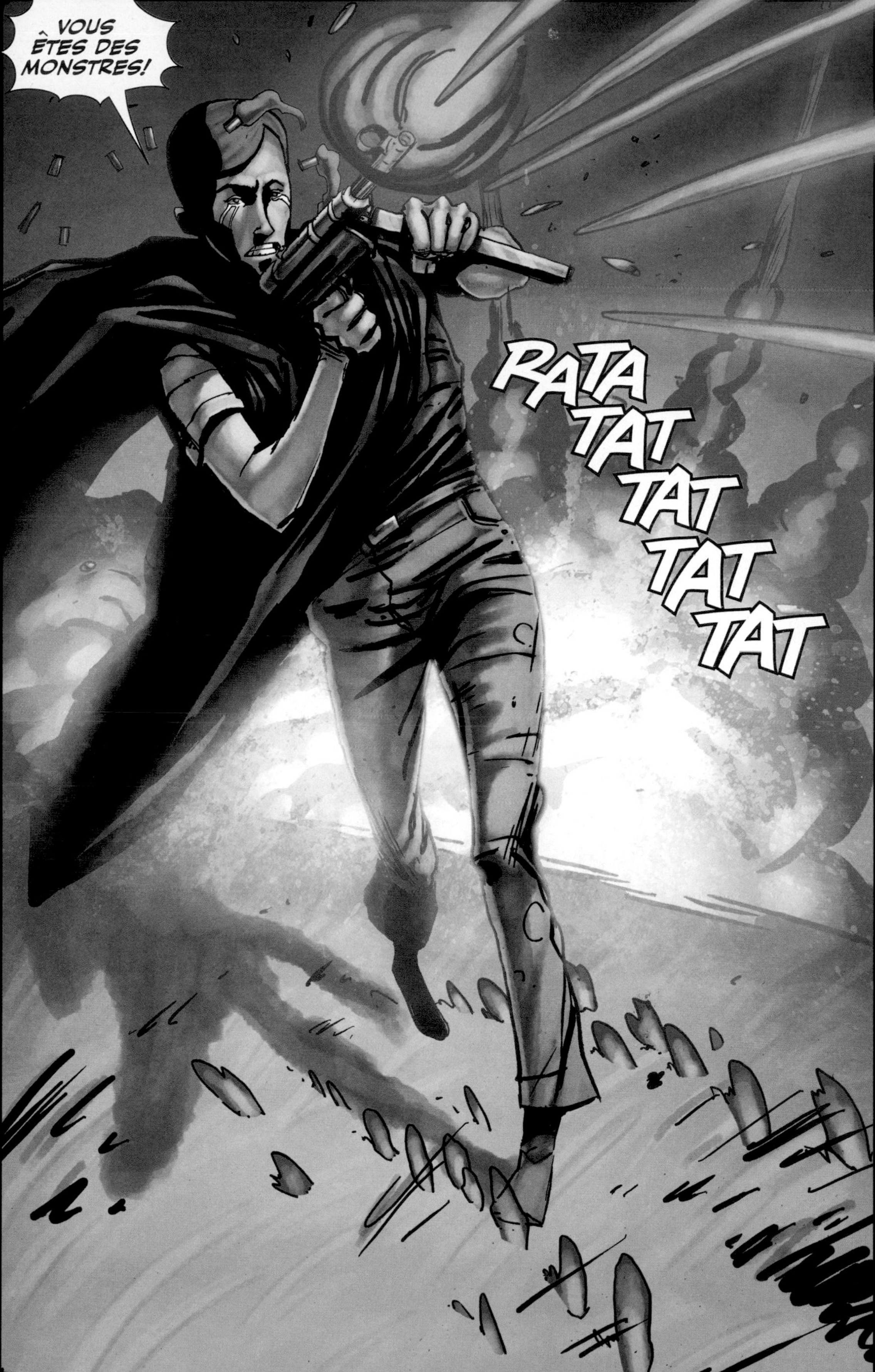
VOUS ÊTES DES MONSTRES!
RATATAT TAT TAT TAT

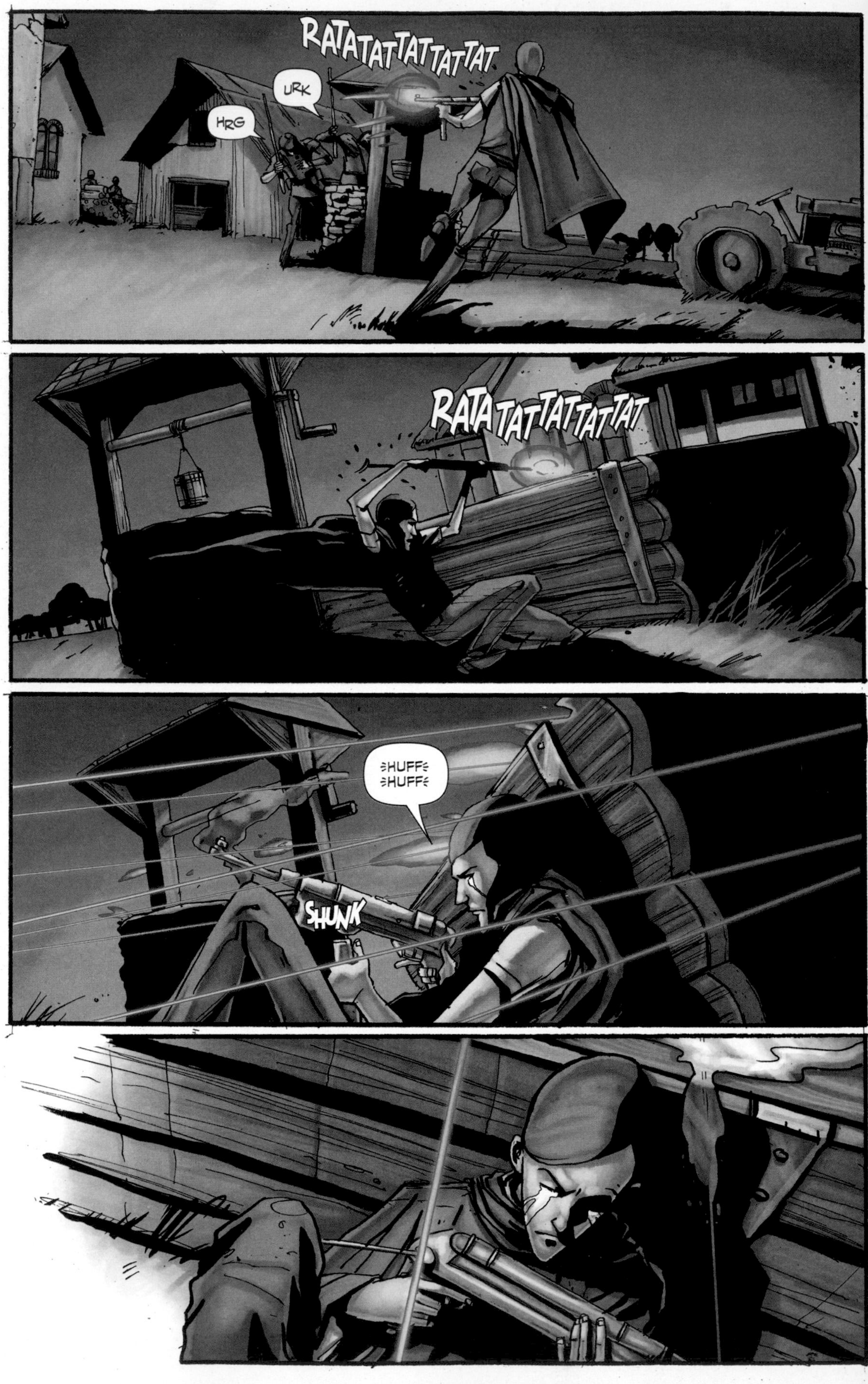
RATATATTATTATTAT
URK
HRG
RATATATTATTATTAT
HUFF
HUFF
SHUNK

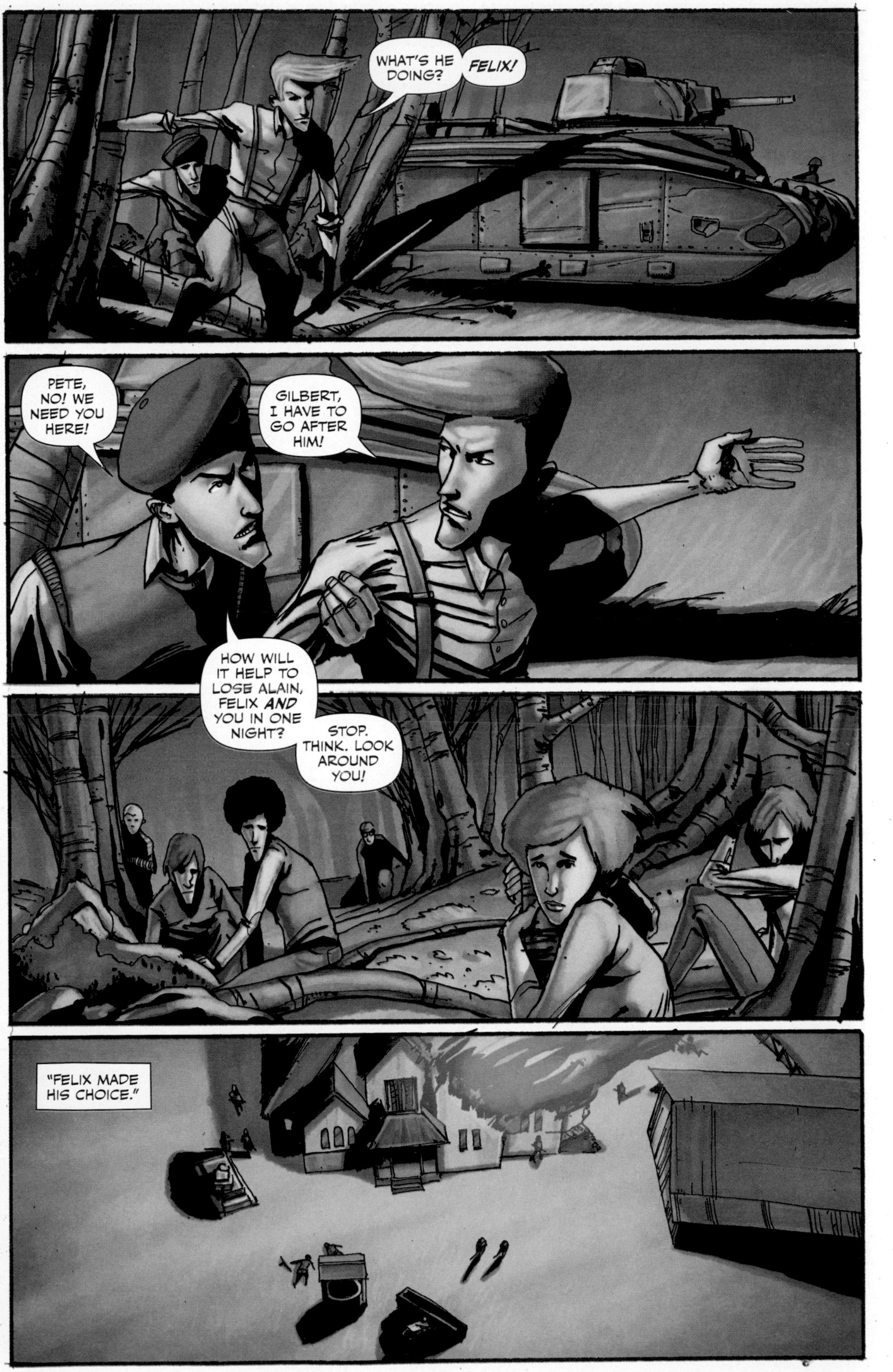
WHAT'S HE DOING?
FELIX!
PETE, NO! WE NEED YOU HERE!
GILBERT, I HAVE TO GO AFTER HIM!
HOW WILL IT HELP TO LOSE ALAIN, FELIX AND YOU IN ONE NIGHT?
STOP. THINK. LOOK AROUND YOU!
"FELIX MADE HIS CHOICE."

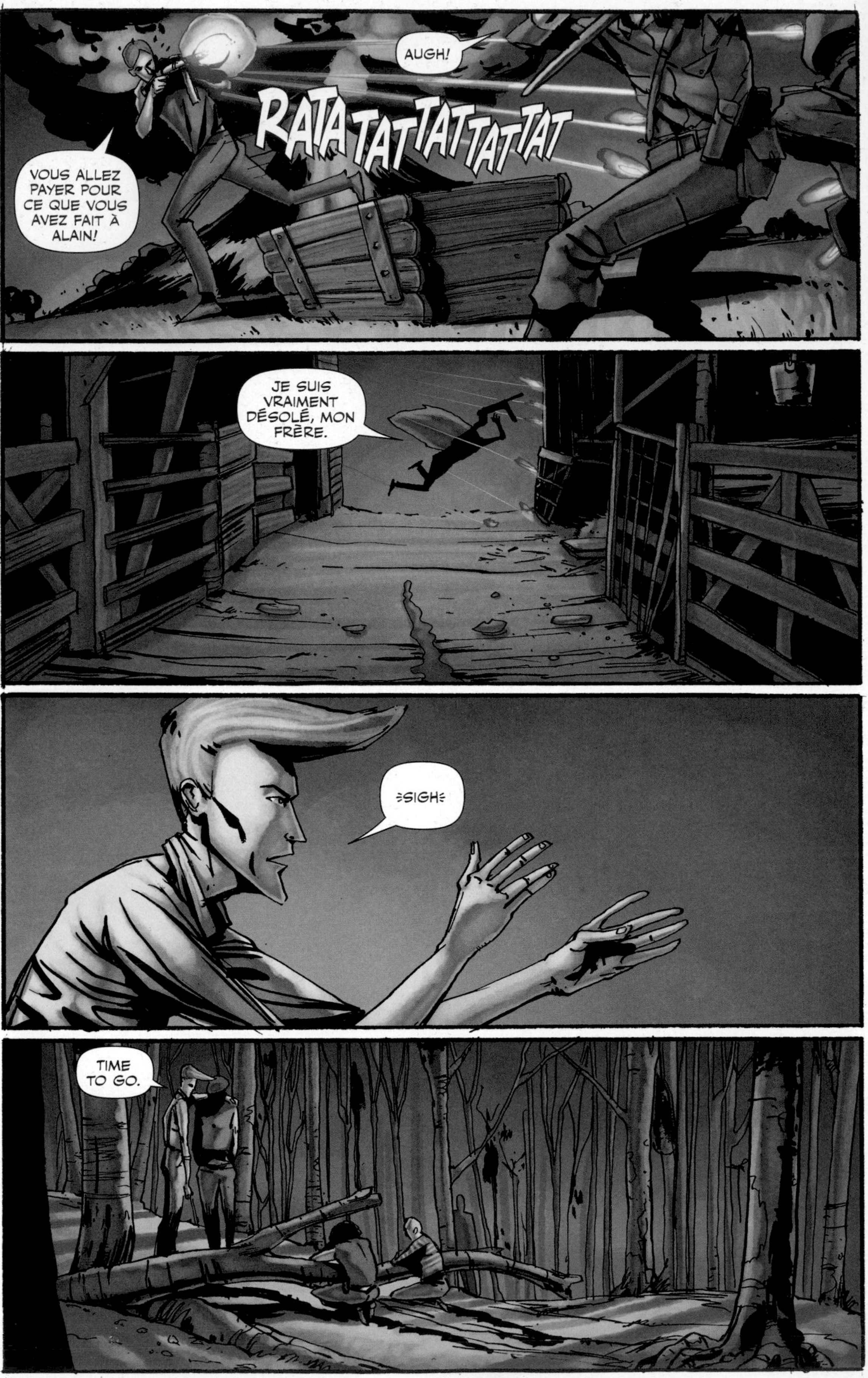

AUGH!
RATATATTATTATTAT
VOUS ALLEZ PAYER POUR CE QUE VOUS AVEZ FAIT À ALAIN!
JE SUIS VRAIMENT DÉSOLÉ, MON FRÈRE.
SIGH
TIME TO GO.

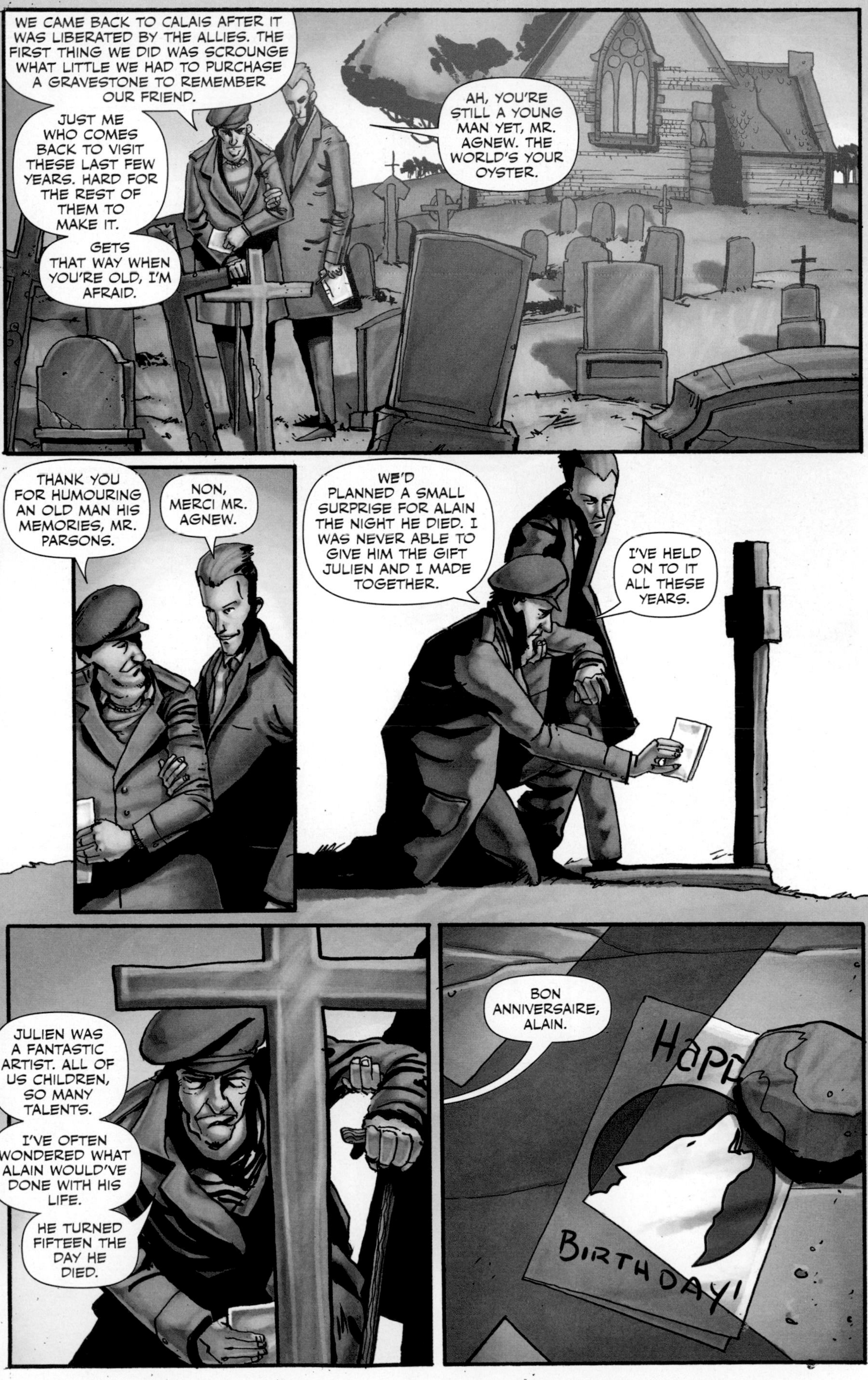
WE CAME BACK TO CALAIS AFTER IT WAS LIBERATED BY THE ALLIES. THE FIRST THING WE DID WAS SCROUNGE WHAT LITTLE WE HAD TO PURCHASE A GRAVESTONE TO REMEMBER OUR FRIEND.
JUST ME WHO COMES BACK TO VISIT THESE LAST FEW YEARS. HARD FOR THE REST OF THEM TO MAKE IT.
GETS THAT WAY WHEN YOU'RE OLD, I'M AFRAID.
AH, YOU'RE STILL A YOUNG MAN YET, MR. AGNEW. THE WORLD'S YOUR OYSTER.
THANK YOU FOR HUMOURING AN OLD MAN HIS MEMORIES, MR. PARSONS.
NON, MERCI MR. AGNEW.
WE'D PLANNED A SMALL SURPRISE FOR ALAIN THE NIGHT HE DIED. I WAS NEVER ABLE TO GIVE HIM THE GIFT JULIEN AND I MADE TOGETHER.
I'VE HELD ON TO IT ALL THESE YEARS.
JULIEN WAS A FANTASTIC ARTIST. ALL OF US CHILDREN, SO MANY TALENTS.
I'VE OFTEN WONDERED WHAT ALAIN WOULD'VE DONE WITH HIS LIFE.
HE TURNED FIFTEEN THE DAY HE DIED.
BON ANNIVERSAIRE, ALAIN.
HAPP
BIRTHDAY!

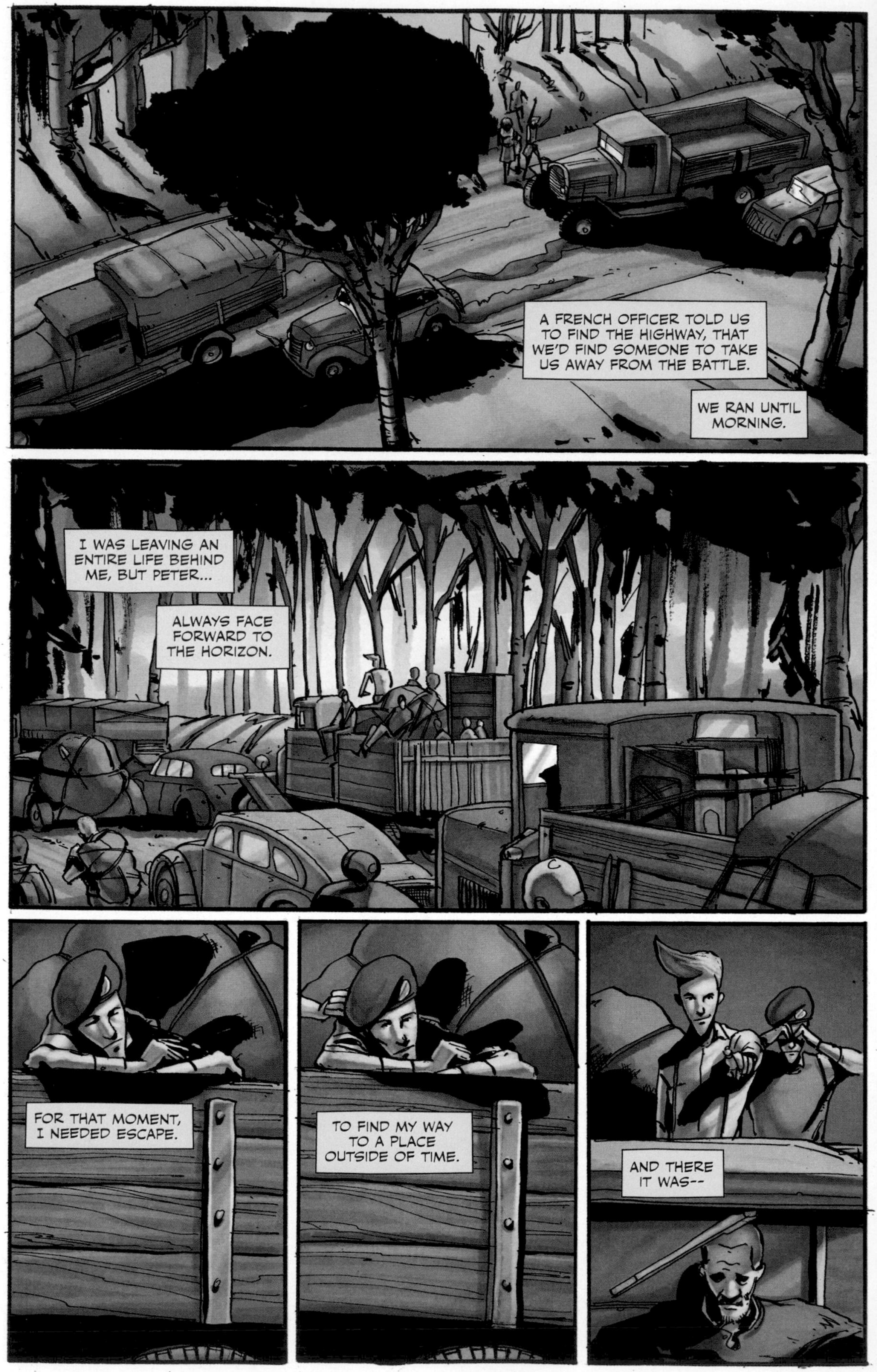
A FRENCH OFFICER TOLD US TO FIND THE HIGHWAY, THAT WE'D FIND SOMEONE TO TAKE US AWAY FROM THE BATTLE.
WE RAN UNTIL MORNING.
I WAS LEAVING AN ENTIRE LIFE BEHIND ME, BUT PETER...
ALWAYS FACE FORWARD TO THE HORIZON.
FOR THAT MOMENT, I NEEDED ESCAPE.
TO FIND MY WAY TO A PLACE OUTSIDE OF TIME.
AND THERE IT WAS--

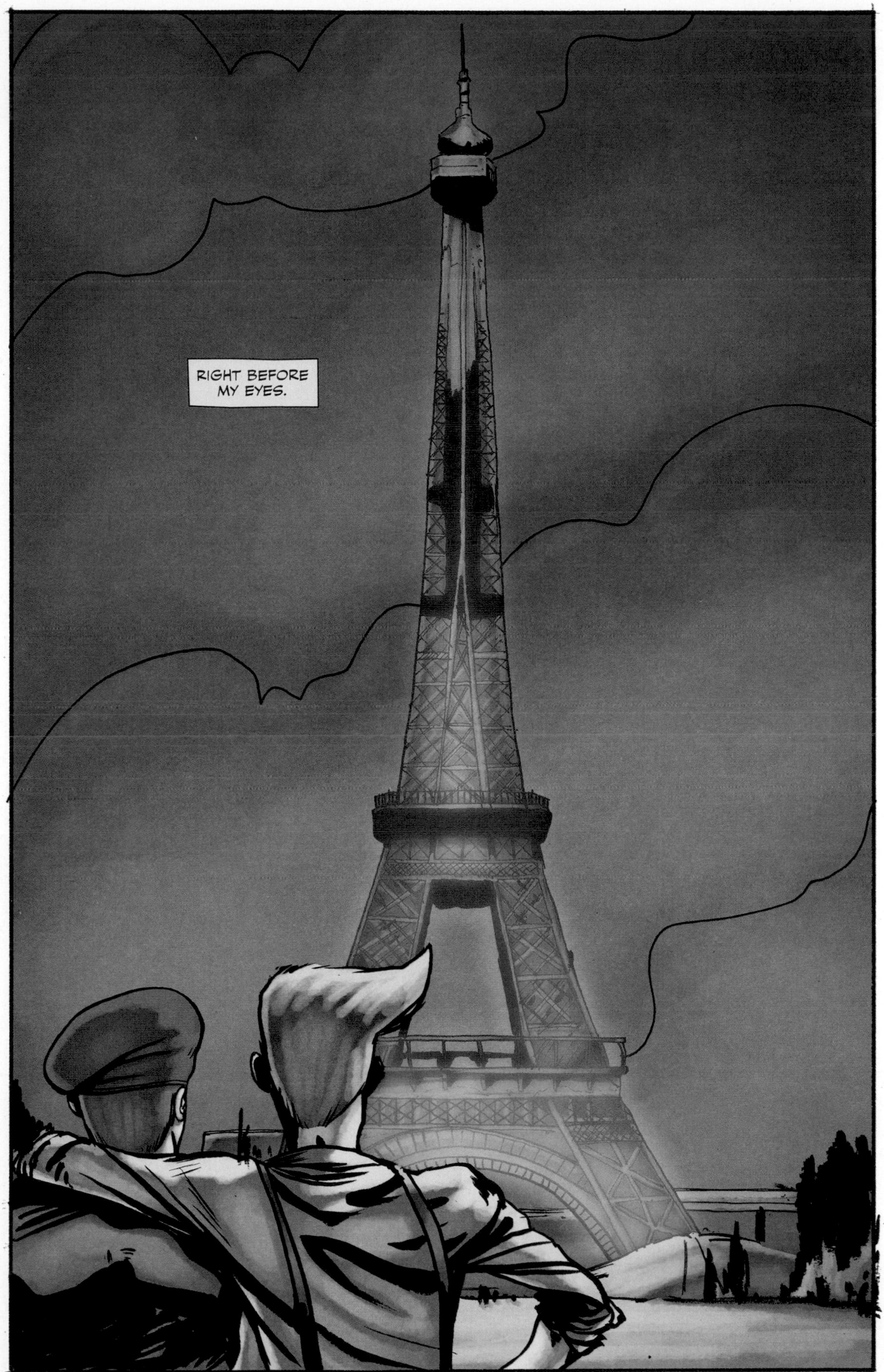
RIGHT BEFORE MY EYES.

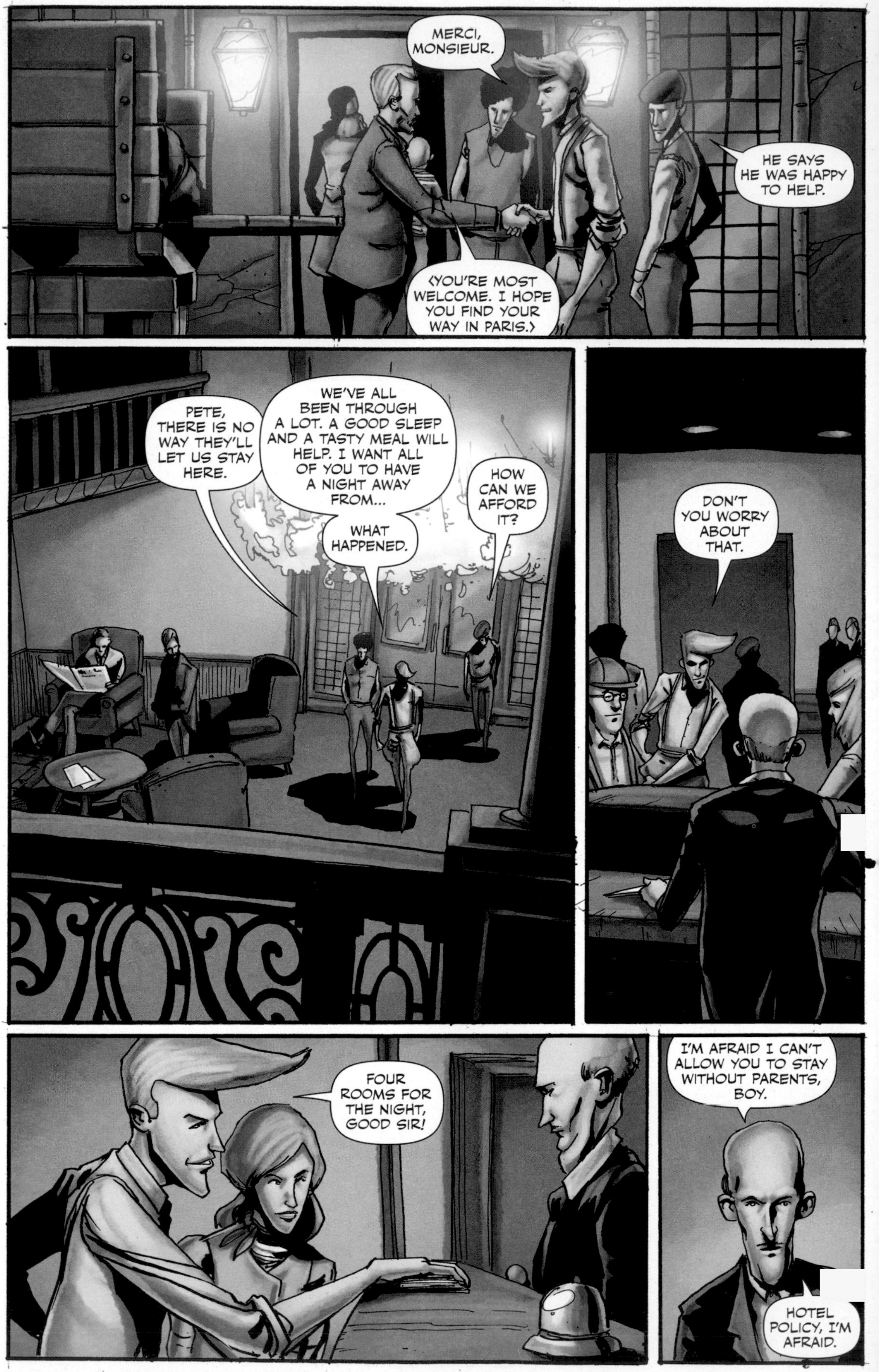
MERCI, MONSIEUR.
HE SAYS HE WAS HAPPY TO HELP.
<YOU'RE MOST WELCOME. I HOPE YOU FIND YOUR WAY IN PARIS.>
PETE, THERE IS NO WAY THEY'LL LET US STAY HERE.
WE'VE ALL BEEN THROUGH A LOT. A GOOD SLEEP AND A TASTY MEAL WILL HELP. I WANT ALL OF YOU TO HAVE A NIGHT AWAY FROM...
WHAT HAPPENED.
HOW CAN WE AFFORD IT?
DON'T YOU WORRY ABOUT THAT.
FOUR ROOMS FOR THE NIGHT, GOOD SIR!
I'M AFRAID I CAN'T ALLOW YOU TO STAY WITHOUT PARENTS, BOY.
HOTEL POLICY, I'M AFRAID.

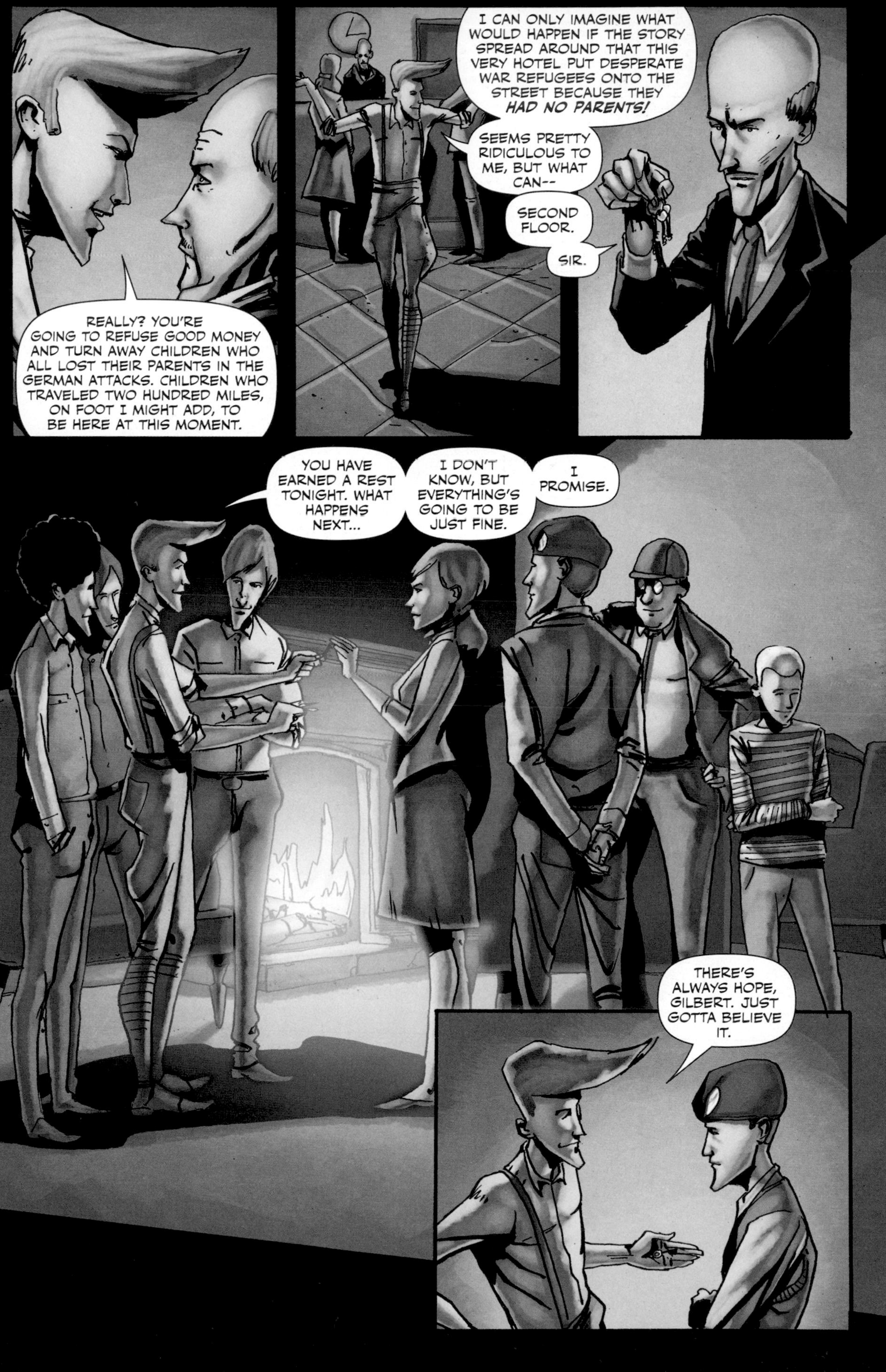
REALLY? YOU'RE GOING TO REFUSE GOOD MONEY AND TURN AWAY CHILDREN WHO ALL LOST THEIR PARENTS IN THE GERMAN ATTACKS. CHILDREN WHO TRAVELED TWO HUNDRED MILES, ON FOOT I MIGHT ADD, TO BE HERE AT THIS MOMENT.
I CAN ONLY IMAGINE WHAT WOULD HAPPEN IF THE STORY SPREAD AROUND THAT THIS VERY HOTEL PUT DESPERATE WAR REFUGEES ONTO THE STREET BECAUSE THEY ***HAD NO PARENTS!***
SEEMS PRETTY RIDICULOUS TO ME, BUT WHAT CAN--
SECOND FLOOR.
SIR.
YOU HAVE EARNED A REST TONIGHT. WHAT HAPPENS NEXT...
I DON'T KNOW, BUT EVERYTHING'S GOING TO BE JUST FINE.
I PROMISE.
THERE'S ALWAYS HOPE, GILBERT. JUST GOTTA BELIEVE IT.

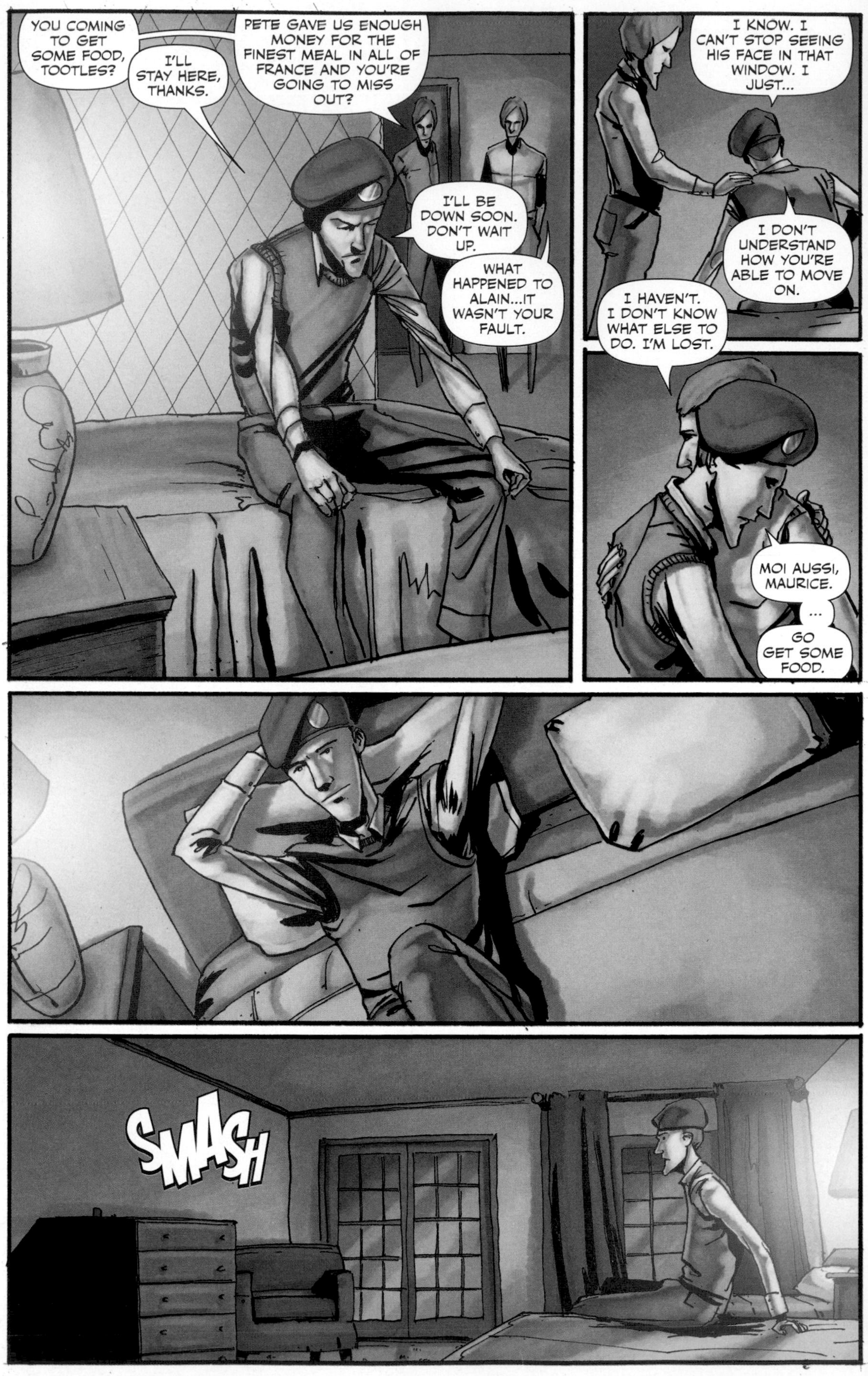
YOU COMING TO GET SOME FOOD, TOOTLES?
I'LL STAY HERE, THANKS.
PETE GAVE US ENOUGH MONEY FOR THE FINEST MEAL IN ALL OF FRANCE AND YOU'RE GOING TO MISS OUT?
I'LL BE DOWN SOON. DON'T WAIT UP.
WHAT HAPPENED TO ALAIN...IT WASN'T YOUR FAULT.
I KNOW. I CAN'T STOP SEEING HIS FACE IN THAT WINDOW. I JUST...
I DON'T UNDERSTAND HOW YOU'RE ABLE TO MOVE ON.
I HAVEN'T. I DON'T KNOW WHAT ELSE TO DO. I'M LOST.
MOI AUSSI, MAURICE.
...
GO GET SOME FOOD.
SMASH

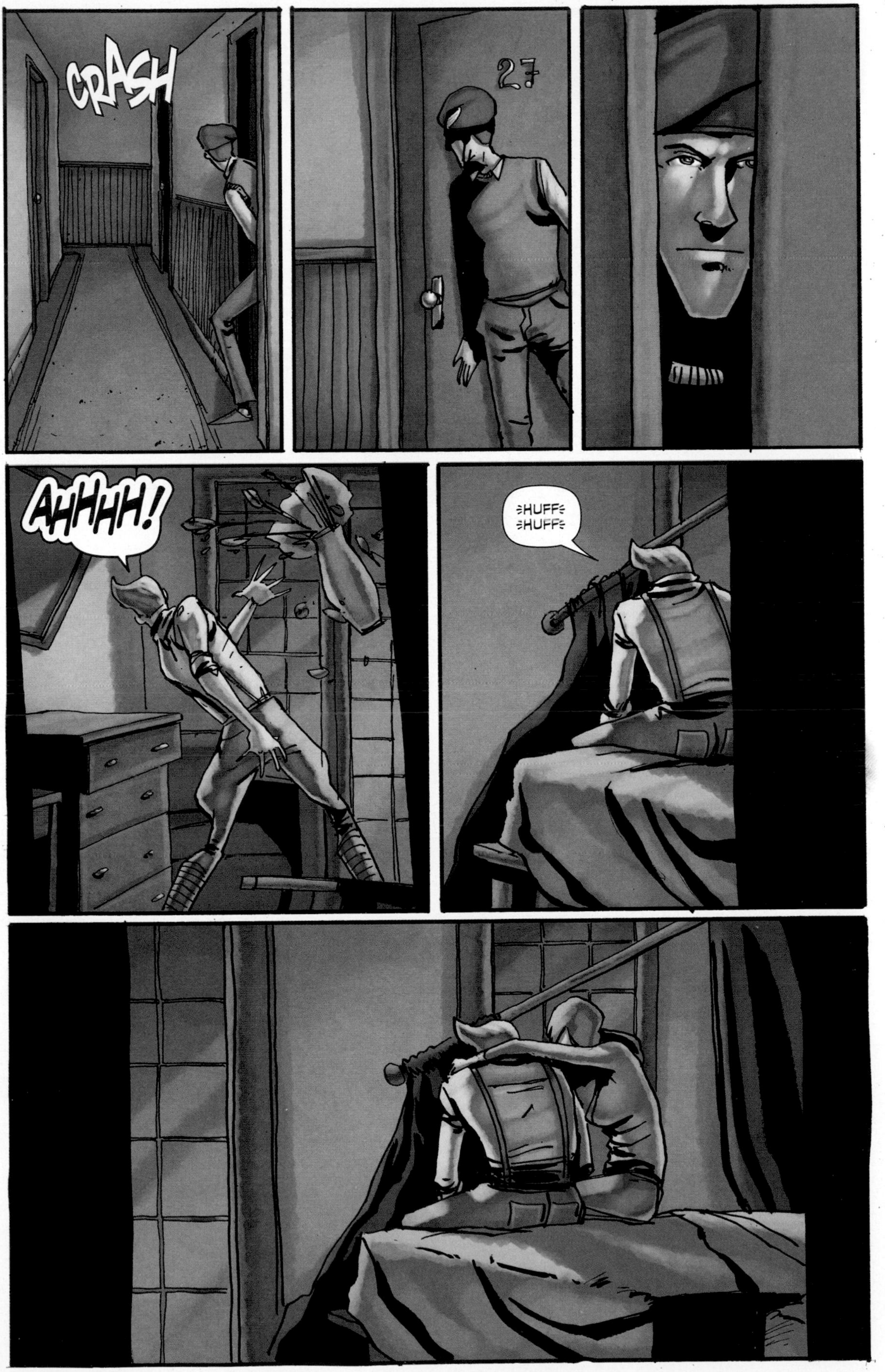
CRASH
27
AHHHH!
HUFF
HUFF

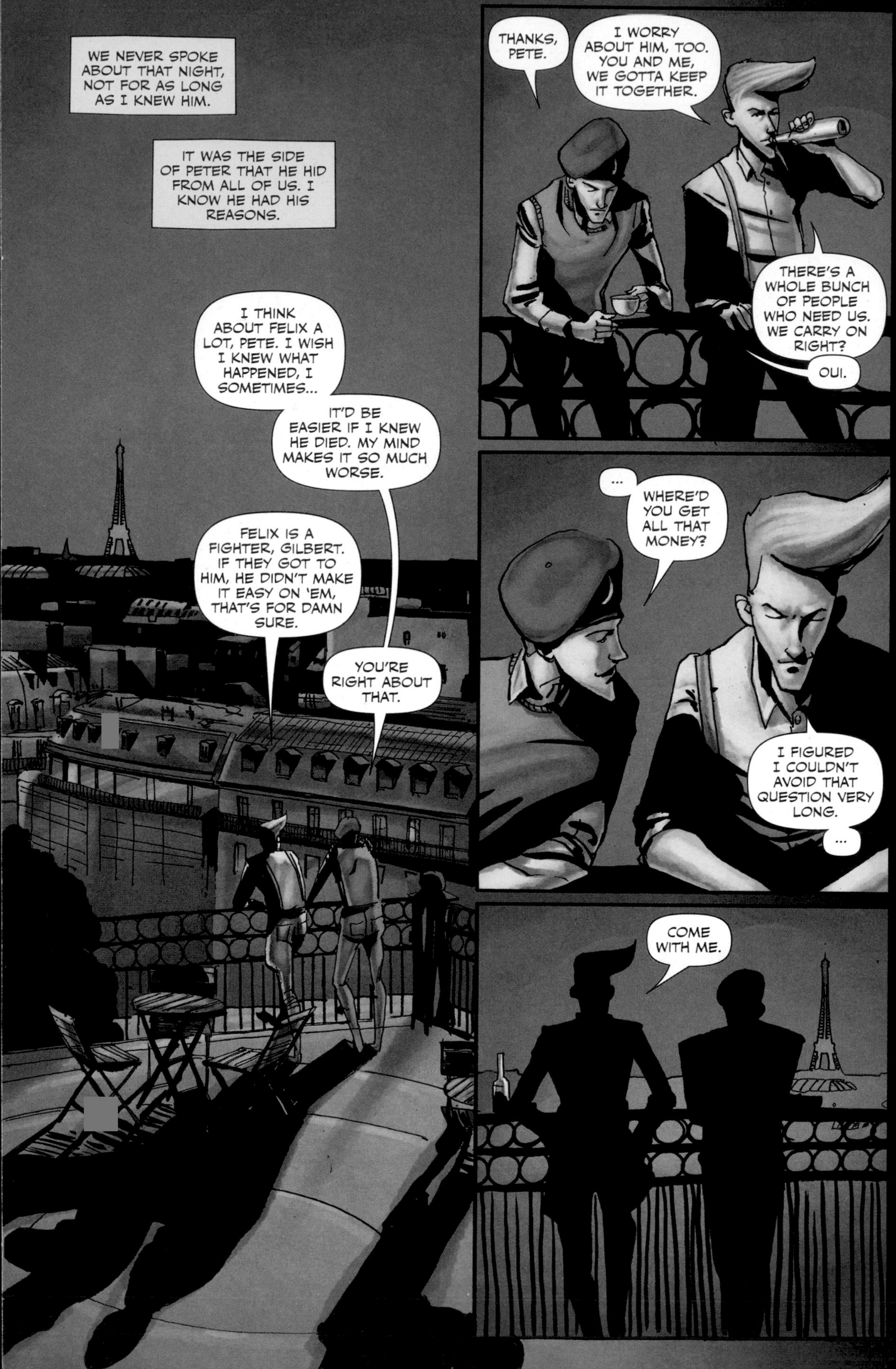
WE NEVER SPOKE ABOUT THAT NIGHT, NOT FOR AS LONG AS I KNEW HIM.
IT WAS THE SIDE OF PETER THAT HE HID FROM ALL OF US. I KNOW HE HAD HIS REASONS.
I THINK ABOUT FELIX A LOT, PETE. I WISH I KNEW WHAT HAPPENED, I SOMETIMES...
IT'D BE EASIER IF I KNEW HE DIED. MY MIND MAKES IT SO MUCH WORSE.
FELIX IS A FIGHTER, GILBERT. IF THEY GOT TO HIM, HE DIDN'T MAKE IT EASY ON 'EM, THAT'S FOR DAMN SURE.
YOU'RE RIGHT ABOUT THAT.
THANKS, PETE.
I WORRY ABOUT HIM, TOO. YOU AND ME, WE GOTTA KEEP IT TOGETHER.
THERE'S A WHOLE BUNCH OF PEOPLE WHO NEED US. WE CARRY ON RIGHT?
OUI.
...
WHERE'D YOU GET ALL THAT MONEY?
I FIGURED I COULDN'T AVOID THAT QUESTION VERY LONG.
...
COME WITH ME.

IT'S IN HERE SOMEWHERE...

AH, HERE WE GO!

WHO'S THIS?

THAT'S MY FATHER. HE DIED SIX MONTHS AGO.

I'M SORRY, PETE.

IT'S FINE, YOU KNOW WHAT THEY SAY. TIME HEALS ALL WOUNDS.

HE WAS A RICH MAN, CAME BACK WITH ALL KINDS OF IDEAS ABOUT INDUSTRY AFTER THE WAR. I WAS HIS ONLY CHILD.

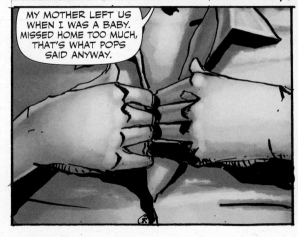

MY MOTHER LEFT US WHEN I WAS A BABY. MISSED HOME TOO MUCH, THAT'S WHAT POPS SAID ANYWAY.

I CAME TO FRANCE TO SEE WHAT THE FUSS WAS ABOUT.

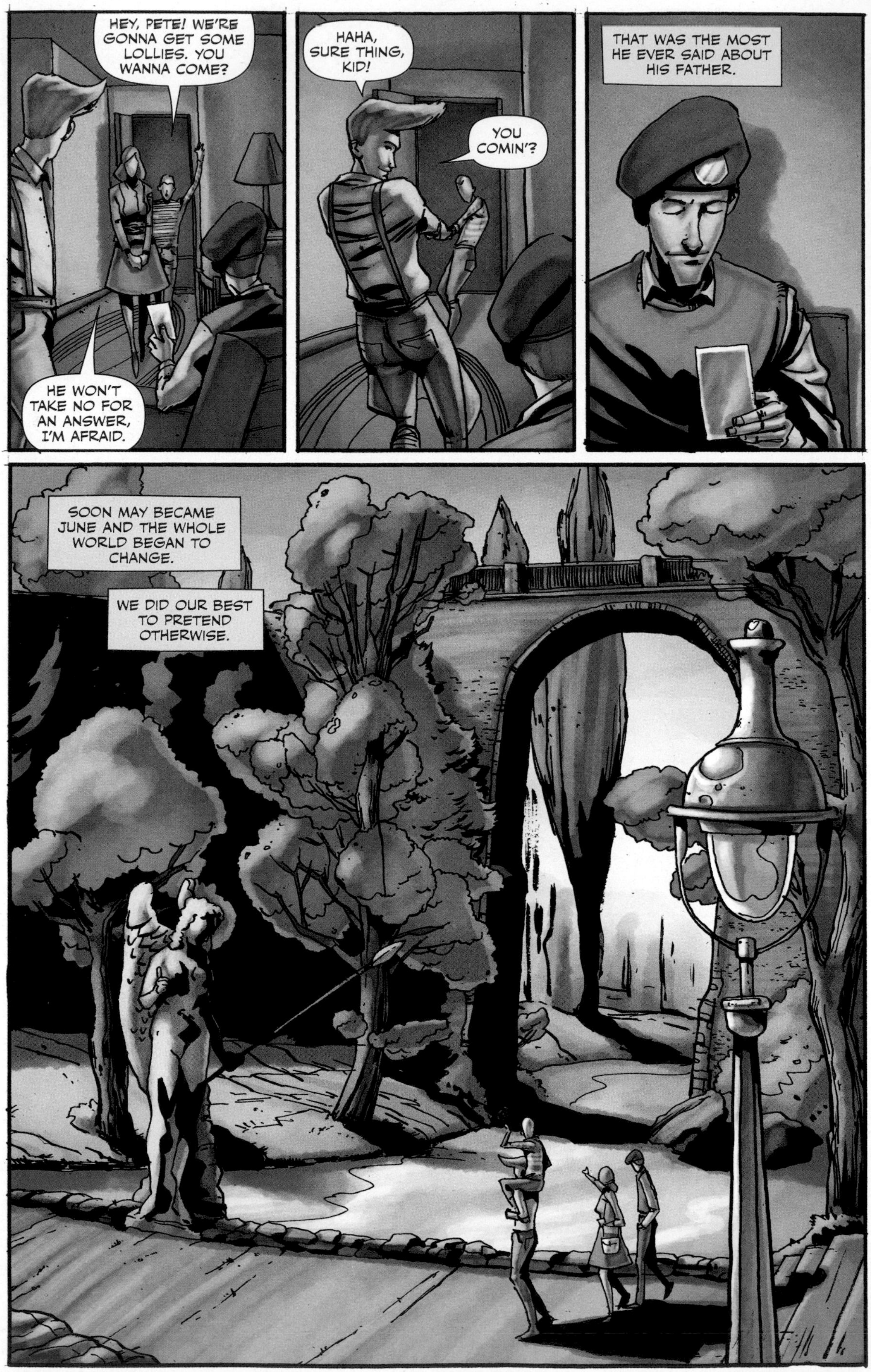
HEY, PETE! WE'RE GONNA GET SOME LOLLIES. YOU WANNA COME?
HE WON'T TAKE NO FOR AN ANSWER, I'M AFRAID.
HAHA, SURE THING, KID!
YOU COMIN'?
THAT WAS THE MOST HE EVER SAID ABOUT HIS FATHER.
SOON MAY BECAME JUNE AND THE WHOLE WORLD BEGAN TO CHANGE.
WE DID OUR BEST TO PRETEND OTHERWISE.

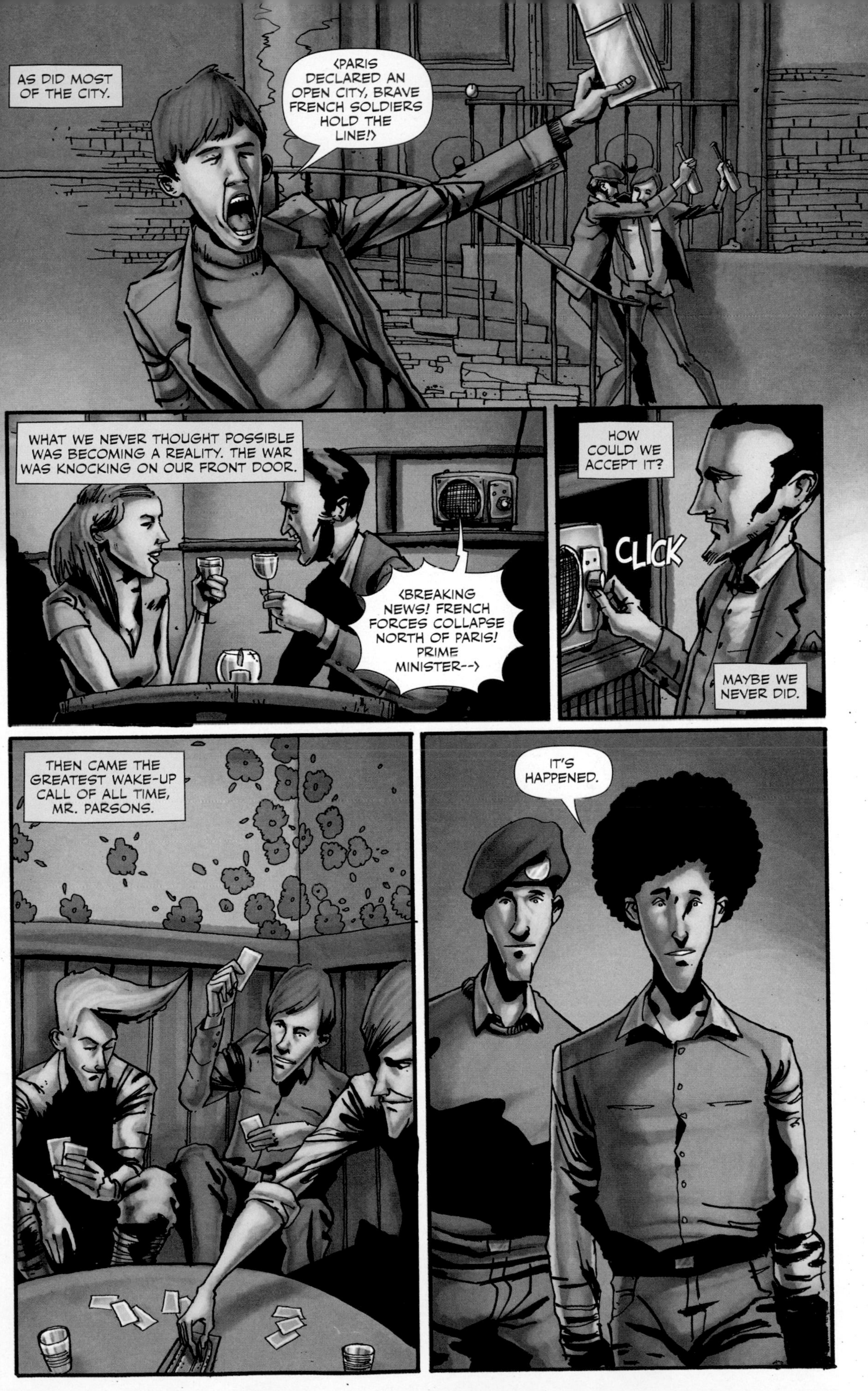
AS DID MOST OF THE CITY.
<PARIS DECLARED AN OPEN CITY, BRAVE FRENCH SOLDIERS HOLD THE LINE!>
WHAT WE NEVER THOUGHT POSSIBLE WAS BECOMING A REALITY. THE WAR WAS KNOCKING ON OUR FRONT DOOR.
<BREAKING NEWS! FRENCH FORCES COLLAPSE NORTH OF PARIS! PRIME MINISTER-->
HOW COULD WE ACCEPT IT?
CLICK
MAYBE WE NEVER DID.
THEN CAME THE GREATEST WAKE-UP CALL OF ALL TIME, MR. PARSONS.
IT'S HAPPENED.

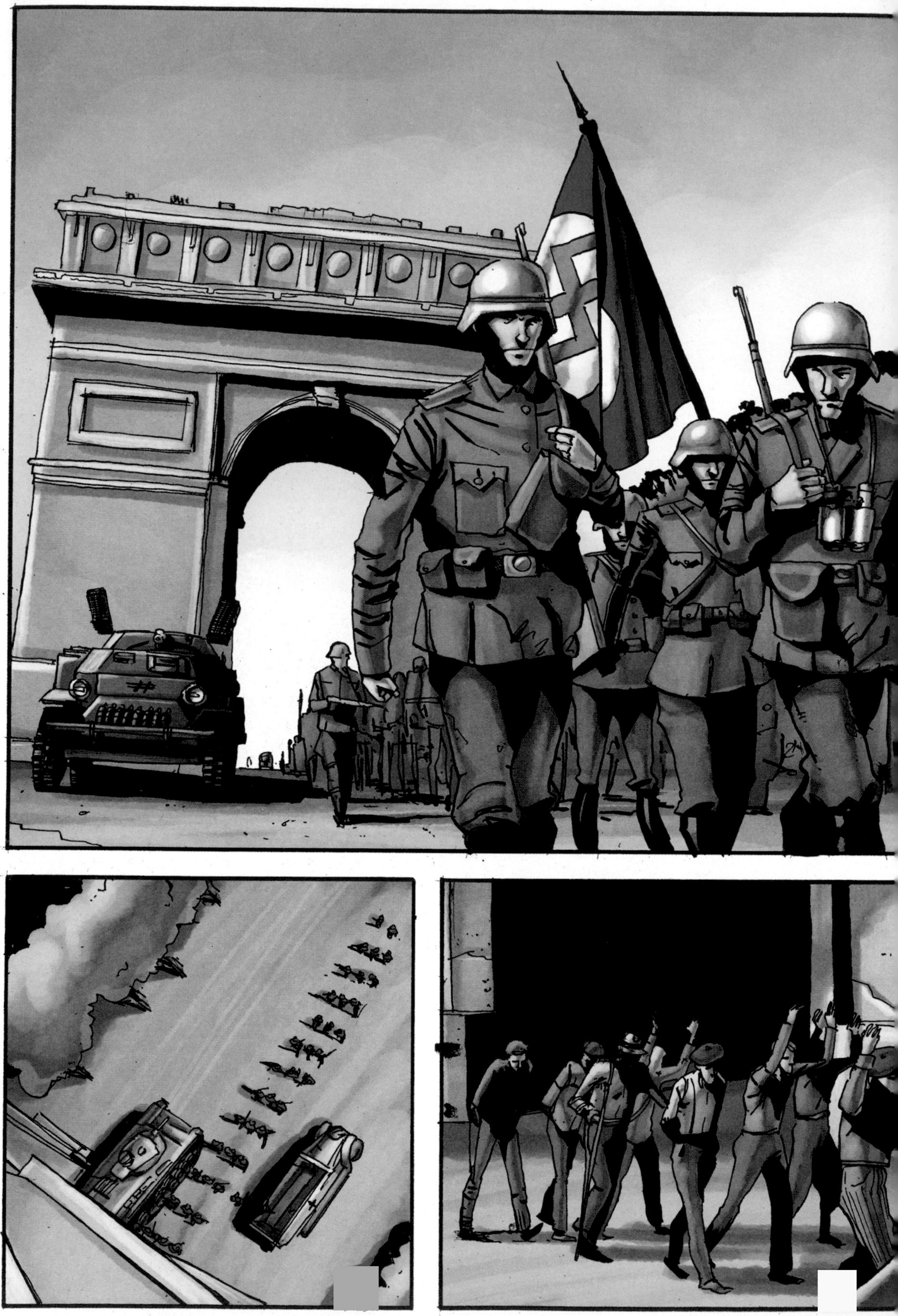

THERE'S... SO MANY.

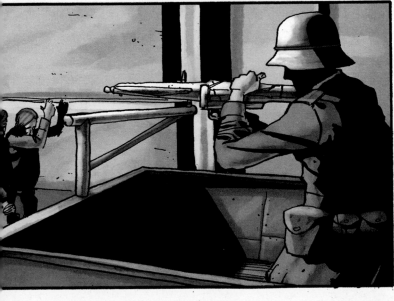

OH MY GOD!

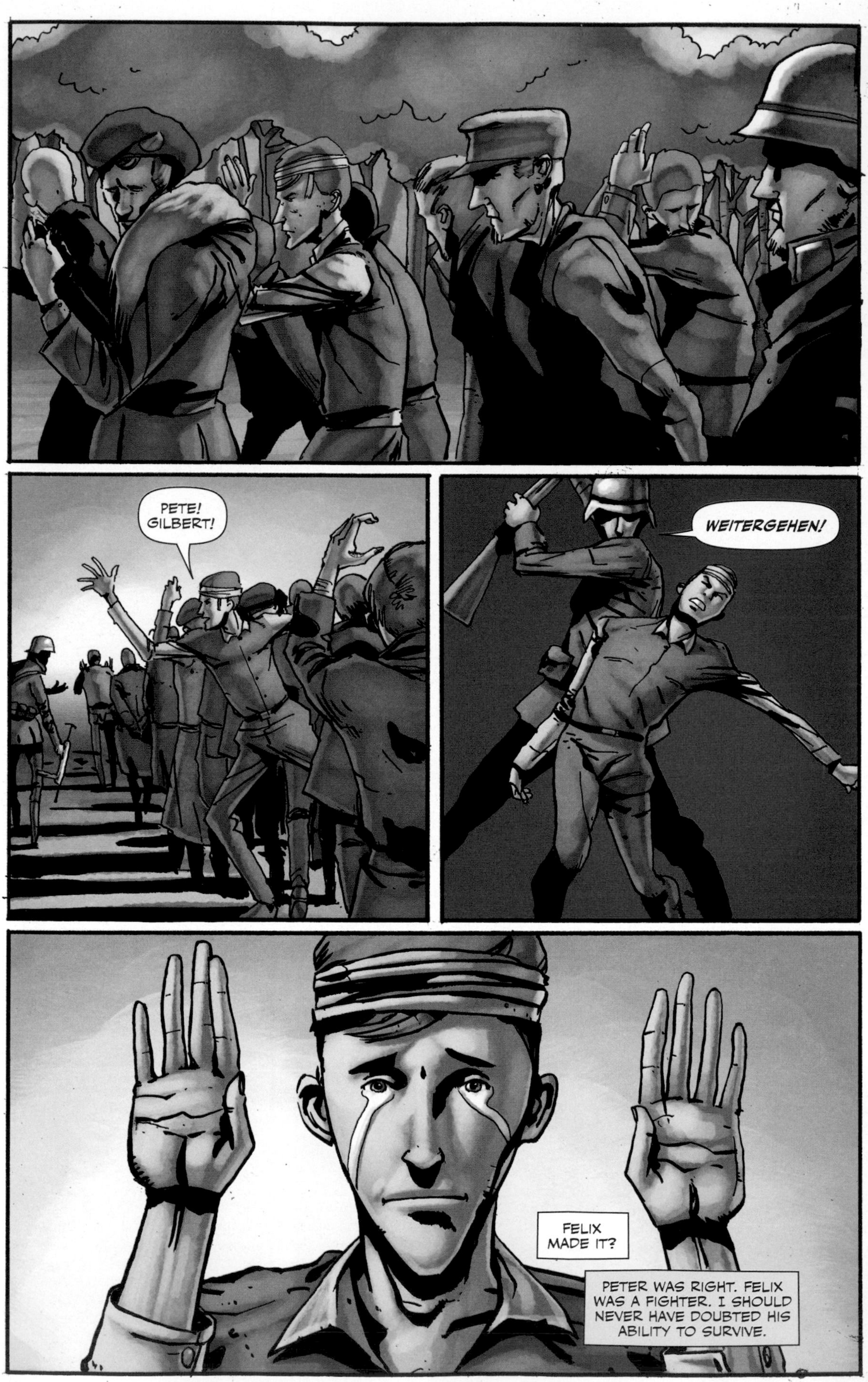
PETE! GILBERT!
WEITERGEHEN!
FELIX MADE IT?
PETER WAS RIGHT. FELIX WAS A FIGHTER. I SHOULD NEVER HAVE DOUBTED HIS ABILITY TO SURVIVE.

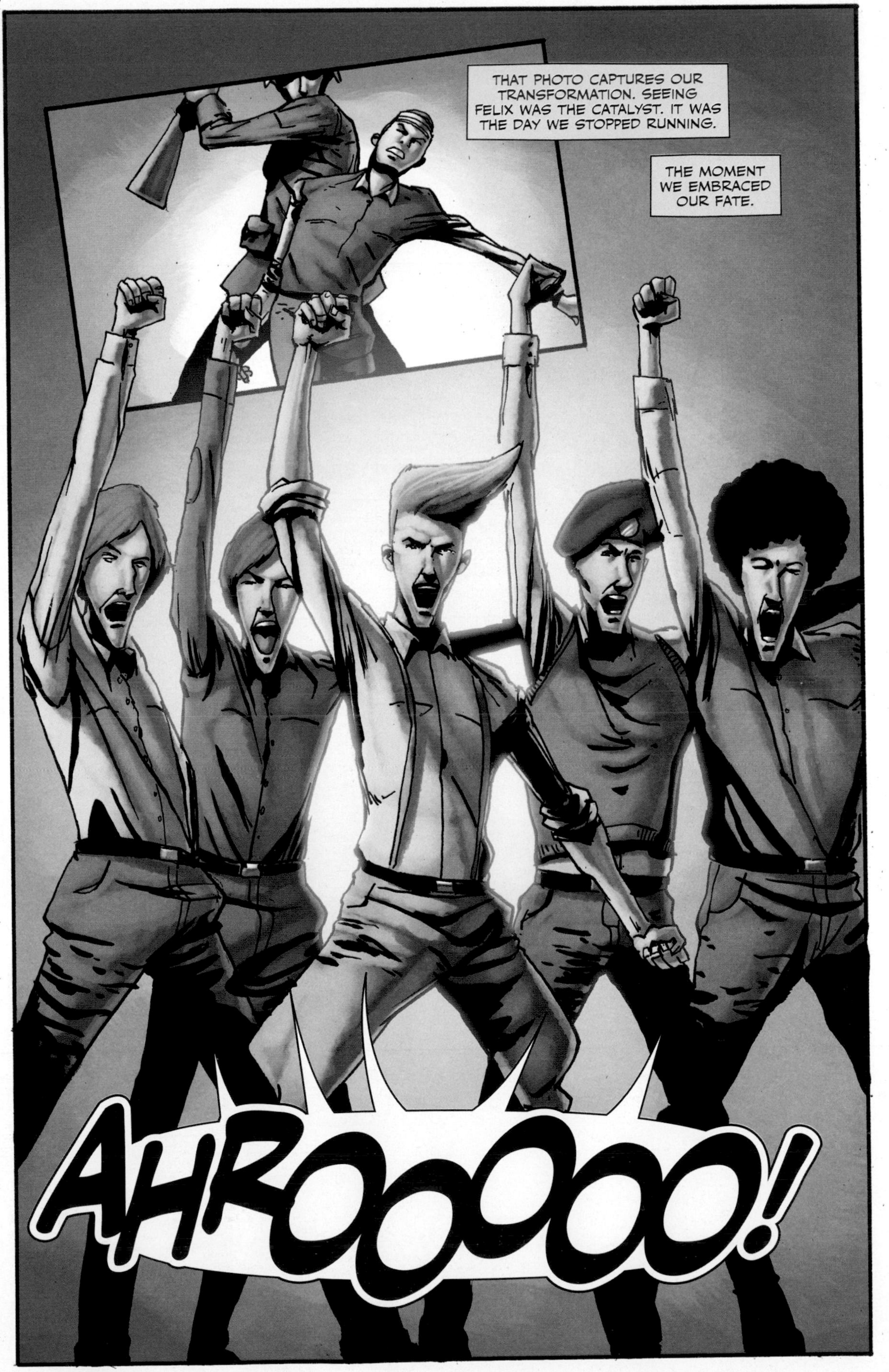
THAT PHOTO CAPTURES OUR TRANSFORMATION. SEEING FELIX WAS THE CATALYST. IT WAS THE DAY WE STOPPED RUNNING.
THE MOMENT WE EMBRACED OUR FATE.
AHROOOOOO!

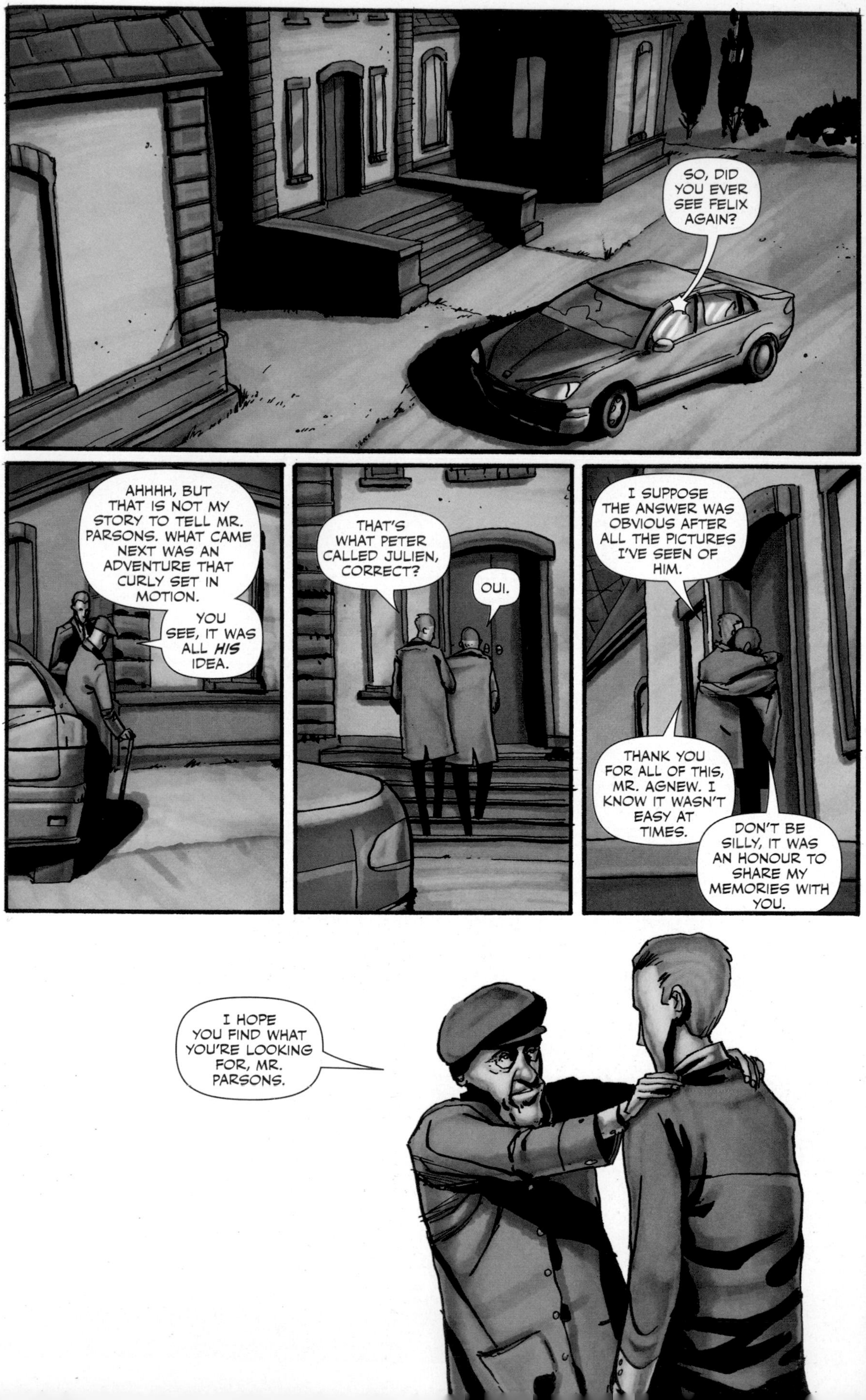
SO, DID YOU EVER SEE FELIX AGAIN?
AHHHH, BUT THAT IS NOT MY STORY TO TELL MR. PARSONS. WHAT CAME NEXT WAS AN ADVENTURE THAT CURLY SET IN MOTION.
YOU SEE, IT WAS ALL *HIS* IDEA.
THAT'S WHAT PETER CALLED JULIEN, CORRECT?
OUI.
I SUPPOSE THE ANSWER WAS OBVIOUS AFTER ALL THE PICTURES I'VE SEEN OF HIM.
THANK YOU FOR ALL OF THIS, MR. AGNEW. I KNOW IT WASN'T EASY AT TIMES.
DON'T BE SILLY, IT WAS AN HONOUR TO SHARE MY MEMORIES WITH YOU.
I HOPE YOU FIND WHAT YOU'RE LOOKING FOR, MR. PARSONS.

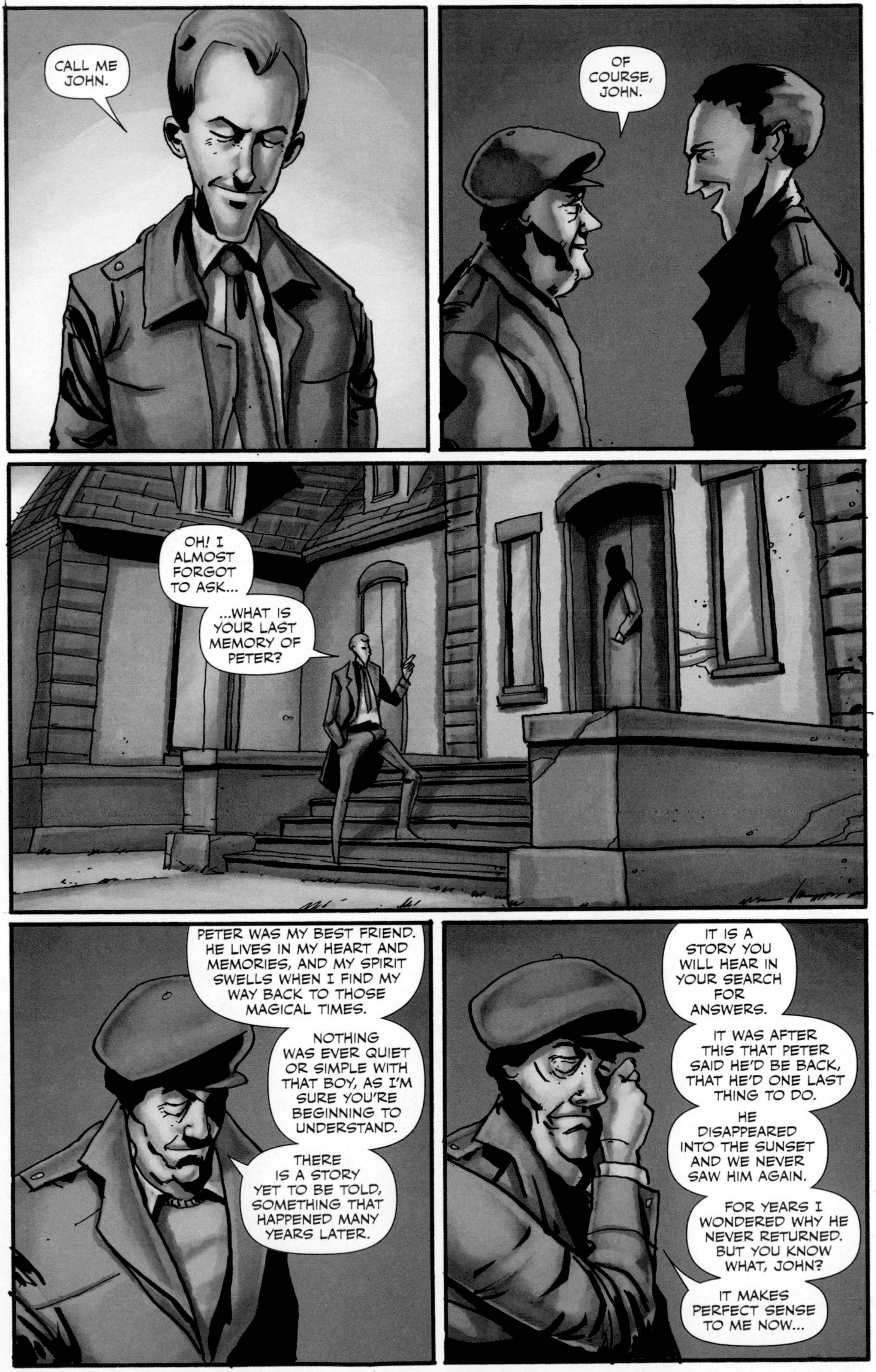
CALL ME JOHN.
OF COURSE, JOHN.
OH! I ALMOST FORGOT TO ASK...
...WHAT IS YOUR LAST MEMORY OF PETER?
PETER WAS MY BEST FRIEND. HE LIVES IN MY HEART AND MEMORIES, AND MY SPIRIT SWELLS WHEN I FIND MY WAY BACK TO THOSE MAGICAL TIMES.
NOTHING WAS EVER QUIET OR SIMPLE WITH THAT BOY, AS I'M SURE YOU'RE BEGINNING TO UNDERSTAND.
THERE IS A STORY YET TO BE TOLD, SOMETHING THAT HAPPENED MANY YEARS LATER.
IT IS A STORY YOU WILL HEAR IN YOUR SEARCH FOR ANSWERS.
IT WAS AFTER THIS THAT PETER SAID HE'D BE BACK, THAT HE'D ONE LAST THING TO DO.
HE DISAPPEARED INTO THE SUNSET AND WE NEVER SAW HIM AGAIN.
FOR YEARS I WONDERED WHY HE NEVER RETURNED. BUT YOU KNOW WHAT, JOHN?
IT MAKES PERFECT SENSE TO ME NOW...

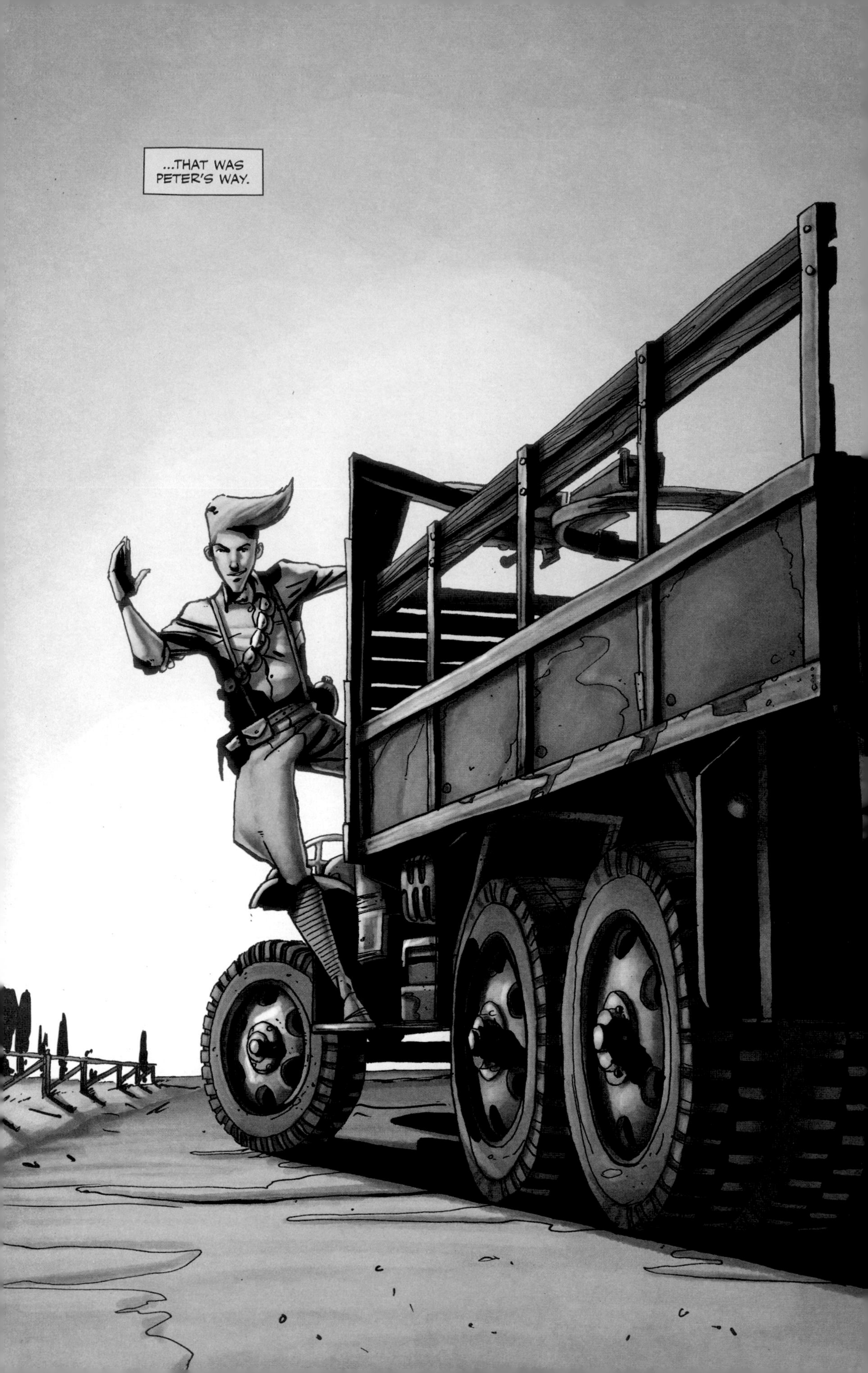
...THAT WAS PETER'S WAY.

EXTRAS

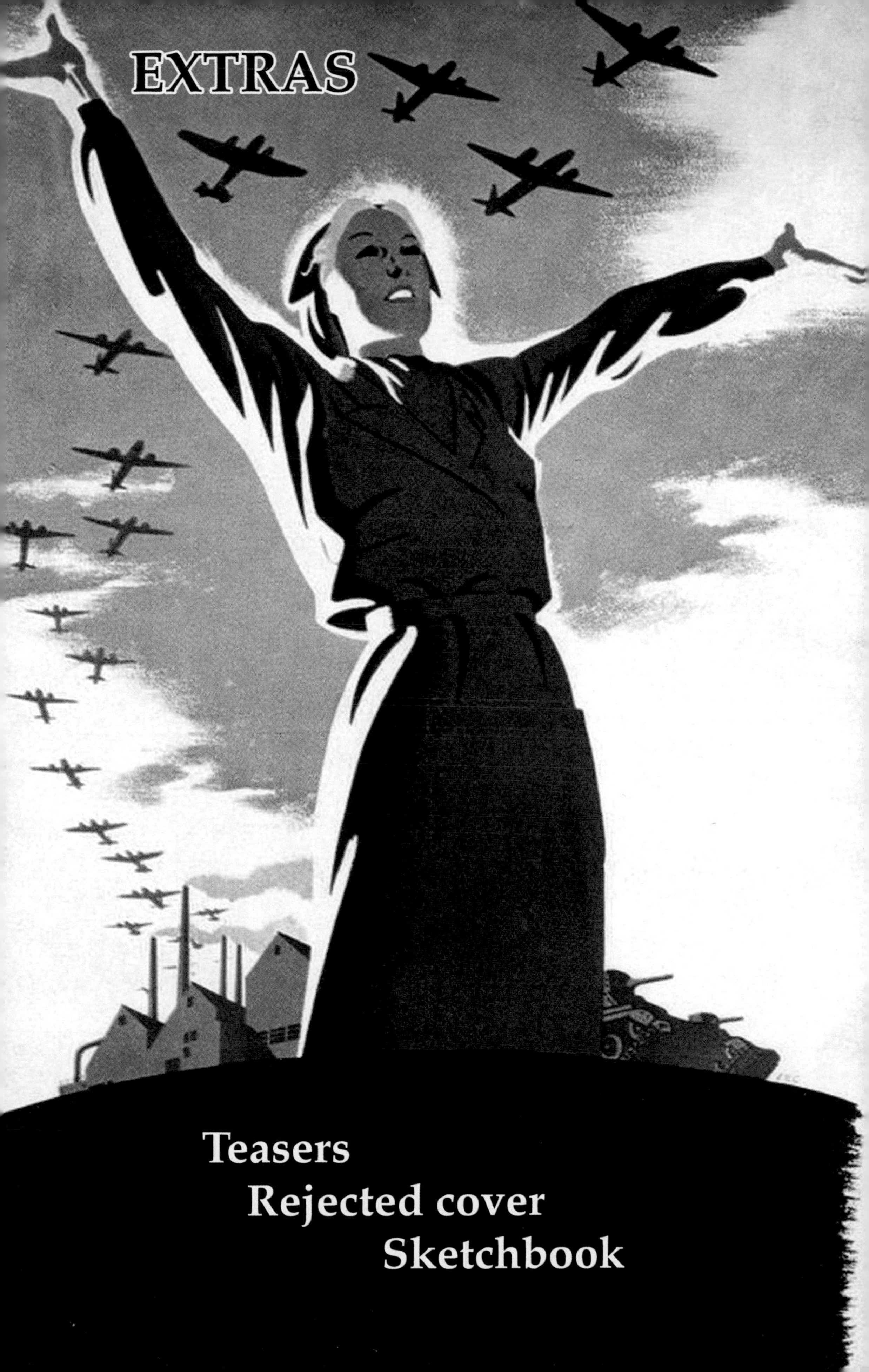

Teasers

Rejected cover

Sketchbook

TEASERS

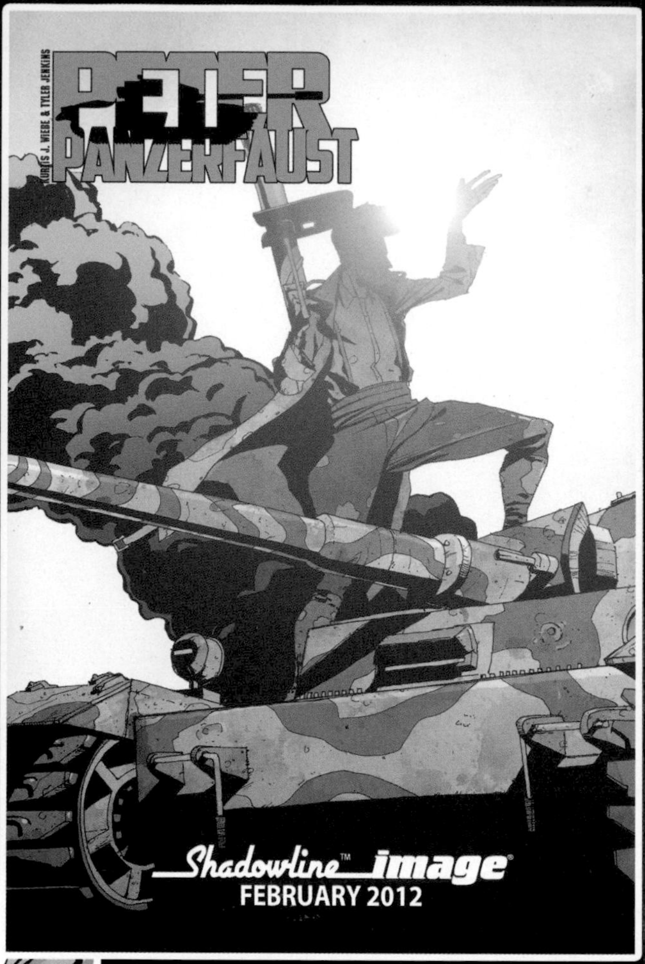
J. WIEBE & TYLER JENKINS
PETER PANZERFAUST
Shadowline image
FEBRUARY 2012

RIGHT:
We've been producing teasers for new books for a couple of years now. These images go over the internet in the hope of enticing readers to try out a new series.
This image is a slightly altered version of the cover for issue number one.

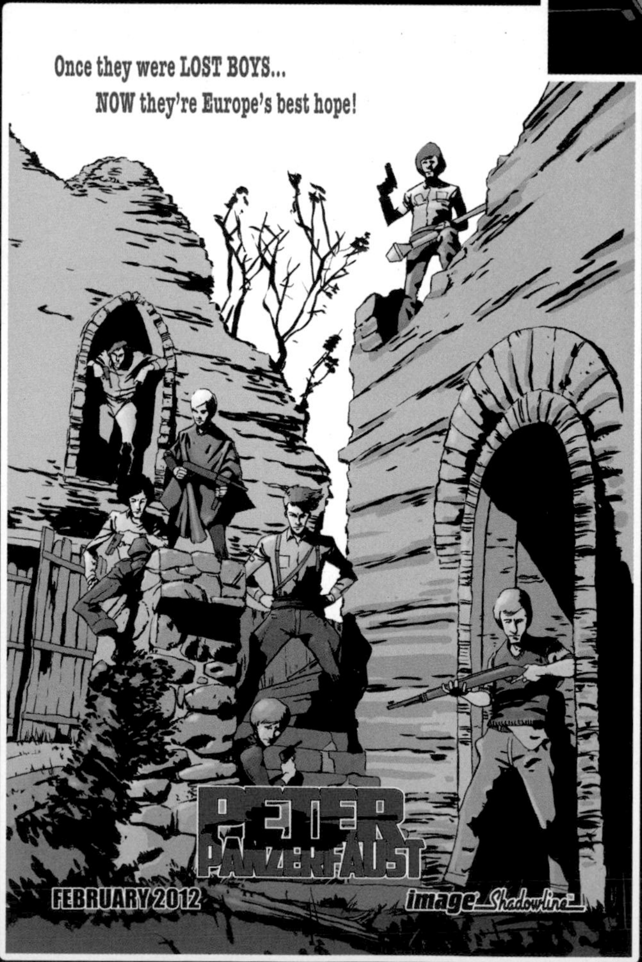
Once they were LOST BOYS...
NOW they're Europe's best hope!
PETER PANZERFAUST
FEBRUARY 2012
image Shadowline

LEFT:
This teaser used the cover art for issue number two and, except for the copy, remained pretty much unchanged for both uses.

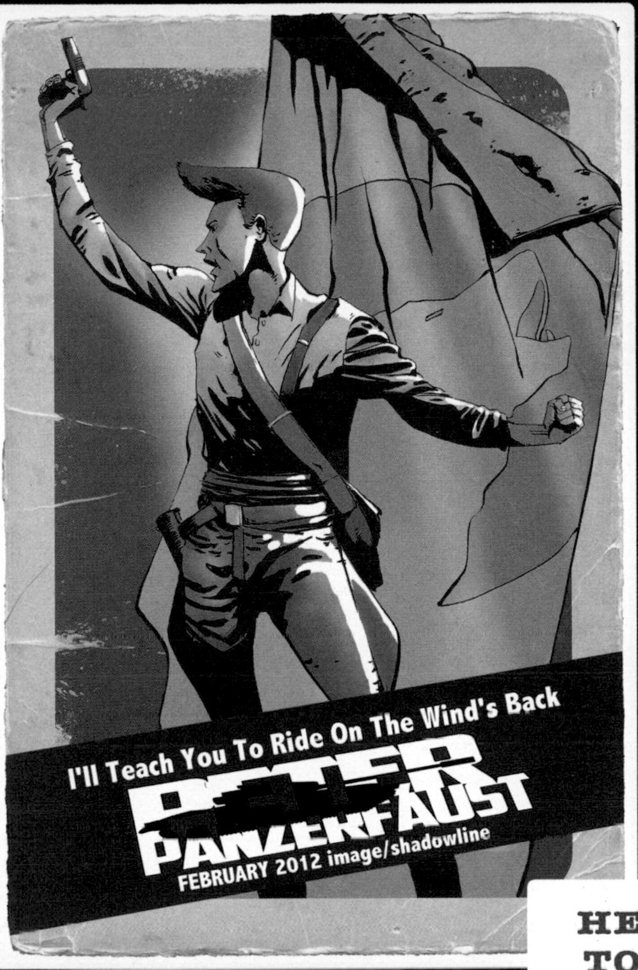
I'll Teach You To Ride On The Wind's Back
PANZERFAUST
FEBRUARY 2012 image/shadowline

LEFT:
In a reversal of the previous two teasers, this image started as an original teaser and became the cover for the second printing of issue number two!
It was inspired by a World War Two poster.

RIGHT:
We all loved this page from issue number one so much that it not only was repurposed as a teaser image, but also served as the illustration for the inside front cover of the series and the credits page for this volume!

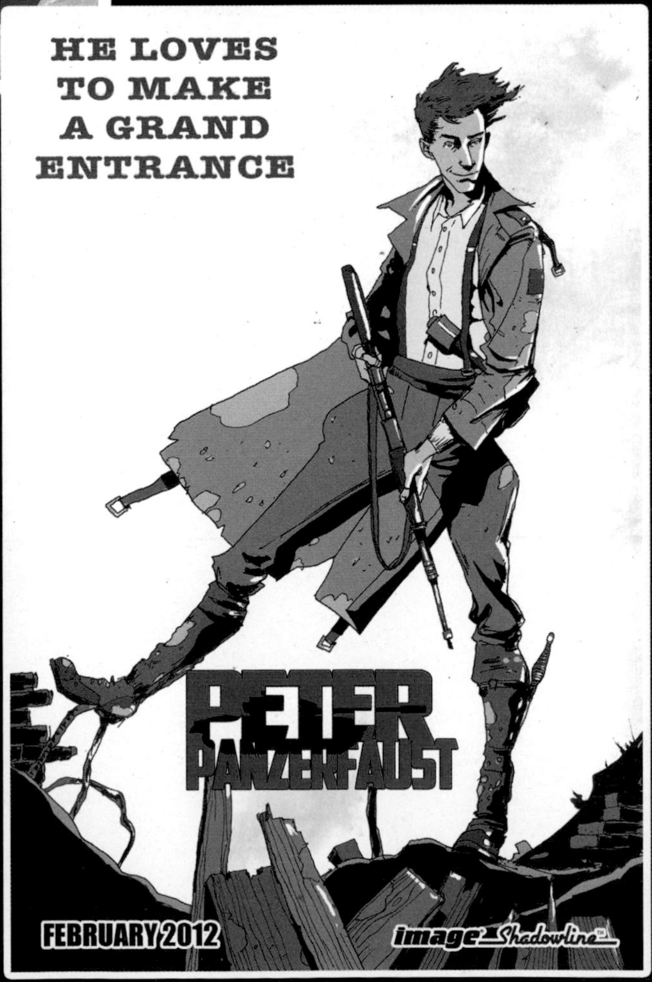
HE LOVES
TO MAKE
A GRAND
ENTRANCE
PETER
PANZERFAUST
FEBRUARY 2012
image Shadowline

RIGHT:
Another teaser image that became a cover! In this case the illustration was used for the second printing of issue number one.

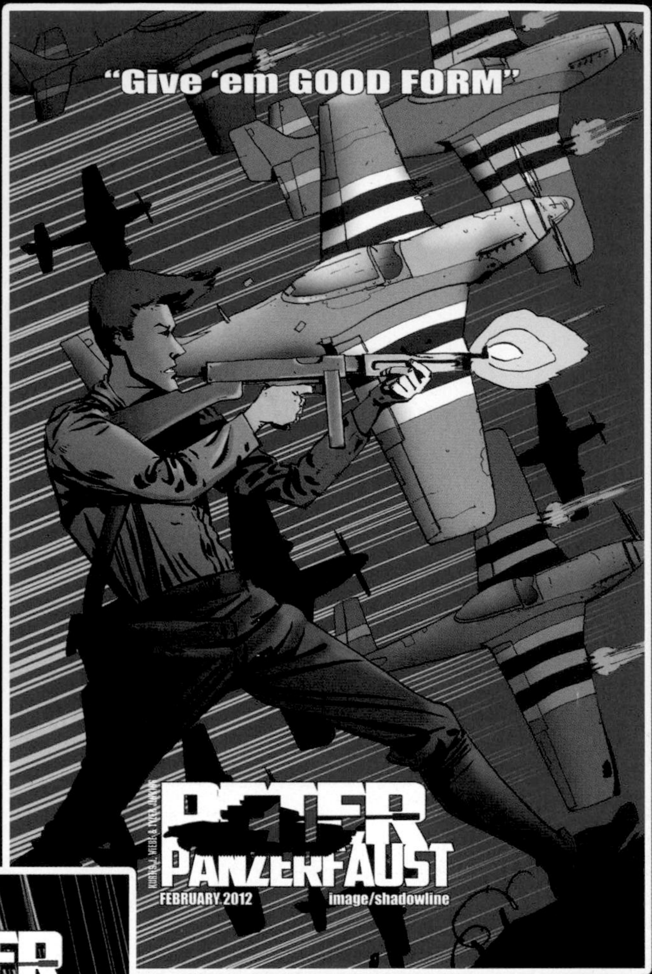

"Give 'em GOOD FORM"
PETER PANZERFAUST
FEBRUARY 2012
image/shadowline

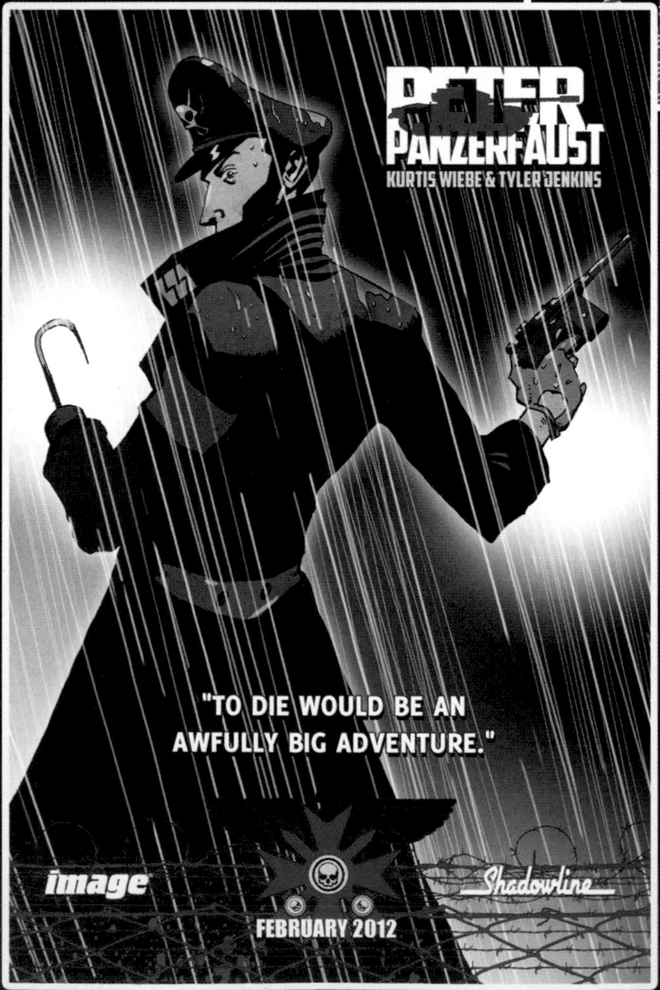

PETER PANZERFAUST
KURTIS WIEBE & TYLER JENKINS
"TO DIE WOULD BE AN AWFULLY BIG ADVENTURE."
image
Shadowline
FEBRUARY 2012

LEFT:
And we close with a teaser image that that has never seen print before! This was the very first appearance of upcoming villain...Hook!
A teaser, indeed.

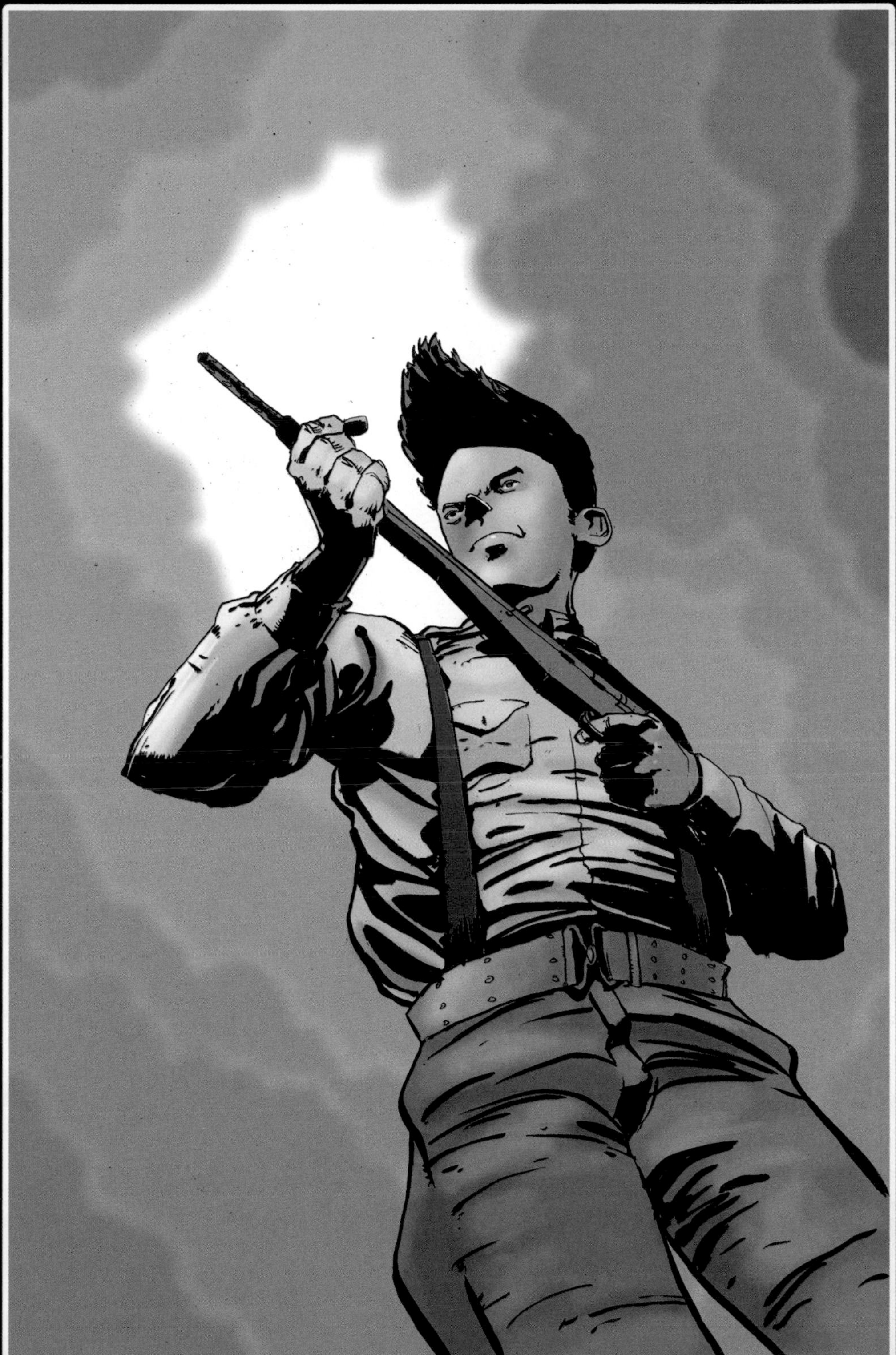

This was the original cover for issue number four. Inspired by a World War Two era poster, Tyler Jenkins worked his tail off to try and get it right, but was never satisfied with the results. He felt he could do a better cover...and he was right! See page 77 for the beautiful cover he came up with on his own.

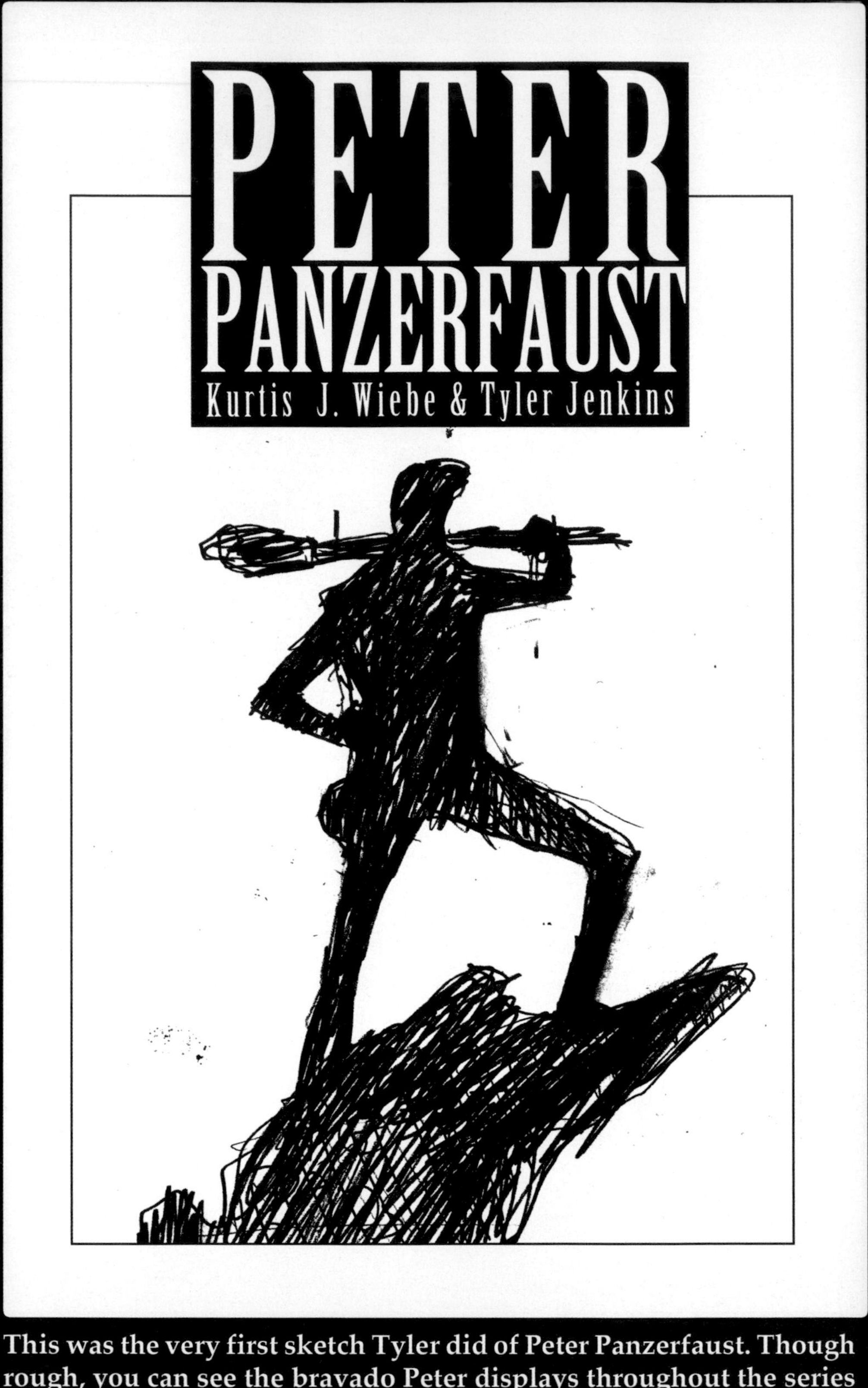
PETER
PANZERFAUST
Kurtis J. Wiebe & Tyler Jenkins

This was the very first sketch Tyler did of Peter Panzerfaust. Though rough, you can see the bravado Peter displays throughout the series in his defiant gesture. Just as a writer has to make copious notes about his plot, characters and pacing, so too does the artist draw uncountable sketches in an attempt to capture gesture, design and composition. Over the next few pages we'll give you a taste of how it's done.

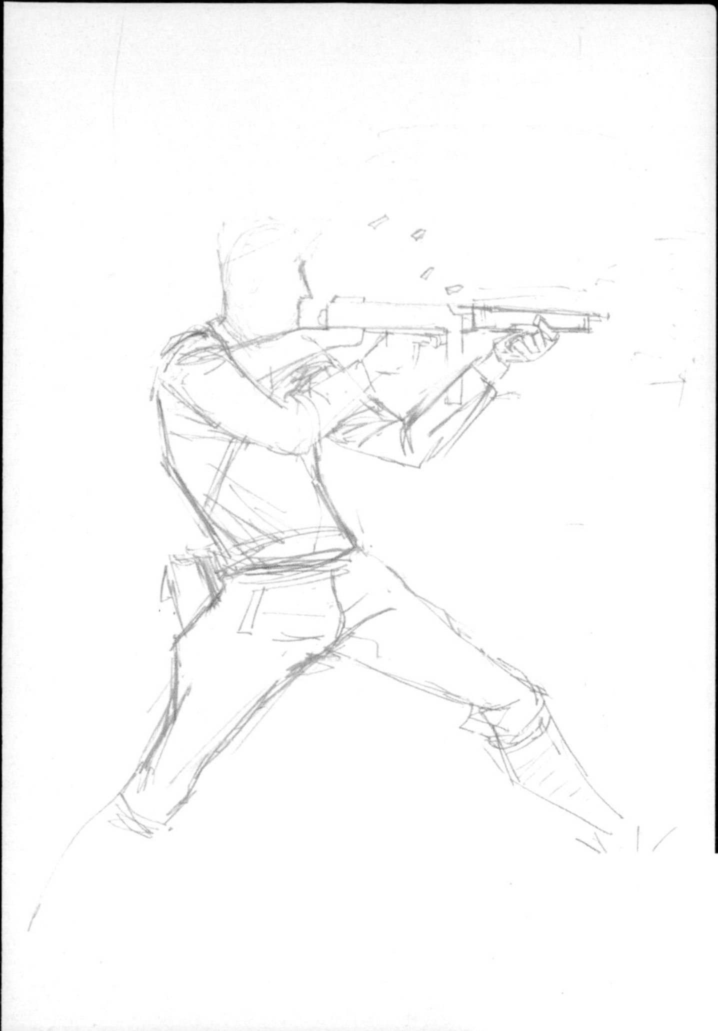

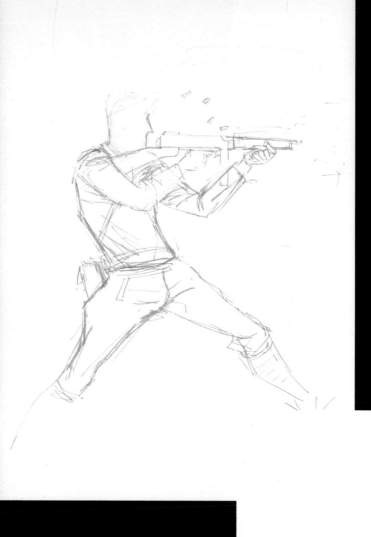

Two studies for the second printing cover of issue one (sans all of the Mustangs).

The one below made it to the final cover.

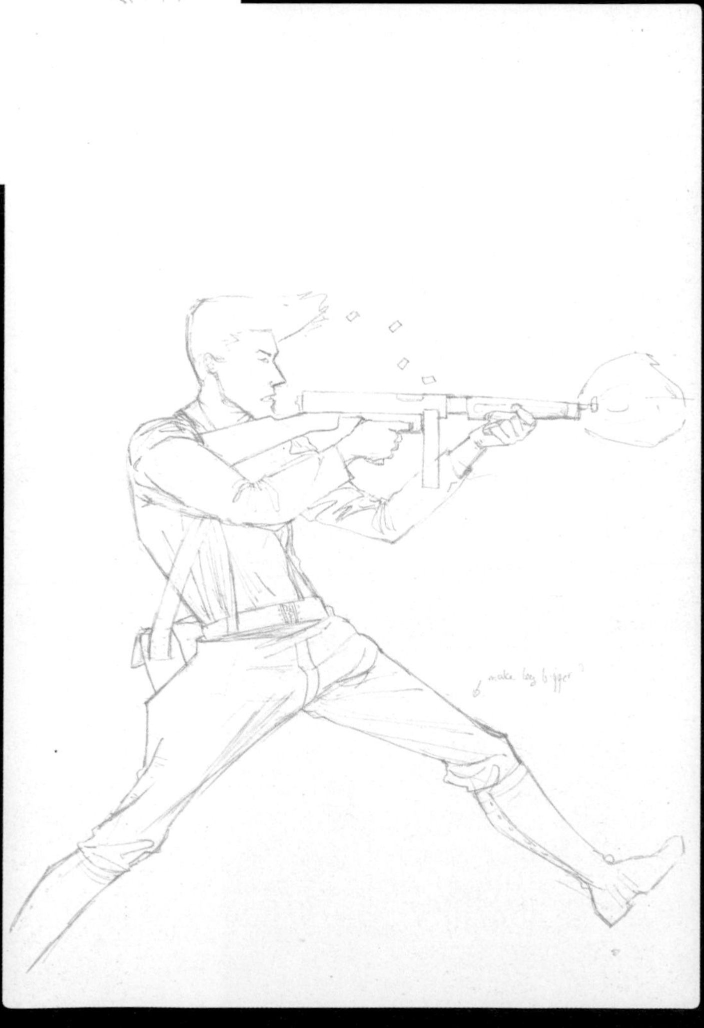
make leg bigger?

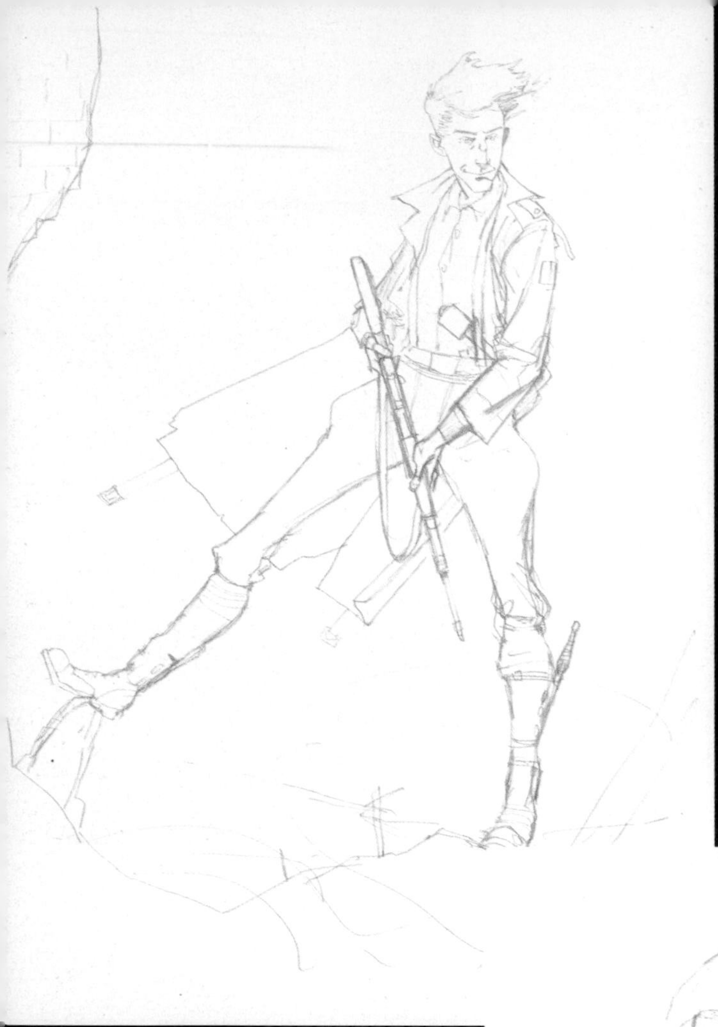

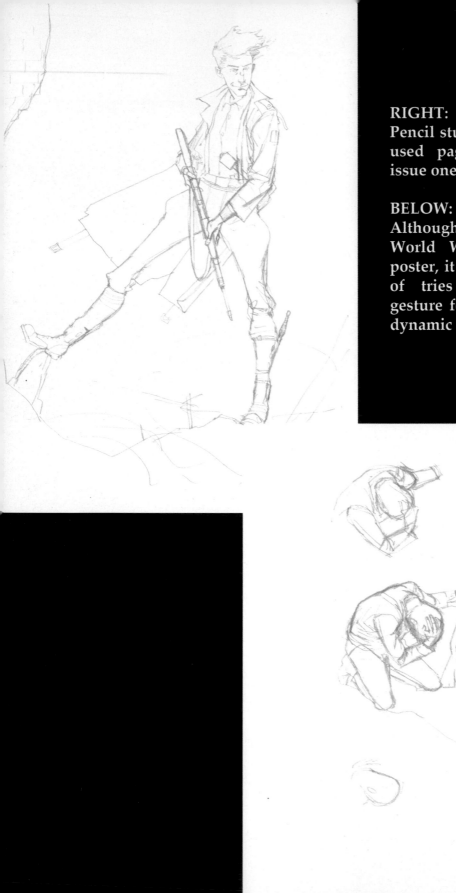

RIGHT:
Pencil study for the oft used page five from issue one.

BELOW:
Although inspired by a World War Two era poster, it took a couple of tries to get the gesture for issue five's dynamic cover.

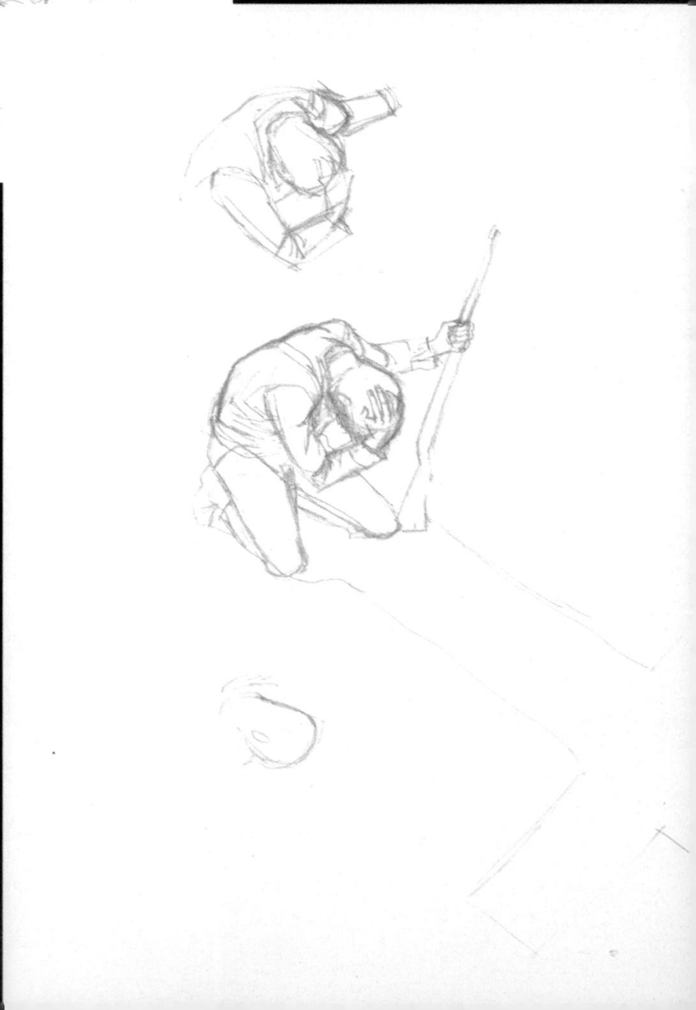

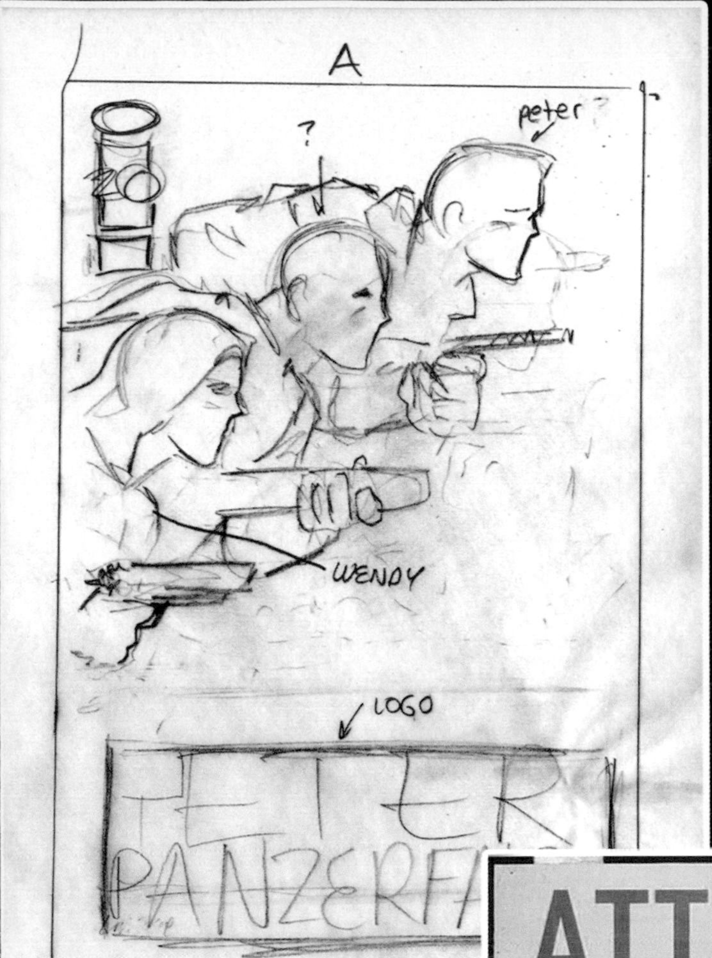
A
peter?
?
WENDY
LOGO
PETER
PANZERFA

Kurtis scoured the internet for World War Two era posters, some of which provided the inspiration for covers, others just didn't work out.

On these next two pages, we're going to show you some of the sketches alongside the posters that inspired them.

All of these sketches were done for issue four.

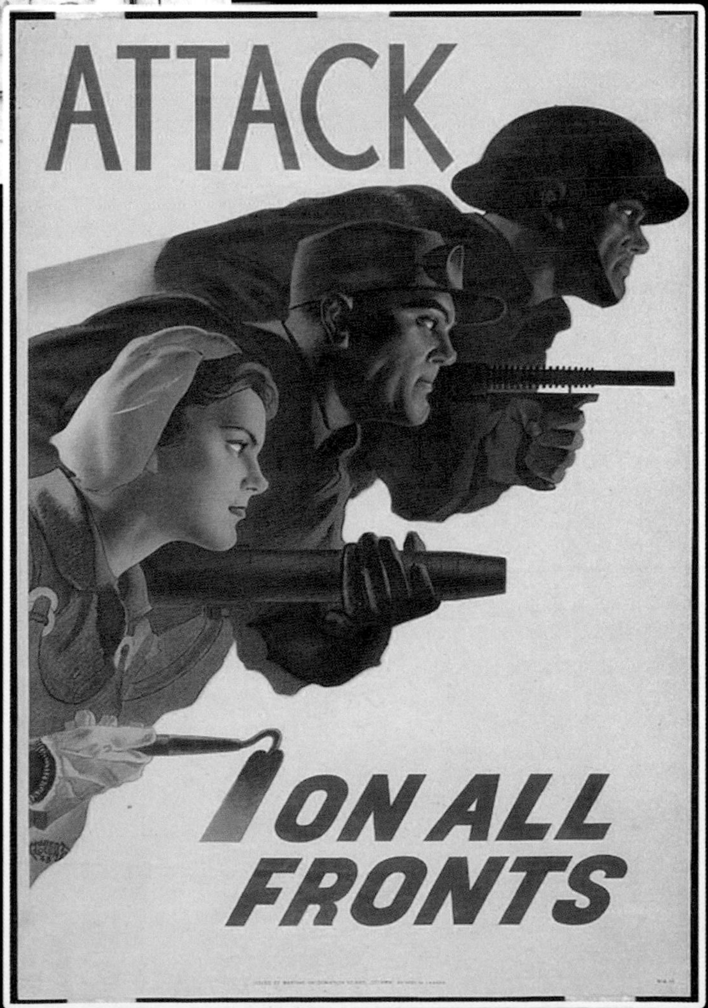
ATTACK
ON ALL
FRONTS

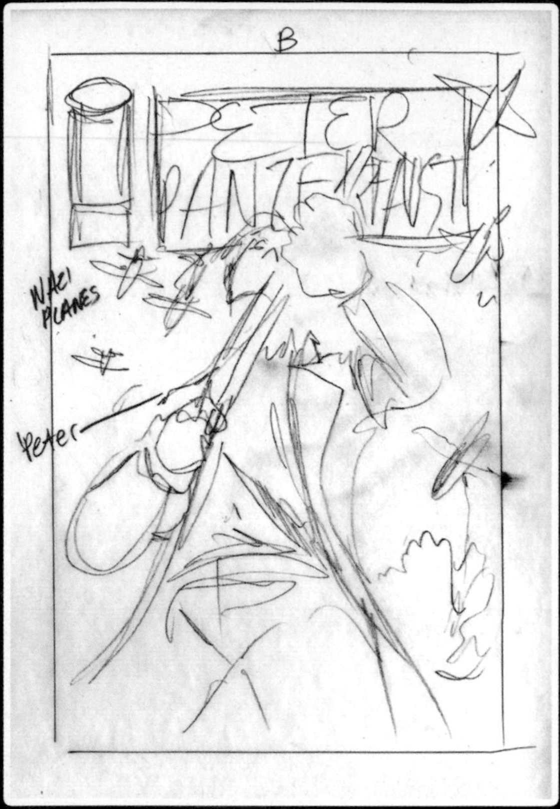
B
PETER
PANZERFAUST
NAZI PLANES
Peter

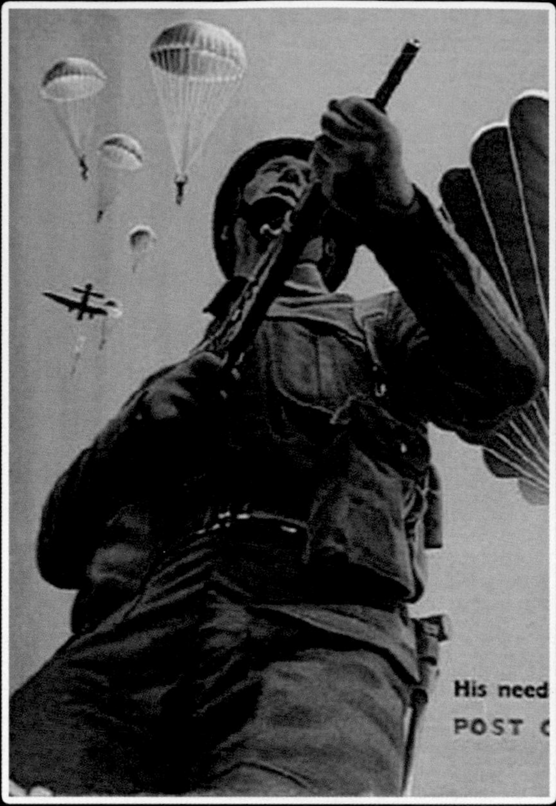
His need
POST

The piece above made it all the way to being colored before artist Tyler Jenkins felt it just wasn't good enough for a cover and rejected it.

The piece below never made it past the sketch stage.

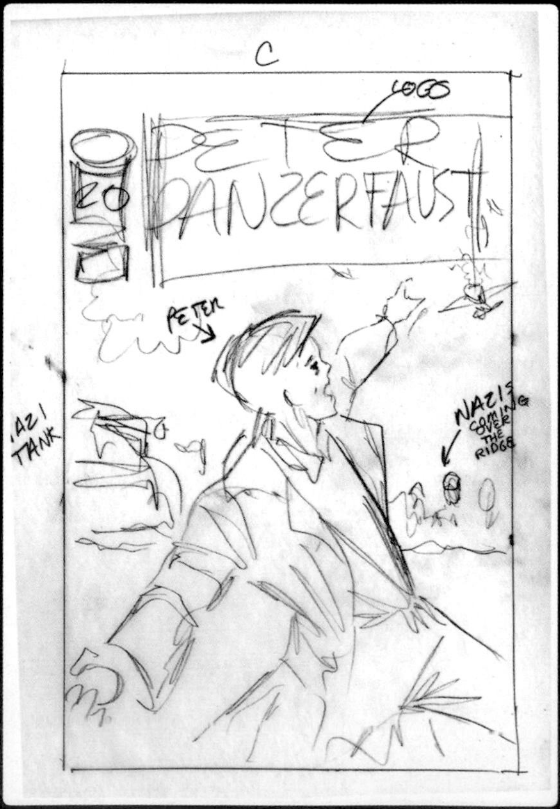
C
LOGO
PETER
PANZERFAUST
PETER
NAZIS COMING OVER THE RIDGE
TANK

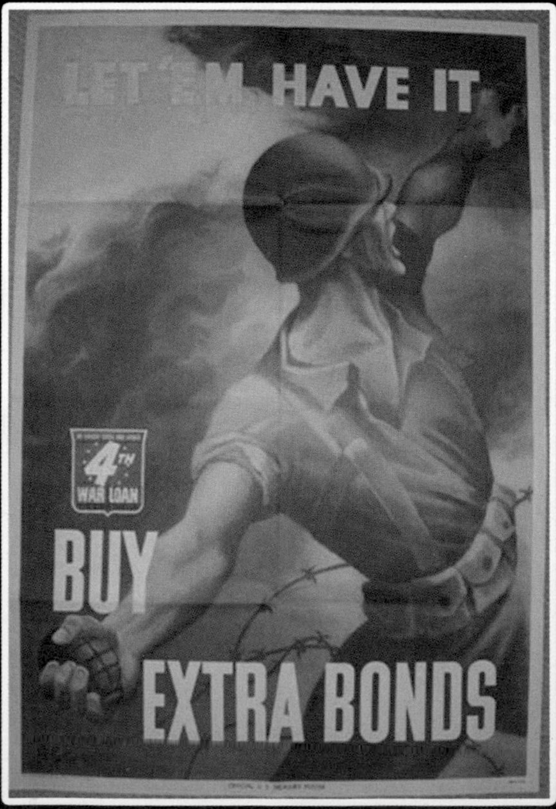
LET 'EM HAVE IT
4TH
WAR LOAN
BUY
EXTRA BONDS

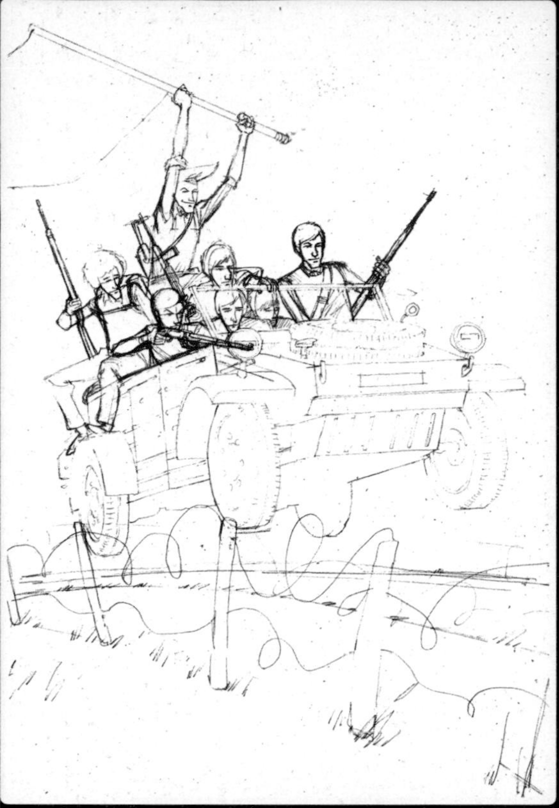

RIGHT:
Tyler's pencil sketch for this volume's cover.

BELOW RIGHT:
The poster that inspired issue five's dynamic cover.

BELOW RIGHT:
We just thought it would be a fun way to close out this section and this volume.
Until next time, keep 'em flying.

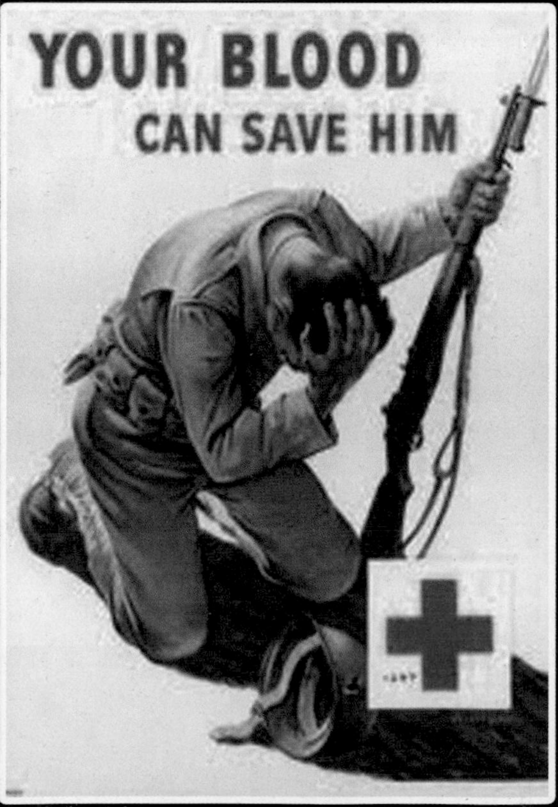
YOUR BLOOD
CAN SAVE HIM

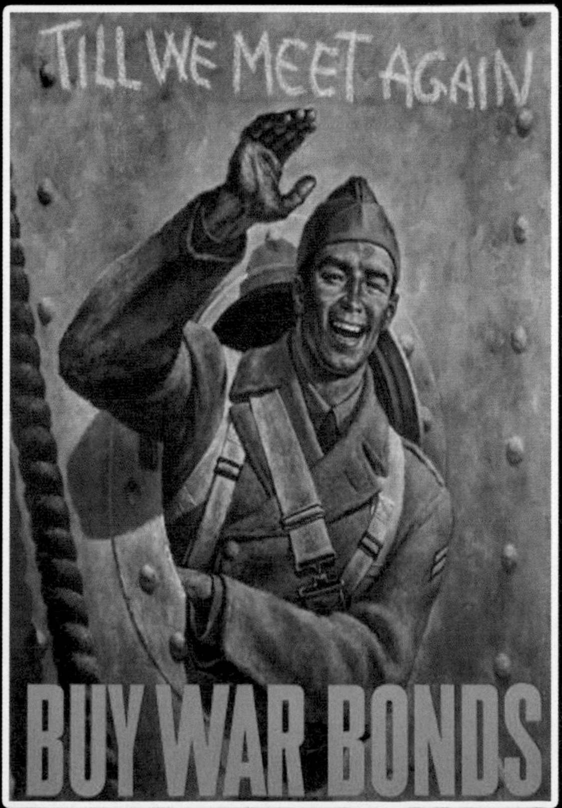
TILL WE MEET AGAIN
BUY WAR BONDS

More books by Kurtis J. Wiebe you're bound to enjoy...

GREEN WAKE
VOLUME ONE
KURTIS WIEBE
RILEY ROSSMO

GREEN WAKE VOLUME ONE
With RILEY ROSSMO

The highly acclaimed, repeat sellout series from writer Kurtis J. Wiebe and artist Riley Rossmo is a riveting tale of loss and horror. In the forgotten town of Green Wake, a string of grisly mutilations leads Morley Mack on the trail of a young woman named Ariel, who is the prime suspect. But when a stranger with startling connections to Ariel arrives under mysterious circumstances, Morley unravels a dark plot with a surprising link to his past.

136 PAGES ISBN: 978-1-60706-432-9

GREEN WAKE
VOLUME TWO
LOST CHILDREN
KURTIS WIEBE
RILEY ROSSMO

GREEN WAKE VOLUME TWO: LOST CHILDREN
With RILEY ROSSMO

The final chapter and the face of Green Wake has been forever changed. A new threat to the city's once quiet shores surfaces when rowboats wash ashore with nothing but fresh blood as a passenger. And a new arrival begins a campaign to unite Green Wake's inhabitants with unknown purpose.

The shocking conclusion to this critically acclaimed series! Collects issues 6-10 plus behind-the-scenes features!

136 PAGES ISBN: 978-1-60706-525-8

THE INTREPIDS

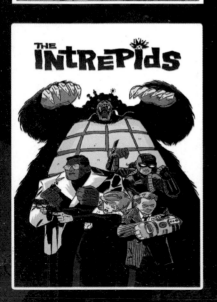

THE INTREPIDS
With SCOTT KOWALCHUK

The Intrepids are a collection of runaway and homeless teenagers that have been taken in and cared for by an aging inventor, Dante. Applying his brilliance, he crafts marvelous technological contraptions. With his vision and help, the teenagers agree to don his technology for the betterment of mankid. Together, they combat tyranny and stop madmen from bringing harm to the world.

144 PAGES ISBN: 978-1-60706-497-9

image Shadowline™